Unions Flying High

ALSO BY TED REED

Carl Furillo, Brooklyn Dodgers All-Star (McFarland, 2011)

BY TED REED AND DAN REED

American Airlines, US Airways and the Creation of the World's Largest Airline (McFarland, 2014)

BY TED REED AND JOHN J. YURECHKO

Kenny Riley and Black Union Labor Power in the Port of Charleston (McFarland, 2020)

Unions Flying High

*Airline Labor Power
in the 21st Century*

TED REED

McFarland & Company, Inc., Publishers
Jefferson, North Carolina

ISBN (print) 978-1-4766-9269-2
ISBN (ebook) 978-1-4766-5457-7

Library of Congress cataloging data are available

Library of Congress Control Number 2024060791

© 2025 Ted Reed. All rights reserved

No part of this book may be reproduced or transmitted in any form or by any means, electronic or mechanical, including photocopying or recording, or by any information storage and retrieval system, without permission in writing from the publisher.

Front cover images: Heads of the biggest unions of flight attendants, airline workers and pilots, Sara Nelson, John Samuelsen and Jason Ambrosi gathered at National Airport in Arlington, Virginia, in October 2023 (Micheal Theis). *Background*: © symbiot/Shutterstock.

Printed in the United States of America

McFarland & Company, Inc., Publishers
Box 611, Jefferson, North Carolina 28640
www.mcfarlandpub.com

For Camila, Luis and Mia.
I hope you read your grandpa's book someday.

Table of Contents

Preface — 1
Introduction — 7

1. A Newspaper Delivery Girl Makes News — 15
2. This Stewardess Likes to Stir Things Up — 21
3. This Union Has Always Punched Above Its Weight — 30
4. The World Discovers Sara Nelson — 37
5. Sara Saves the Airline Industry — 44
6. Sara Fights Goliath at Amazon — 53
7. She Wanted to Work for Hillary Clinton: Maybe She Did Better — 59
8. In 2024, Flight Attendants Unite, UAW Helps and Sara Looks Ahead — 66
9. Child of Brooklyn — 72
10. Rock Bottom at Rikers — 78
11. "The transit authority did not give a rat's ass" — 84
12. Mike Quill and the Strike Culture of TWU Local 100 — 92
13. Who If Anybody Won the 2005 New York Subway Strike? — 99
14. Battling New York's Organic Green Tea–Drinking, Neo-Liberal Hipsters — 105
15. Transit Union Brings Tough Tactics to the Airline Industry — 112
16. Jason Ambrosi Moves to the Left Seat — 118
17. How the Allied Pilots Association Made the World Safer — 123

18. How ALPA Fights for Airline Safety 130
19. U.S. Airways Leads the Parade to Bankruptcy 136
20. Saying No Is Easy; the Hardest Thing Is Getting to Yes 142
21. How Labor Enabled the American–U.S. Airways Merger 147
22. From a Freedom Flight to the Airline of the Stars 153
23. Sito Takes a Seat at the Table 160
24. "Going into a war zone, you're not giggling" 165
25. Flight Attendant Leader Treasures Her Dad's Union Pins 171
26. The Not So Strange Case of Laura Glading 178
27. Unions Big and Small Find Spots in the Airline Industry 183
28. Justice for Janitors Cleans Up at Airports 190

Chapter Notes 197
Bibliography 205
Index 207

Preface

When I became the airlines reporter for the *Miami Herald*, I was assigned to cover Eastern Airlines and Pan American World Airways. At both, nearly every group of employees was represented by a labor union, and I very quickly realized that covering the airline industry meant covering the unions. In fact, this conclusion was inescapable: At the time, in May 1989, the three largest unions at Eastern were on strike.

The Eastern strike was perhaps the best known and most significant labor action in airline industry history. In its aftermath, Eastern collapsed and airlines became far less willing to reach the point in contract talks where a strike could occur, knowing that such an event could lead to extinction. The three unions that struck Eastern were the Air Line Pilots Association (ALPA); the International Association of Machinists (IAM), which represented mechanics and fleet service workers; and the Transport Workers Union (TWU), which represented flight attendants.

I have covered these three unions, off and on, ever since; they all play key roles in this book.

After Eastern shut down in January 1991, I focused on Pan Am, which, in fact, would only fly until the end of the year. At Pan Am, I covered ALPA; an independent flight attendants' union; and the International Brotherhood of Teamsters (IBT), which represented many employee groups—including even the accountants.

When Pan Am shut down in December 1991, American Airlines, which had purchased Eastern's Latin American routes, became Miami's dominant carrier. At American, ground and maintenance workers were in the TWU, while pilots and flight attendants were represented by the Allied Pilots Association (APA) and the Association of Professional Flight Attendants (APFA), respectively. Thus, by 1991, I was familiar with all but one of the airline industry's leading unions.

1

I added the Association of Flight Attendants (AFA) when I moved to Charlotte in 1996 to cover U.S. Airways for the *Charlotte Observer*. It was a time when airlines were covered primarily by the newspaper reporters in their hubs. We all formed strong relationships with labor leaders. Sadly, the decline of the newspaper industry has resulted in diminished coverage of the labor movement, not only at airlines, but also in other unionized industries.

Labor unions are democracies that represent people. In this book, I provide a behind-the-scenes look at the union leaders who have led the key constituencies of the twenty-first-century airline industry. Each of these leaders started out at the bottom and worked their way up—first in their job and then in their union's hierarchy. To know them is to know their craft. Their stories are critical when it comes to understanding the role labor plays in shaping the airline industry and the broad swath of workers employed by it.

In this preface, I want to briefly describe my relationship with each major airline union; they and their leaders are the principal characters in this book. Like unions in other industries, they are generally known by their initials, so perhaps this preface can serve as a reference point for the alphabet soup of union names.

I will start with ALPA. It is the largest airline pilot union in the world and has long represented pilot interests. It has a national office, skilled in lobbying Congress and the airline-related federal agencies, such as the Federal Aviation Administration. However, I have often worked primarily with ALPA chapters at individual airlines. This began with the Eastern pilots, whose ALPA office was in Coral Gables, Florida. They were members of the bankruptcy committee, which regularly conducted closed telephone discussions. They would let me listen. This was probably illegal, but it was also 35 years ago. During negotiations with Eastern management, a pilot negotiator would take breaks to call me and update me in time for my deadlines. Today, when reporters quote sources, I like to think those sources are as close to the subject as this one was.

I also worked closely with the ALPA chapter for U.S. Airways pilots. In 2007, the U.S. Airways pilots broke away from ALPA to form their own union, the U.S. Airways Airline Pilot Association, based in Charlotte. It lasted six years. After a 2013 merger with American, U.S. Airways pilots became part of Allied Pilots Association. Once I became a national airlines reporter for *The Street* and *Forbes*, I covered APA at American and ALPA chapters at United and Delta and ALPA national.

Jason Ambrosi, ALPA's national president and a former Delta pilot, once told me that the MD-80 requires more manual involvement than Boeing planes. "Boeing builds airplanes. McDonnell Douglas builds character," he said in 2020. This is how reporters remember people—by their best quotes. Since he took over as national president in 2023, Ambrosi has already become one of ALPA's most accomplished leaders.

The TWU has long held my attention. As a child in New Jersey, I read New York newspapers and I decided early on to become a newspaper reporter. I envisioned covering Mike Quill, who led Local 100, which represented New York subway workers, and who was very quotable. Fifty years later, in 2017, John Samuelsen was elected TWU international president. By that time, the union's largest membership was at American Airlines. Samuelsen had started as a subway track inspector, worked his way up to president of Local 100, and then became international president. To me, he is the second iteration of Mike Quill, whom he considers a hero. In May 2019, at a memorable public meeting with Robert Isom, who later became American's CEO, Samuelsen said if TWU were ever to strike American, it would "engage in absolutely vicious strike action against American Airlines, to the likes of what you've never seen, not organized by airline people but organized by a guy that came out of the New York City subway system that's well inclined to strike power and who understands that the only way to challenge power is to aggressively take it to them."

The IAM led the Eastern strike. It struck the carrier after being locked out. Within days, the other unions followed. The leader of IAM Local 100, which had 10,000 members, was Charlie Bryan. Initially, he refused to talk with me, so I worked with his chief lieutenant. In 1996, five years after Eastern shut down, I wrote a story on Bryan and got to know him. I wrote his obituary for *Forbes* in 2013. It began: "The labor movement has produced its share of heroes, but it's hard to say whether Charlie Bryan was among them. Bryan was a leader of the most dramatic labor conflict in the history of the airline industry, but 24 years later it is impossible to say whether he won or lost." I tell people to be nice to me because someday I may write their obituary.

Later, I came to know Sito Pantoja, IAM's general vice president for transportation, and Joe Tiberi, his chief of staff. The transportation division had about 100,000 members. For a time, Pantoja was the top labor dealmaker in the airline industry. He was known as the person who could come in at the end of negotiations and close a deal. In 2020, working jointly with TWU leaders, Pantoja signed his greatest deal, worth $4.2 billion and covering about 30,000 mechanics and fleet service workers. Within weeks after the tentative agreement, the pandemic began. Union members moved quickly to ratify the contract. The following year, in a political dispute with IAM national leadership, Pantoja was ousted. Unfortunately, because I covered Pantoja so closely, I could not convince IAM's current leadership to talk with me for this book.

Pat Friend led AFA for 16 years. During her four terms as president, she was an early leader in the battle for equal rights for women in the workplace. She retired in 2010, and four years later, Sara Nelson took her place. Since then, I have covered Nelson closely. Even before she arrived, AFA punched above its weight, partially because it helped to lead the movement of women into the workforce. But Sara—she is known throughout the industry by her first name—has taken this small union to the top tier of the labor movement. Before becoming union president, she developed the skill of working with reporters in the courtroom where United Airlines' bankruptcy proceedings dragged on for three years. She often sat next to *Associated Press* reporter Dave Carpenter, who is a longtime friend of mine.

The Teamsters, also known as IBT, were the major union at Pan Am. They were led by another colorful New Yorker, Bill Genoese, one of the early labor organizers in the airline industry. In those days, Pan Am was the world's leading airline, occupying a landmark New York skyscraper. By the time I covered Pan Am, however, it was dying. Its competitors began to serve transatlantic routes from interior hubs like Atlanta and Dallas, but Pan Am was not permitted to expand its domestic system. Its last hope of survival evaporated in December 1991, when Delta walked away from a deal to finance Pan Am's emergence from bankruptcy. Early the next morning, a Delta spokesman called me to ask if Pan Am flights were operating. I called Miami IBT leader Joyce Hardy to find out. She said no. That was how it ended. It was said that Eastern died of cancer, while Pan Am died of a heart attack.

American CEO Bob Crandall came to Miami in 1989 to announce that he had acquired Eastern's Latin American routes, the first step in establishing the airline's Miami hub. I began to cover APA, the American pilots' union. The union's spokesman, Dave Bates, would occasionally come to the *Miami Herald* newsroom to chat. He later became APA president. When U.S. Airways wanted to acquire American in bankruptcy, it worked with American union leaders including Bates and Laura Glading, president of APFA. In 2007, Dennis Tajer became principal AFA spokesman. I have talked with him hundreds of times since then. One thing I want to make clear in this book is that because spokespeople like Tajer and Taylor Garland of AFA work so hard, their unions' views are included nearly every time a serious discussion of the airline industry occurs in the media.

I want to thank all the people I have mentioned here and a few others. The ALPA spokeswoman Corey Kuhn and IBT spokeswoman Kara Deniz helped me arrange interviews. Alan Saly, chief of publications for TWU Local 100, worked closely with me on photos. Gary Mitchem, senior editor at McFarland, has helped me on all four of my books, particularly this one. My editor is Audrey Williams June, a longtime friend from the *Charlotte Observer* who is now a senior reporter for the *Chronicle of Higher Education*. Audrey also introduced me to Michael Theis, a Washington, D.C., photographer. We spent a morning taking photos at the old terminal at National Airport in October 2023.

In this book, I have attempted to make clear that part of a union leader's job is to engage with reporters. I have always felt that if you position yourself as someone who leads thousands of people, you ought to be capable of taking a few minutes to answer a couple of questions from a reporter.

Introduction

Labor unions help workers. The advantages of labor unions are particularly evident in the airline industry, one of the most heavily unionized industries in the United States. At three of the four largest airlines—American Airlines, Southwest and United—between 80 percent and 85 percent of the workforce is unionized. This compares to a rate of about 11 percent in the rest of the country. At Delta, the fourth of the big four carriers. only pilots and dispatchers are unionized. To maintain its non-union status in the face of recurrent organizing drives by various airline unions, Delta pays as well as or better than competitors.

Some statistics from the industry trade group, Airlines for America, make the benefits of union representation clear. The A4A, as the group is known, sometimes works with the unions in coalitions of convenience. At other times, it battles them. In any case, according to A4A, the industry had about 750,000 employees in 2023. Their average salary in 2021 was $102,100 annually, 38 percent higher than the $74,000 earned by the average private sector employee.[1] Additionally, union membership often brings benefits such as better health care and a grievance procedure where disagreements can be addressed by equal parties, rather than by management acting alone. Beyond salary and benefits, unionized airline employees typically have a say in their scheduling, an essential component to their quality of life. However, airlines' 24-hours-a-day, seven-days-a-week operations mean that workers who have low seniority will likely have to work during holidays when most people just want to be at home with their families.

Perhaps the most impressive recent display of the advantage of union membership came when the airlines and their unions worked together to secure $60 billion in payroll support from Congress during the pandemic. The assurance of regular paychecks from employers provided a lifeline during a period of intense uncertainty. In seeking support from Congress for the funding, A4A and labor worked together. Their most essential partner was AFA President Sara Nelson. At one crucial moment in the spring of 2020, when the industry was faltering in the early days of the pandemic, American Airlines CEO Doug Parker told his fellow CEOs they were not going to get the Congressional help they needed if they did not work with Nelson and the unions.

At the time, Nelson—president of a relatively small union of 50,000 members, most of whom were women—was perhaps the country's most prominent labor leader. By 2023, the labor movement was reasserting its importance, and Teamster President Sean O'Brien and United Auto Workers President Shawn Fain had also ascended in national prominence. But in 2020, Nelson was better known than either. Additionally, she had a presence in Washington, D.C., the home of two major unions that are composed entirely of airline employees: AFA and ALPA. While then–ALPA President Joe DePete, a former FedEx pilot, was also heavily engaged in lobbying Congress, it was Nelson who led.

For ALPA, it wasn't until January 2023 that Jason Ambrosi ascended from Delta ALPA president to national ALPA president, giving the union a prominent and recognizable leader who has worked to become well-known in Washington.

Nelson, a United Airlines flight attendant since 1996, often dresses in a United flight attendant uniform. She has long been willing to do the hard work of a union leader, which includes traveling constantly to labor events, engaging regularly with Congress and other labor leaders, and being available whenever reporters call. Ask Nelson to appear on your 10 p.m. cable news TV program or your Sunday morning program or your evening network news program, and she is likely to say yes. Ask for an interview for your newspaper story or your blog, and she is likely to say yes to that as well. Or ask for an off-the-record explanation of some airline industry practice, and she will explain that, because she is steeped in the passenger airline industry.

As a result, no one else from the airline industry has been so ubiquitous in industry coverage. Of course, it helps that Nelson is attractive and articulate and understands the value of media interaction. Long well-known within the industry, she emerged as a national presence in 2019, when her call for a national strike overwhelmed social media and galvanized opposition to a 35-day government shutdown. It is probably beside the point that United Airlines flight attendants, the primary component of AFA, might have been unable to participate in a strike, given

Introduction 9

United Airlines flight attendant Sara Nelson led the airline industry out of the pandemic (Michael Theis).

the constraints of their contract. What mattered is what happened: Nelson, largely enabled by some audacious air traffic controllers who called in sick, seized control of the moment. "Few people had a better shutdown than Ms. Nelson," Lane Windham, a labor historian at Georgetown University, told *The New York Times*. "How many moments have there been when labor leaders have taken over social media in that way?"[2]

The prominence she gained in 2019 put Nelson in a good position to try to save the airline industry in 2020. "There are many people who played important roles in the process," Parker said later. "But there is one leader who deserves more credit than anyone else—Sara Nelson, the president of the Association of Flight Attendants."[3] The $60 billion came in three tranches: the first was $34 billion, part of the $2.2 trillion Cares Act, which was approved by Congress in March 2020. At the time, the U.S. economy had largely collapsed, the airline industry had totally collapsed, and fear gripped the world. Yet, only the airline industry was singled out by Congress for payroll protection for its workers.

Said Nelson, "We were the only ones putting forward a plan that put workers first. It showed that when we set the agenda and use our power, we can make the corporate elite come in our direction, rather than allowing them to determine the world's economic fate. We were the only industry not to have an increase in inequality during the pandemic. In every other industry, workers and executives grew further apart in average pay. That's because unions are the best countervailing force against the greed of capitalism. Capitalism is about profits and unions are about people. In a democracy, you can form unions and can fight against the worst forces of unchecked capitalism in order to make a more fair society."[4]

(From left) Sara Nelson, John Samuelsen and Jason Ambrosi gathered at National Airport in Arlington, Virginia, in October 2023 (Michael Theis).

Besides being heavily unionized, the airline industry has some other unusual characteristics. For one, it is particularly insular, populated largely by people who are in love with it. At every airline, internal newsletters regularly include stories about pilots or flight attendants who have worked flights with their children acting in the same capacity. Stories about people who hold different types of airline jobs getting married—such as a flight attendant and a fleet service worker or a flight attendant and a pilot—are also common. The stories of the occasional conflicts between pilots and gate agents are generally untold. Individual airlines take on vast personal importance to their employees, as well as to their passengers. For some passengers, the carriers are a component of their self-identity, embodying the freedom to travel; to visit loved ones; to explore new worlds and to go home. The personal importance of travel gives airlines outsized importance in the world.

U.S. airlines carried 931 million passengers in the peak year of 2019. A year later, due to the pandemic, the number fell by 60 percent to 372 million, the lowest since 1984. Traffic has rebounded since 2020, reaching 858 million in 2023.[5] These travelers have broad access to airline industry information. Performance statistics, videos on social media, and blogs devoted to the particulars of airline credit cards and frequent flier programs are all easy to find. Additionally, many celebrities discern that there is intense interest in where they are seated on an aircraft and in whether flight attendants fail to cater to them. Meanwhile, social deviance on aircraft is widely tracked by social media as well as traditional commercial media. Stories, tweets and videos focus on industry failures such as stranded passengers, cancelled flights, occasional safety failures and regular instances of passengers abusing flight attendants and gate agents. Also, airline performance is widely tracked by websites, regulatory agencies and airport monitors. If your doctor is late to see you, only you know, but if your flight departs late, the whole world knows.

Opinions about air travel are never in short supply. An adage, sometimes attributed to former American Airlines CEO Robert Crandall, maintains that extremely large numbers of people consider themselves to be experts on how to run baseball teams, restaurants, and airlines. This level of pseudo-expertise increased markedly as airlines became enmeshed in the culture wars that stemmed from flight attendants being put in the uncomfortable position of enforcing mask mandates between June 2020 and April 2022. Nelson viewed the battle over masks as one that "lifted the profile of flight attendants at a critical time. What we were experiencing was what every worker on the front line—postal workers, grocery workers, retail workers—was experiencing, but we had a plane full of witnesses. Overwhelmingly, the public supported us. The disrespect from bad actors was horrific and unbelievable, but 99% of people showed us more respect, and flight attendants tell me all the time that our union is so out there in the public view, and that allowed us a platform to do something about it. We were in the mix, fighting for people."[6]

As corporate entities, airlines engage with the media at a relatively high level. Most have active, accessible communications staffs, issue frequent public statements, conduct quarterly earnings calls, participate in investor conferences, which are webcast, and maintain a presence on social media. Years ago, a friend who had worked in corporate communications at Pan American World Airways moved to a hotel chain. She told me that at Pan Am, she had answered calls all day. At the hotel chain, she told me, she begged for coverage.

Despite its high visibility, the U.S. airline industry is relatively small. Its biggest companies—Delta, United, American and Southwest—generated total 2023 revenue of $188 billion, less than a third of Walmart's fiscal 2023 revenue of $611 billion. Not only are airline revenues comparatively small, but also the airline industry has historically been unprofitable. From 1979, the first full year that the industry was deregulated, to 2022, the industry lost about $11 billion, according to A4A figures.

Airlines compose a classic boom or bust industry. From 1990 through 1994, a period that included bankruptcies by Eastern and Pan Am, the industry's loss was about $11 billion. Airlines made about $21 billion from 1995 through 2000, then lost $60 billion, including paper losses associated with multiple bankruptcies. From 2001 through 2005, every major carrier except for Southwest sought bankruptcy protection. The profitable years of 2006 and 2007 produced $23 billion, followed by recession-related losses of $27 billion in 2008 and 2009. Then the industry was up again, with 10 consecutive profitable years from 2010 through 2019, producing $103 billion.[7] "I don't think we're ever going to lose money again. We have an industry that's going to be profitable in good and bad times," American's Parker declared in 2017, at a Dallas meeting of analysts and reporters.[8]

Parker, of course, did not anticipate the pandemic. The industry lost $35 billion in 2020 and $3 billion in 2021, before returning to a $1.6 billion profit in 2022. The pandemic's day-to-day impact was tracked most prominently by the Transportation Security Administration, which each morning posted the number of people (including airline crew members) who cleared security the previous day. The practice began in March

(From left) John Samuelsen, Jason Ambrosi and Sara Nelson head the biggest unions of flight attendants, airline workers and pilots (Michael Theis).

2020, soon after the coronavirus began to affect travel. On April 13, 2020, the number shrank to 87,534, which turned out to be its pandemic low. What struck TSA spokeswoman Lisa Farbstein at the time was that "on an average weekday prior to the pandemic, airports like JFK or LAX would see volume of 100,000 by themselves, and nationwide you had less than what one airport would do—that was quite eye-opening."[9] The last time the entire U.S. averaged fewer than 100,000 passengers a day was in 1954, A4A said at the time.

Travel suddenly started to pick up in March 2022, a month when Bank of America analyst Andrew Didora wrote in a report that "leisure demand is 'insatiable.'"[10] Subsequently, the summers of 2022 and 2023 became periods known for "revenge travel," when passengers sought to reclaim the travel experiences they had been deprived of in 2020 and 2021 because of the pandemic. On Friday, June 11, 2021, the TSA screened 2,028,961 people, marking the first time more than two million were screened since March 2020. Sadly, the industry was not well prepared for them. Although the payroll support program succeeded in keeping the industry marginally intact, the sudden recovery drew attention to a misjudgment: Some airlines used a portion of the money to pay for lump sum retirements, contributing to understaffing when travel returned. Throughout the summer of 2022, airlines never seemed to catch up with the demand, having retired hundreds of airplanes and thousands of employees. In the summer of 2023, travel—especially international travel—continued to grow. On Friday, June 30, 2023, the TSA screened 2.9 million people, the highest number through checkpoints in its history. Yet, the industry still had too few pilots to serve all the markets that existed before the pandemic and too few air traffic controllers to adequately staff airports, particularly in New York and Florida.

A phenomenon occurred as the airline industry recovered. Most of its contracts with its unions had become "amendable," a term reserved for contracts negotiated under the Railway Labor Act that don't have expiration dates, but are instead up for renegotiation after a set time. The act, a federal law enacted in 1926 to govern relations between railroads and their unions, was amended in 1936 to include air carriers. It generally enables employees in the two essential transportation modes to unionize, but also makes it difficult for them to strike, setting up a long process that can include extensive mediation before either side can engage in "self-help" in the form of a lockout or a strike. Under certain circumstances, the National Mediation Board can even ask the president to establish an emergency board to recommend settlement terms. During the pandemic, various sets of contract talks—particularly talks with pilots' unions—were delayed as the carriers struggled with the mountain of problems they were encountering. Meanwhile, as demand suddenly contracted and then suddenly expanded, the industry found itself short-staffed in nearly every category, increasing union leverage as contract talks restarted.

1

A Newspaper Delivery Girl Makes News

As a child, Sara Nelson delivered newspapers—*The Corvallis Gazette-Times* to be exact. I say this not because having a paper route was unusual for a child growing up in a medium-sized Oregon city in the 1980s, when widely-circulated newspapers still bonded communities—or because it establishes any particular relationship between Nelson and newspapers—although she is skilled at forming positive relationships with reporters. Rather, Nelson has been written about so often that this seems a noteworthy detail to highlight, because it represents an episode in her life that has not been written about elsewhere.

Nelson was born in Corvallis, Oregon, on March 11, 1973. Subsequently, her parents had two boys: Scott, who is two years younger than Sara, and Andy, who is five and a half years younger. Her late father, Don, was a millworker who later went into lumber sales, while her mother, Carol, worked as a music teacher in the public schools. Sara recalls a bucolic childhood, growing up in an Oregon city that hosts a major university and is often described as extremely livable. Her home on Dixon Street was a block from her grade school, and roughly equidistant from her middle school and high school. She started her paper route while in the seventh grade. "When I got enough seniority for the route with my house on it, I could roll out of bed and walk the paper route, basically around my block, in my pajamas," she recalled. "I had to deliver it no later than 7 a.m. Half the time it was raining, so I had to poly bag everything before I could go out. A lot of the time I would go back to bed afterwards, then get up and ride my bike three blocks down the street, park at a neighbor's house, and run across the creek bridge to school."[1]

Some mornings, she had to be at school early for jazz choir. She also played tennis and ran cross country and track, although she declined when the cheerleading squad sought to recruit her. "I wanted to watch the games," she said. "Cheerleaders don't get to watch the games." Sara was a big fan of high school and Oregon State sports, and she fondly remembers early 1980s Beaver basketball stars AC Green, "my first hero" and Charlie Sitton, as well as coach Ralph Miller. She saw Beavers basketball games because her family shared season tickets with another family from church. "My two brothers and I would rotate going with mom and dad," she said.[2]

Sara's parents instilled a social conscience in their only daughter, who especially remembers two incidents involving her mother. "My mom was very direct, she taught me through her actions," she said. Once, when Sara was in the first grade, she and her mother went to Richeys' Market, a neighborhood grocery store that, when it closed in 2010, was described by the *Gazette-Times* as "the last mom and pop."[3] Outside the store were mechanical ponies for children to ride.

"I was standing there, looking at the ponies and looking at my mom, thinking I'm not going to get on one this time because she's not going to spend money on that, when this girl from my class walked past me.

Sara Nelson grew up in Corvallis, Oregon, with two brothers, Scott (left) and Andy (courtesy Sara Nelson).

This girl was not someone who was popular in school. Looking back, you would say today that she was bullied. My mom saw the girl and said hello, but I didn't say anything. Then the girl went into the store and my mom pulled me over by my arm and said in an angry whisper, 'What was that?' I said, 'None of the kids say hi to Cheryl.' And my mom said, 'Not my daughter. You don't ever treat someone like that.' My mom didn't get stern very often, but when she did, she was very direct, and I remembered it and I remember thinking then that I'm never messing with this woman."[4]

A second incident involved the high school prom at Corvallis High School, which had 218 seniors in the graduating class of 1991. Sara went with the son of her mother's friend, a single mother of modest means who lived on a farm. "My mom knew that he didn't have a lot of money to go to a restaurant for dinner, so she dressed up as a conservative French maid and served us dinner overlooking the backyard garden," she said. "It wasn't romantic; we were family friends. She wanted us to have a good time, she didn't want him to feel any financial pressure, and she took ownership of it."[5]

Carol was a third-generation Christian Scientist. She raised her daughter as a church member, even though Sara is not practicing today. Nevertheless, "You can't take the Christian Scientist out of the girl," her daughter said. "Even though I do not go to church regularly, it still shapes the way I approach life. The biggest example is that in Christian Science, I was taught to believe that your being is godlike, that God is perfect and that humankind is perfect too, in God's image. That means any problem is an illusion and it is solvable. I think knowing that allows me to pivot a lot faster in strategic planning."[6]

Additionally, religion was an early influencer shaping Sara's thoughts about gender. She learned through Christian Science that "There's a full array of different qualities of God. There are male and female qualities, but those are not defined by your body. Seeking to express God means expressing all of the qualities of God. Marriage is a metaphor for this because marriage brings male and female qualities together. That is an expression of God. There is no differentiation that says one quality is more important than the other."[7]

In life, Sara has encountered the perception that men and women should be treated differently, but that is not what her religion taught her. "Take your pick; there is a broad range of ways in which women are treated horribly," she said. "But I wasn't aware that there was any notion that men and women aren't equal. I had to learn that existed." Sara acknowledges that she ignored an early indicator. When she was in the fourth grade, a teacher asked what each child wanted to become, and she said, "President of the United States." the teacher responded, "You want to be the first woman president of the United States." Looking back, Sara says, "I can see now that it was a sexist comment. In my fourth grade mind, I just wanted to be president. I didn't have to be the first. Now I wonder, in retrospect, 'Why did she want to make it hard for me?'"[8]

Don Nelson grew up in Los Angeles. "He drank and smoked, but that changed after he met my mom," Sara said. Don was drafted into the Army and was expecting to go to Vietnam after basic training. But he somehow ended up being shipped to Alaska, where the Army was preparing for a northern invasion by the Russians. "He drew a lottery ticket on that," his daughter said. "He ended up having the thrill of his life, training for biathlon,"[9] a winter sport that combines cross-country skiing and rifle shooting. Later, the training inspired Don to earn a master's degree in physical education, as he hoped to become a high school physical education teacher. But while he was studying, Oregon reduced funding for public schools, the number of jobs diminished, and lumber sales beckoned. Don died in June 2004.

Growing up in Oregon, Sara was well aware of the state's liberal traditions. The counterculture of the late 1960s flourished on the West Coast and seemed alive for high school students in the late 1980s. "Marijuana was pretty ubiquitous in Oregon, although I was hardly what you would consider a stoner," she said. "When I look back on it, I think of myself as a hippie chick, but that was more about being a free spirit than about being a serious hippie. I was exposed to a lot of the spirit that came from the hippies and the anti-war movement and I went to coffee shops to do my homework. Oregon had hundreds of independent coffee shops way before Starbucks became a thing. One exciting moment for me in the 1990s was when my mom took me to the Esprit factory in San Francisco. It all seemed pretty chic to me."[10]

At the time, Esprit was a youth clothing brand marketed with a message of liberal harmony. When it came time to go to college, Sara selected Principia College, a small, private liberal arts college with a Christian Science affiliation in Elsah, Illinois, a village about 40 miles north of St. Louis. That meant she eschewed the in-state schools where dozens of her classmates went. "I grew up going to Beaver games, and at my high school we all thought of Oregon State or even University of Oregon as a continuation of high school. But I was pretty sure I didn't want to stay at home," Sara said. "I wanted to explore."[11]

When the Principia College theater program presented *The Sound of Music,* **Sara played Maria (courtesy Sara Nelson).**

Sara thought about becoming a teacher, but she did not want to do the same thing her mother did. The college's theater program soon attracted her interest. The theater professor was Richard Morse, the brother of movie director Robert Morse. "Theater was a natural for me," she said. "I liked getting up in front of people; I never had a hard time with that. People think that theater means playing a part, but that's not what my theater training was. My training was in telling the truth. We would do improvisation skits, where you would come on stage and you had to have a story with urgency behind it. You had to convey why you were there. I learned a lot about communicating. I remember my theater director saying, 'Why are you on the stage?' and another student not having an answer, and he said, 'If you don't know why you are there, get off. Come back when you have something to say, something that matters.'"[12]

She graduated from Principia in 1995. Although early on she dreamed of an acting career, her studies quickly reverted to teaching high school English, with some Shakespeare. But in order to make ends meet and start paying off her student debt, she worked four jobs: substitute teacher, waitress, linen salesperson and temp worker at an insurance agency. She planned to teach school in the fall, but what happened next is among the best-known parts of her story. A friend who had joined United Airlines as a flight attendant called one day from Miami, where she was on layover at the beach. The friend had majored in physics, yet had chosen a career as a flight attendant. The union job provided flexible schedule, health care, a pension, a higher salary than teaching, and the option to take early retirement at 50. "Our moms were around 50," Sara said. "I thought I could do that until I'm 50 and then I could go do something else." Moreover, she said, "I was miserable in St. Louis and I was dog-tired and my friend was razzing me about how she was living it up. She said she was in a bikini and she had her toes in the sand."[13]

Sara was convinced. The next day, she drove to Chicago for a United recruitment open house. She was asked to return for a second interview. At the time, United required that flight attendants speak a second language; Sara had studied German in high school and college. For some reason, she was able to have her second language interview over the phone, rather than in person, and she passed. Then she flew back to Chicago for a physical. Flight attendants had to be at least 5'2". She was 5'4" and weighed about 120 pounds. "I thought I was fat," Sara said.[14]

2

This Stewardess Likes to Stir Things Up

In October 1996, at the age of 23, Sara Nelson reported to work as a United flight attendant in Boston, after completing a six-week training class. Flight attendants had yet to shake the term "stewardess," although the union made the name change official in the late 1970s. They were still required to wear two-inch heels, makeup and nail polish. Such restrictions would soon disappear, largely due to the influence of the Association of Flight Attendants, the union Nelson would eventually lead. But to start, Nelson was a rulebound Boston-based United flight attendant, living in an apartment two stops from the airport with seven other flight attendants.

Like many beginners, she started out working reserve, which is to say that she was essentially on call during her working time. After a few months, she acquired enough seniority to bid for trips and to put together her schedule one month out. This enabled layovers in cities with beaches or mountains, as well as in small Midwest towns. Like many flight attendants, Nelson appreciated the contrast to jobs with redundant schedules and constant oversight. During her time in Boston, Nelson—totally independent for the first time—married another Boston-based flight attendant. Her marriage to Rico Dela Cruz took place in October 1998. It didn't last. The couple separated in January 2001 and divorced in 2004, but remain friends. Nelson said in 2022 that she still visited his mother and texted with his sisters.

At first, Nelson didn't know much about labor unions. She learned about them early in her Boston career, when her paycheck didn't arrive as scheduled, leaving her near penniless. But a more senior flight attendant and union member offered to loan her $800 and advised her to call the union, which helped her to get paid immediately. Nelson took notice. She became part of a group of AFA members, mostly women, who felt kinship with one another. She began to attend meetings of the Boston domicile, which had about 300 members. Just before she arrived, AFA had voted down a tentative agreement. "I recognized right away that people didn't know what was happening in bargaining," Nelson said. "I wanted to know and to share what I knew."[1]

She became involved in internal communications. Jeff Zack, AFA's national communications director, saw Nelson's communication skills and began to turn to her for newspaper and TV interviews. "He recognized that I was good at this, so when local media needed a comment from a flight attendant, they would come to me," Nelson recalled. "At first, I really didn't know what I was doing."[2] An early battle came in the late 1990s, when United inaugurated a nonstop Boston/London flight, staffed entirely with London-based flight attendants. The Boston local fought for and won the right to staff some of the flights. Why would United insist the flight be staffed in London? "Hotels were cheaper in Boston than in London," Nelson said.[3]

The September 11, 2001, terrorist attacks had a particular impact on United's Boston base. United Flight 175, a Boeing 767, departed that morning from Boston Logan International Airport, headed for Los Angeles. It crashed into the South Tower of the World Trade Center. The second of four flights to crash that day, it carried 56 people, including five hijackers and nine Boston-based crew members. "It was a small, tight base," Nelson

Sara Nelson started out in 1996 as a United Airlines flight attendant based in Boston (courtesy Sara Nelson).

said. "Everyone knew and loved everyone. We would vacation together." The passengers include two Boston-based customer service agents who were Nelson's friends. As she named them during a phone interview, her voice choked. "We were very tight," she said.[4]

On September 10, the day before the attacks, Nelson was on the West Coast with a friend. She boarded a red-eye to Chicago, where the union had scheduled a training session. She planned to sleep on the plane because, she said, "I could save a hotel night for the union. It was an empty flight, so I found a spot where I could stretch out across five seats in the middle. I got a strange feeling, right before we took off. Something didn't feel right, so I got on my hands and knees to see if there was something under the seats. Then I thought, 'You're being an idiot, just go to sleep.' I've never really told anyone about that."[5]

The flight arrived at Chicago O'Hare International Airport early on September 11. Nelson had a few hours before the training session, so she headed for the gym at the airport Hilton, where she had purchased a gym membership. She had frequent layovers in Chicago and she knew she could sleep on the gym's massage table. That morning, a gym staff member woke her and told her that a plane had crashed into the World Trade Center. It was American Flight 11, which had departed Boston for Los Angeles and crashed into the North Tower at 8:46 a.m. Nelson walked over to the TV. At 9:03 a.m., United Flight 175, which had also departed Boston for Los Angeles, crashed into the South Tower. Said Nelson, "I stood in the Hilton and watched the next plane hit. Although I didn't know it at the time, that was my friends. Then I stared at the TV. I said, 'I gotta go.' I went to the office. We set up a crisis center, we got printouts of all of the flights in the air or already diverted, and tried to figure out what was going on. The next day, there were no flights, so I drove back to Boston with another flight attendant and customer service agent."[6]

The terrorist attacks intensified an economic slowdown that shattered the airline industry. By the end of 2002, United had sought bankruptcy protection. Earlier in the year, Nelson was elected to be communications chair for the United chapter AFA chapter. It was a key role, made all the more important by the bankruptcy, which brought reporters, United employees, United executives, and United attorneys together in a courtroom on a regular basis. United sat in Chapter 11 for 38 months, until February 2006, as CEO Glenn Tilton took longer than any previous airline CEO to present a plan of reorganization. In the bankruptcy, United's unions were asked to make substantial wage and benefit concessions. They were obliged to speak out and fight to save decades of bargaining gains worth billions of dollars.

The bankruptcy marked an intense period for Nelson, both personally and professionally. Working around the clock in the union's Chicago-based field office, Nelson commuted regularly from Boston. She spent most days in the bankruptcy courtroom, in union strategy sessions, and handling all internal communications with members and external communications with the media and public. In 2003, she recalled, she spent just 12 nights in Boston. Then, in June 2004, her father died, and she moved home to Corvallis to be with her mother, commuting from there to Chicago.

A night in March 2005—when Nelson reconnected with David Borer, a former attorney for the AFA—marked a personal turning point. She and Borer had first met at a local council meeting in Denver in 1997. "We had a respectful working relationship; we never talked about anything personal during all that time. But in 2004, both of our fathers died, right in the middle of the United bankruptcy, and when we came back from funerals or memorials, time with our families, it opened the door to more personal conversations. It took another year before our first date. At the time, we didn't admit it was a date. We were working at our union office in Rosemont, near O'Hare. I usually worked until ten or midnight; he always took off a little earlier. But one night, when I thought I was the last person walking out of the office, I saw a light on in his office and I said, 'David, you're still here!' and he said, 'Yeah,' and then he said, 'Do you want to get a bite to eat?' and I thought

Sara Nelson is pictured at an AFA meeting shortly after the September 11, 2001, terrorist attacks (courtesy Sara Nelson).

'This is different.' We went to Pine Grove Restaurant, down the street from O'Hare, and we had ham and cheese omelets at midnight."⁷

The couple married in 2006 and had a son, Jack, in September 2009. In 2010, after Nelson was elected AFA international vice president, Borer became general counsel for the American Federation of Government Employees, which represents 600,000 federal and Washington, D.C., government employees. In 2024, Jack was attending middle school in Bethesda and was described by his mother as "extremely smart, creative and artistic," someone who "could go into arts or design or become a tech developer, although he's always said he wants to be a marine biologist, bringing together his love of animals and the water."⁸

Nelson's AFA responsibilities continued to increase. After Zack left his post at AFA in 2004, Nelson took over the task of devising media strategy for United flight attendants without the benefit of having a mentor by her side. "That's when I really got my training," she said. "There was so much going on. I was really involved, all the time. Jeff said 'You just need to take the lead on this.' Today, most of our media interface is done from the DC office, but it wasn't then. We had our attorneys in Chicago. Everything was happening right there. I was working round the clock."⁹

Tilton, a longtime oil executive who oversaw the 2001 merger of Texaco with Chevron Oil, was brought to United to turn it around. He had a typical corporate persona, but Nelson said Rosemary Moore, the corporate communications person who came from Texaco to United, "was good at dressing him up, having him roll up his sleeves."¹⁰ Among the reporters who covered Tilton and United was Dave Carpenter, an Associated Press veteran. Carpenter had been the AP's Moscow correspondent for four years and East Europe news editor for two. He thought Tilton and Moore were aggressive in their efforts to manage media coverage.

"Tilton was sharp, but was a bit of a fish out of water in the airline industry as an oilman brought in to rescue a troubled company," Carpenter said. "I found him a bit overly cagey. He invited reporters to meet with him, but everything he said was required in advance to be off the record. I wouldn't agree to such terms and I did not attend. I didn't want to be tied to United as a sort of insider who couldn't write what I learned." When United corporate communications didn't like a story, someone would call AP to complain. "They would call to complain about my lede if they thought it didn't portray United in the proper light, especially if it related to criticism by one of their unions," Carpenter said.¹¹

In the courtroom, Nelson often sat next to Carpenter. "I talked to him all the time," she said. "I wanted to know him because he was respected, he was a good reporter. I remember he said he wasn't too happy sitting in a courtroom every day and covering a bankruptcy hearing."[12] Carpenter had covered Boris Yeltsin in Moscow and he had covered wars and now he sat for days on end. He could see that Nelson communicated well.

"She stood out for her savvy, inquisitiveness and willingness to engage honestly with reporters," he said. "Probably just being a good, friendly person who wasn't fearful or distrustful of the media helped her cause. Obviously, she had something to gain by getting her union's side across to the public. But she was not afraid of the media and didn't try to spin the facts. No union spokesperson that I dealt with—or company spokesperson, for that matter—was more responsive to questions or better at articulating their side's cause than Sara. She was so good at that, and so available, that I think we all had to be careful not to give the flight attendants more than their fair share of coverage."[13]

Carpenter wasn't the only person who came to know Nelson during the bankruptcy. Another was Craig Symons, a United dispatcher who at the time was a shift representative for his union, the Professional Airline Flight Control Association. (Symons would later become union president.) The two were part of the union coalition that met regularly to determine joint strategies. Nelson was selected to be communications chair. "She was young and I was young," Symons said. "It was easy to see that she had a commitment to unions, she commanded respect, she was competent and she didn't step on toes. She was animated and active. Even then, she had a personality that took command of the party."[14]

At times, the interactions with Tilton brought out the theater major in Nelson. One day, in 2003, Tilton presided over a meeting of United employees at the O'Hare Hilton to introduce what was then termed Project Starfish, a low-cost, low-fare airline within United. At the time, the concept was popular within the industry. United's unions were opposed. "We were in a huge ball room at the Hilton, all lit up," Nelson said. "They wanted to sell this thing to the pilots, and a lot of pilots were there in uniform. I found out about it about a half hour before it began, so I grabbed our vice chair and we went to the hotel and we walked in, through a sea of pilots. I headed for the front row, I always sat in front. During the presentation, I was making faces and mouthing my opposition: I knew it was a bad idea. A lot of United execs were there. They could see me because I was in front. So could Tilton, and he was getting annoyed. He had his sleeves rolled up and he was going for it.

Nancy Pelosi (third from left, in front), Peter DeFazio (in light suit) and Sara Nelson (right) remember the September 11, 2002, attacks in a 2019 Capitol memorial (courtesy AFA).

When it came time for questions, they had someone in the audience with a mic. Someone said 'Don't give it to her,' but I got hold of it and I gave a long, blistering speech on why it wouldn't work. I said it would cannibalize our operation, undercut our jobs, and be bad for passengers. The pilots were all cheering. After a while, Rosemary Moore cut me off. But we killed it. We got the creditors to vote it down."[15]

The victory meant United had to run the new brand, called "Ted," under the existing union contracts, rather than with a lower tier, Even so, United moved forward. Ted started flying in February 2004 and lasted until January 2009. "We called it 'CheaTed' as we fought to save retiree healthcare,'" Nelson said. Five years turned out to be a long time in the captive airline business. Earlier, U.S. Airways had tried MetroJet operated from 1998 until 2001. Delta introduced Song on April 15, 2003. It shut down in May 2006.

The Starfish showdown wasn't the only time Nelson and Tilton engaged in face-to-face conflict. During the bankruptcy, United management developed a plan to terminate retiree health care. One day in 2004, Nelson went to United headquarters in Elk Grove Village, along with about a half dozen retirees who were being forced to retire. As it happened, the fire alarm went off—that was due to an act of God, Nelson said—and the building largely emptied out. But Tilton remained in his office. Nelson and her companions climbed the stairs—the building only had a few floors—and entered the office.

"We had him cornered," she said. "This gave us almost an hour alone with Tilton. He had to listen to the retirees and hear what this would mean for their lives. After decades of service to United, they had to retire early to preserve their health care. He tried to explain it. Retirees asked him how he slept at night. As other management came to his rescue and ushered us out, I turned on my heels and looked him in the eye—he was a short man—and he said, 'You know, Sara, I get e-mails from people who say I'm doing the right thing.' And I said, 'Of course Glen, but you're taking what you want to hear because you run a dictatorship. I run a democracy, and the vast majority are with me. And democracy is more powerful than dictatorship, and we're not going to let you end retiree health care.'"[16] After the incident, retiree health care remained in place and United enhanced the security at Tilton's office.

Nelson won't deny it; she likes to stir the pot. She recalls another employee meeting in 2005. This one was to discuss proposed cutbacks in employee pensions. Again, most high-ranking United executives were in attendance. Again, Tilton had his sleeves rolled up; he made a presentation, with a chart on a board behind him. Again, Nelson sat in the front row. The expectation, clearly anticipated by management, was that Nelson would raise questions about pension reductions. But she knew then, and now, that the best questions are surprise questions. "He was ready to shoot me down on pensions," she said, of Tilton. "But I said, 'What I would like to talk about today is our meteorologists. You talk about relationships; the thing that I am most proud of, when I walk through our world headquarters, is that United has its own meteorologists. We have respect and meaningful relationships because of this all over the world. The FAA counts on us and that comes in handy for the airline when we need them. Why are you firing the meteorologists?"[17]

3

This Union Has Always Punched Above Its Weight

The AFA is a small union, but doesn't act like it. Founded by United flight attendants in 1945, it has long been in the vanguard of the women's movement, battling restrictions—many regarding women's appearance and clothing—that seemed increasingly senseless as women moved into the civilian workforce in the years following World War II. Early on, airlines had age limits for "stewardesses," prohibited them from working if they were married or pregnant, and governed the minutiae of their appearance. Beyond navigating those restrictions, flight attendants also had to deal with incidents of sexist treatment, which have historically been legion.

Most notably, they were regularly touched inappropriately by male passengers. Nelson herself has multiple stories. Once, around 1998, during a redeye transcontinental flight, she said, "I woke up in the window seat when a man was fondling my breast. He was drunk. I was entirely on my own to work it out. No one took this stuff seriously and the message across the industry was that we were just supposed to take it." In another incident in her early days, a male passenger approached her from behind, ran his hand down her hip and asked, "What, no girdle?" Said Nelson, "Passengers regularly tapped us on the rear end to get our attention. They thought we were there to serve them and they acted as though they had every right to touch us where they wanted to."[1]

Nelson had not grown up in a sexualized environment and did not, at first, feel confident in her ability to respond. Today, sexual harassment still occurs, but the frequency has diminished, partially because the union pushed management to denounce sexist past practices, lift up flight attendants as safety professionals, and communicate a zero tolerance at the airlines for sexual harassment and assault. "There is so much

3. This Union Has Always Punched Above Its Weight   31

more focus on it now," Nelson said. "Now, thanks to the me-too movement, there is the narrative in society that this is not acceptable, and flight attendants know that if they report incidents, they are more likely to be taken seriously." In 2018, she said, she asked United CEO Oscar Munoz to set a zero tolerance policy for bullying and sexual harassment and sexual assault. "He responded immediately," she said. "He set a different tone."[2] Efforts continue to secure similar policies at other airlines.

Before Nelson, the most prominent AFA leader was Pat Friend. Born in 1946 in Benton Harbor, Michigan, Friend grew up outside Tulsa, Oklahoma, the daughter of a career Army officer. After two years of college, she decided to become a flight attendant. "My father claims my early years made me a gypsy," she said. She applied at Braniff, United and TWA and fortunately was hired in 1966 by United, the only one of the trio to survive. Friend became interested in the union and started at the bottom. During a round of contract talks, "I called the local office to see what I could do," Friend said. "I started stuffing envelopes. I always tell young activists that the union hierarchy hooks you in. They always say 'It's not a lot of work—it won't take much time at all.'"[3] Friend was elected president of United's AFA chapter in 1984, stepped down in 1990 to fly full time, then took over as union president in January 1995. She served four four-year terms before retiring at the end of 2010. At the time, 84 percent of the union's 50,000 members were women.

Friend tirelessly fought regulatory and legislative battles, often to

U.S. Airways flight attendants protest slow contract talks at the Charlotte airport in February 2011 (Ted Reed).

alter policies that affirmed gender inequality in the workplace, and she was often victorious. In one effort she led, the AFA convinced the Federal Aviation Administration, in 2003, to issue certificates to flight attendants who complete training at an airline. "We worked for that for years," Friend said. "It recognizes that this is a profession and requires a certain amount of competence."[4] Another achievement came in 2004, when AFA merged with the far larger Communications Workers of America, which had 700,000 members, providing a much larger institutional infrastructure.

Additionally, Friend lobbied to improve the Federal Medical Leave Act, which protects workers' jobs by requiring large employers to offer unpaid, job-protected leaves for reasons such as illness or care of a newborn. When the law passed in 1993, it defined the number of hours required to qualify in a way that shut out flight attendants. The method by which their hours are calculated creates an appearance that they don't work enough hours. But in 2010, Congress passed legislation ensuring that flight attendants would be covered. Friend also battled to have flight attendants covered by OSHA. Under the law, if another federal agency—in this case the FAA—had jurisdiction over a workplace, OSHA does not apply. In 2014, after she retired, OSHA gained limited authority over the working conditions of flight attendants, imposing its standards for noise, hazard communication and bloodborne pathogens on aircraft in operation.

When Friend joined United, she had to agree to step down when she turned 32 or got married. Eventually, the courts found both requirements illegal. But to the end, Friend fought to overcome the perception that flight attendants were ornaments, not professionals. Weight checks continued at some airlines until the early 1990s. Friend had a chance to reflect on the changes when she spoke to a class at Cornell University in 2010, as she was retiring. "I told the class that I lived through that period, and I wasn't willing to accept the limitations the industry put on women,"[5] she said then.

"Pat Friend was our longest serving AFA president," Nelson said. "She was revered across the labor movement for her no-nonsense approach and she was respected for it. We couldn't be more different in leadership style, and she's not known for giving compliments. So when she backed me for president, I was honored and maybe even a little surprised. And when she said I would serve as AFA president longer than she had, I was deeply touched."

Starting in 2002, Nelson served three terms as United's communications chair. In January 2010, she was about to return to work from maternity leave when friends urged her to run for AFA international vice president. "They asked me to run," she said. "I said 'When is the election? Next year?' And they said, 'No, in four months.' I remember thinking, I just had a baby. But David and I had planned a short vacation to Barbados and I said, 'We'll talk about it then.' Jack was four months old. The hotel gave you two hours a day of free babysitting with a nurse. The last night, we took advantage of that to talk about me running for vice president. We decided that it's not the right time, so don't do it. But I woke up the next morning thinking that was the wrong decision. How would I look my son in the eye and say 'I thought it was the wrong time? So I ran."[6]

In the April 2010 AFA election, the candidates for president were Bill McGlashen, a former America West flight attendant who had become executive assistant to Friend, and Veda Shook, an 18-year Alaska Airlines flight attendant who had served as AFA's vice president since 2007. The AFA board of directors, approximately 75 people who are directly elected by local presidents of bases at each airline, chooses its national officers in a vote. Each delegate carries the voting strength of the members of their local council, or geographical and airline base location.

Initially, McGlashen had Friend's support and appeared to have the votes to win. But "Several people changed their votes, and Veda won and was certified as president," recalled Mike Flores, who was chairman of the U.S. Airways AFA chapter. Shook's election was a bit of an oddity, since she had support from neither the national president nor the Northwest flight attendants nor the United flight attendants. "Veda was considered an outsider to the tried-and-true AFA people," Flores said. One reason, he noted, was that she was very closely aligned with CWA President Larry Cohen following the AFA/CWA merger. "Anybody aligned with CWA was unpopular," Flores said.[7]

On January 1, 2011, Shook and Nelson took office as president and vice president, respectively. "Sara was very popular with the United rank and file," while her husband had been a well-respected general counsel for the union, Flores said. Borer had left AFA in 2008, two years before the election, but he and Nelson "were both very good at what they did, and also, they knew everything about everybody," Flores said.[8]

In 2012, American and U.S. Airways announced their intent to merge. That represented a potential loss for AFA, since American's flight attendant union, the Association of Professional Flight Attendants, was larger. Six months earlier, the National Mediation Board had changed the rules to trigger a union election from 35 percent to 50 percent. U.S. Airways had only one third of the total flight attendants in the merger and the numbers seemed to indicate APFA would be the surviving union.

But Nelson took up the cause of advocating for the U.S. Airways flight attendants, who in many ways had a better contract than the American flight attendants. "We wanted to have equal representation on the bargaining committee and expedited bargaining to get the benefits of the new revenue generation of the merger as soon as possible," Nelson said. "And we wanted to get rid of a conditional agreement that APFA had negotiated with airline executives that would have meant serious concessions for US Airways flight attendants."[9]

In September 2013, the AFA board passed a resolution that gave Nelson, rather than Shook, the right to negotiate with APFA. Nelson benefited from having backed the U.S. Airways flight attendants so strongly, and opposing a deal Shook had supported in the United/Continental merger. That deal furloughed pre-merger United flight attendants, while hiring was allowed to continue on the Continental side of the merger. Nelson's stance on the merger also gave her a leg up when it came time for the 2014 national elections. Given Nelson's position at the union's largest airline, her advocacy for the U.S. Airways group and her concerns that CWA wasn't living up to its merger obligations with AFA, it should not surprise anyone that the ambitious, forceful vice president with a big personality and a gift for media interaction was viewed as a potential president. Is there a vice president anywhere in the world who doesn't envision themselves as the next president?

Nevertheless, Shook contended that she was surprised that Nelson ran against her in 2014. In a 2019 interview with *Politico*, Shook said, "I was still working and undergoing chemotherapy and then all this other stuff happened," Shook said. "I didn't see it coming until it was too late because I'd never met anyone like that before."[10] Said Nelson, "I had no intention of running for president, but people begged me to. The future of the union was at stake."[11]

As Nelson gradually emerged as a flight attendant leader, she won various battles, but the war for the profession was ongoing. "When I started, flight attendants were an afterthought," she said. "They were 'the girls in the back.' The women who mentored me told me, 'No one is going to give you a seat at the table.' I had to muscle it out and I worked diligently. I knew that it was a huge problem, and I went to work at changing it."[12] One effort that Nelson joined was to shift how flight attendants were perceived, so that people would realize that they did not just serve drinks but were also first responders to safety and health crises. Additionally, in the aftermath of the September 11 terrorist attacks, when aircraft security rose to become a paramount concern, Nelson beat back a move to allow airline passengers to carry pocket knives on board. And in 2023, she was leading an effort to enable flight attendant mothers to pump breast milk while airborne.

Talking with reporters regularly may look easy. Beyond a most basic level, it is not. It requires not only a willingness to engage but also a sizeable time commitment. Reporters have expectations and often work under tight deadlines.. They want designated communicators to know their subject matter, speak freely, share information off the record and be constantly available—essentially, to always answer the phone. Nelson figured that out in the Chicago courtroom. She is comfortable with doing that, and she realizes that to advance the cause she believes in, it must be done. She averages about 15 interviews a week.

"It's not magic; it's hard work," she said. "It's been hard work for 25 years. But we try to be available." People say the AFA gets an inordinate amount of media attention, Nelson said. She attributes that to AFA responding to every media request. "That might mean only sending someone a statement back, which is what we have to do when I am booked solid, but we always respond. Sometimes I have to write and review a statement at the same time as I am taking a call, which saves time, but it's not easy," Nelson said. "A lot of reporters have my personal cell phone

During United bankruptcy, Sara Nelson talked regularly with reporters (courtesy AFA).

number. They call me directly. You have to put yourself out there and you're taking a risk every time you do an interview, but I do it."[13]

Reminded that many labor unions lack interest or expertise in responding to the media, Nelson said, "I don't think most labor leaders really understand the value of it. They would say that's not why they ran to be president. From the outside, what we see a lot of times is that the union president says 'Dealing with the media is not my job.' It's never been done, they don't know what to do and they might not have a staff that understands. Also, in recent decades, labor density and influence declined, and there was less interest in coverage. Labor had become irrelevant, and it had become comfortable in its own irrelevance. Not only that, but newspapers have declined too; labor reporters disappeared. We work hard to combat this. We know that when there's an event, people want to know about it. And I feel it's something I have to do."[14] In 2023, a new generation of press savvy labor leaders with knowledgeable communications staffs emerged. They include Sean O'Brien, who was elected Teamster president in 2021 and Shawn Fain, elected UAW president in 2023.

It's no secret that Nelson is attractive, or that it benefits the labor movement to have an attractive, articulate woman—who often wears her flight attendant uniform—as its most public spokesperson. During a phone interview, when Nelson and AFA spokeswoman Taylor Garland were on the phone, I asked Nelson whether she thinks it helps her to be attractive. "I don't think of myself that way," she said, "Taylor can tell you that the last thing I think of myself is that I'm attractive. She will tell you that there are thousands of photos of myself I wish I could erase because I think I look terrible in them."[15]

"But I suppose I learned it along the way. Early on I was gregarious and outgoing, but I was innocent about all of that: I didn't really understand. It was something I had to learn. Now I understand that as much as it shouldn't matter, and it can also be a disadvantage if I don't deal with it, I simply need to figure out how to use every tool available to get in the room, get to the table, be able to engage, to speak up and get solutions. One advantage is that people often underestimate you and invite you to spaces where you can make a difference." I asked Nelson if she is secure and she said, "I am a secure person when I understand my purpose. Absent that, I am extremely hard on myself."

4

The World Discovers Sara Nelson

It would be wrong to say that Sara Nelson burst on the scene in January 2019, when she emerged as the most visible leader of the effort to end a 35-day government shutdown. She had been known in the airline industry long before then. Still, her visibility soared after the shutdown. Less than a month after its conclusion, she was the subject of a story entitled "The Shutdown Made Sara Nelson Into America's Most Powerful Flight Attendant," that ran on the front page of *The New York Times* business section. The subhead said, "A rising star of the labor movement, she's made a career of getting unruly people to do what she wants."[1]

In reality, by the time the story was published on February 22, 2019, Nelson had been the nation's most powerful flight attendant since 2014, when she was elected AFA president. For years she played an active role in advancing the legislative interests of her union and the industry, which involved regular appearances before Congressional committees. She also appeared frequently on TV. Yet the winter of 2019 was the moment when Nelson, then 45 years old and well into her second term as AFA president, was discovered at the highest level of national reporting.

Moreover, her shutdown stardom was just a start. A little more than a year later, when the pandemic suddenly shut down the airline industry in the spring of 2020, Nelson emerged not as a movement leader whose influence was often idealistic, inspiring people and shaping their thoughts, but rather as a skilled political strategist. She used her influence to shape a multi-billion-dollar federal spending program that is widely credited with keeping the airline industry from collapsing. And there was yet more to come.

By 2022, the airline industry was largely back in business, the labor movement was gaining the sort of momentum and favorability it had

Sara Nelson returns to National Airport, site of 2019 speech that contributed to the end of the government shutdown (Michael Theis).

lacked for decades, and Nelson was among the movement's most visible leaders. She bridged the gap between aging, hidebound, organized labor and the semi-organized young people who were shaking up new economy businesses—like Amazon and Starbucks—which had worked hard to keep employees in their modern, post-industrial global enterprises from recognizing the benefits of union representation.

The federal government shutdown began on December 22, 2018, and lasted until January 25, 2019, making it the longest government shutdown in history. The primary issue was that President Donald Trump wanted a $5.7 billion appropriation to build a border wall between the U.S. and Mexico. In the divided United States of the early 21st century, this was enough to muddle passage of a trillion-dollar budget. In December 2018, the Senate unanimously passed an appropriations bill that did not fund the wall, while the Republican-controlled House passed one that included wall funding, setting the stage for the usual sort of Congressional standoff. Of course, various efforts at resolution periodically emerged, especially after major agencies began on December 22 to curtail spending, each time exposing instances where a slowdown or shutdown could be seen and felt by the public. For example, on December 30, the National Park Service suspended trash collection and road maintenance at national parks.

In the critical airline industry, the issue was not that any particularly

4. The World Discovers Sara Nelson 39

visible service was halted, but rather that workers who were not getting paid reached a hard-to-dispute conclusion that if they were not getting paid, they should not go to work. Each day, increasing numbers of security screeners who work for the Transportation Security Administration didn't make it to work, shutting down various locations in airport screening. On January 11 about 800,000 federal employees missed their first paycheck. The next day, the shutdown entered its 22nd day, breaking the previous shutdown record of 21 days, set in 1995.

One particularly visible impact was that a terminal at Miami International Airport closed because security screeners called in sick at twice the normal rate. On January 15, the FAA recalled thousands of workers to perform needed safety inspections and other essential tasks; they had been furloughed since they could not be paid. They still weren't getting paid, but they were nevertheless deemed "essential" and required to come to work. In Congress, a newly seated Democratic-majority House took office and approved the Senate bill that excluded funding for the wall. But that didn't resolve anything. The bill sat because Senate Majority Leader Mitch McConnell (R.-Kentucky) declined to schedule a vote on a bill that Trump was going to veto. Words like "gridlock" and "impasse" and "standstill" rose in popularity.

Nelson stepped into the breach. On January 20, the thirtieth day of the shutdown, she spoke at an AFL-CIO event honoring Martin Luther King, Jr. She was there to accept the organization's MLK Drum Major for Justice Award. She gave a rousing speech, summoning the memory of King's final 1968 visit to Memphis in support of striking sanitation workers. "We need to follow Dr. King's lead and think big," she said. "Think big, like the hotel workers who took on the largest hotel chain in the world and won. Think big, like the teachers in Los Angeles who this very minute are taking on powerful hedge funds to save public education for our children." She advocated for other unions to join the 800,000 unpaid federal workers in staging a general strike. "Almost a million workers are locked out or being forced to work without pay," she said. "Others are going to work when our workspace is increasingly unsafe. What is the Labor Movement waiting for? End this shutdown with a general strike."[2]

Within a week, a January 25 headline in *The Atlantic* read, "Is a General Strike What's Needed to End the Shutdown?" while a January 27 headline in *Salon* said, "The single most important pro-labor speech of the shutdown was not given by AOC," a reference to New York Congresswoman Alexandria Ocasio-Cortez, an even better-known star of the left than Nelson. The subhead read, "The country was convulsed by shutdown finger-wagging and one lone voice called for a general strike. It wasn't AOC."[3]

As the shutdown went on, commercial aviation continued to unravel under the weight of mounting sick calls. In fact, part of Nelson's argument in support of a general strike was that employees' contracts did not require them to work under unsafe conditions. On January 23, the three principal unions representing air traffic controllers, flight attendants and pilots issued a warning. They called the shutdown "unconscionable" and declared that safety concerns were mounting.

"We have a growing concern for the safety and security of our members, our airlines, and the traveling public due to the government shutdown," said the statement. "In our risk-averse industry, we cannot even calculate the level of risk currently at play, nor predict the point at which the entire system will break. It is unprecedented. Due to the shutdown, air traffic controllers, transportation security officers, safety inspectors, air marshals, federal law enforcement officers, FBI agents, and many other critical workers have been working without pay for over a month. Staffing in our air traffic control facilities is already at a 30-year low and controllers are only able to maintain the system's efficiency and capacity by working overtime, including 10-hour days and 6-day workweeks at many of our nation's busiest facilities. Due to the shutdown, the FAA has frozen hiring and shuttered its training academy, so there is no plan in effect to fill the FAA's critical staffing need."[4]

That day, *The New York Times* reported that one in every 10 airport security workers was not showing up for work. Additionally, sick calls by air traffic controllers were causing delays at major airports, including LaGuardia, Washington National and Atlanta Hartsfield-Jackson.

The next day, January 24, Nelson spoke at a media event at National Airport, where she again advocated action to end the shutdown. "Many of these people are our veterans," she said, her voice wavering. "Many of these people are fighting for our country right now, and we are not paying them."[5] A video of the speech "blanketed the lefty internet."[6] The next day, East Coast flights were briefly grounded when about a dozen air traffic controllers at FAA oversight facilities in Jacksonville, Florida, and Washington (they oversee planes already in the air) called in sick, saying they could no longer do their jobs safely.

Nelson shot out a media statement saying, "Leader McConnell, can you hear us now?" Hours later, Trump announced a deal to reopen the government. How big a role did Nelson play? "Few people had a better shutdown than Ms. Nelson," said Lane Windham, a labor historian at Georgetown University, quoted by *The New York Times*. "'How many moments have there been when labor leaders have taken over social media in that way?' People love flight attendants, and they have a special affinity and affection for her."[7]

Was there ever going to be a general strike? It's hard to see how that would have happened. Employers might have argued that workers couldn't strike over an issue that had nothing to do with their companies. In fact, a United executive sent a letter to Nelson asserting that a strike by United flight attendants would be illegal. Nevertheless, about 20 days after the shutdown ended, labor writer Kim Kelly wrote that Nelson's call for a general strike "was widely credited for jump-starting the endgame of President Donald Trump's brutal five-week shutdown."[8] Kelly's story, entitled "Sara Nelson's Art of War," appeared in *The New Republic* on May 13. Kelly wrote, "The most powerful labor leader in the country right now is about 5'5" in sneakers, though her work uniform generally adds an extra inch or two," and noted that "Nelson is no stranger to wearing heels—but after spending some time with her, one gets the distinct impression that she'd be just as comfortable in combat boots."[9]

It was not just that Nelson made a meaningful speech that embodied the thoughts of millions of people at a critical time, but also that the speech's importance to the national dialogue was widely reported. Of course publications like *The Atlantic, Salon, The New Republic,* and writers like Kelly, who has specialized in covering labor issues, may lead coverage. But often it's *The New York Times* that legitimizes everyone else's reporting. This reflects a long-established pattern.

For decades, media in every city re-reported whatever appeared in that city's morning newspaper. Although the local newspaper industry has largely collapsed in the internet economy, on a national level the model remains, giving a single newspaper an outsize influence on what other outlets choose to cover. Thus the *Times'* coverage was followed by laudatory Sara Nelson stories in other respected media outlets. On May 30, 2022, *The New Yorker* published an 8,300-word Nelson biography, the longest to date, entitled, "Flight Attendants Fight Back." The subhead was: "Sara Nelson, the head of the largest flight attendants' union, leads her members through turbulent times and mounts a major organizing drive at Delta."[10]

Months later, on September 1, 2019, the day before Labor Day, the CBS News Sunday night TV show "60 Minutes" returned to the subject of Nelson and her speech. The segment began with a film clip and

Sara Nelson poses for a *New Yorker* story in a Washington, D.C., photo studio (courtesy AFA).

reporting by Lesley Stahl: "The woman dancing around the picket line is Sara Nelson, president of the Association of Flight Attendants-CWA. Don't be fooled by her playfulness; She's been called 'the most powerful labor leader in the country.' Her steeliness came through in a speech she gave—a call to arms, really—to the AFL-CIO on January 20, 2019, in the midst of the federal government shutdown."[11] Another clip showed Nelson singing "This Land Is Your Land." Stahl noted that the last general strike in the U.S. occurred in 1946 and that Nelson was calling on all 12 million members of the AFL-CIO to walk out en masse. On camera, Nelson declared, "We have real power as workers. If we decide not to participate in this economy, it stops. Everything stops."[12]

On the weekend of March 10–12, 2023, Nelson celebrated her 50th birthday in Rochester, New York, at a retreat set up by Richard Bensinger, the former organizing director of the AFL-CIO. About 80 people, representing organizing campaigns in Canada, Europe, and the United States, attended, as did Nelson's husband and son. On Saturday morning, when she walked into the "Inside Organizer School," every person there wore a pin that said "Flying with Sara." Said Nelson, "They turned my birthday into a solidarity campaign and, at the end of the day, they thanked me for spending the day with them and for being outspoken in support of labor and for being an inspiration for them and for other workers to stand up in the workplace. I was very humbled by this."[13]

5

Sara Saves the Airline Industry

A year after the shutdown, in the early days of the pandemic that created a far more dramatic situation for the airline industry than the seven-week shutdown of the U.S. government, Sara Nelson's leadership preserved the industry. That is, in fact, what American Airlines CEO Doug Parker said in a speech to the Wings Club, a non-profit, high-profile organization of aviation professionals that meets at the Yale Club, which is across the street from Grand Central Station.

In October 2021, the club met to award Parker its annual Distinguished Achievement Award. In his speech, Parker paid tribute to Nelson. During the pandemic, he said, the airline's leaders put employees first. "We fought for them and we worked collaboratively together with your union leaders, on behalf of those we all represent. And because of that, with the goal of saving our people's jobs, first and foremost, not just saving our companies, we were able to accomplish things no other industry accomplished."[1]

Then Parker said, "I owe something to someone here tonight. There are many people who played important roles in the process I just described. But there is one leader who deserves more credit than anyone else: Sara Nelson, the president of the Association of Flight Attendants. Many times over the past year and a half, I told Sara, 'I'm going to figure out a way to make sure everyone knows what you did for them.' This seems like as good an opportunity as I'm ever going to have. I've got 1,300 aviation professionals in a room. If it weren't for Sara Nelson and her leadership, we U.S. airlines would [still] have received our federal support. We would have received it, but it would have been entirely in the form of low interest loans, rather than what we did receive: payroll support to keep our teams employed. Without that payroll support, the

U.S. airlines would have shut down back in April 2020, furloughed virtually everyone, and then waited for demand to return until we started bringing people back and flying again."[2]

"As it turns out, that probably would have been this summer at the earliest. Sara didn't make that happen just once; she did it three times. So if keeping several hundred thousand airline industry professionals employed and the U.S. airline industry flying over the past year and a half was important to you, please join me in thanking Sara Nelson." The tribute was greeted with applause and Nelson, in the audience, stood up to more, as Parker cited her "incredible commitment to working people everywhere and a wonderful example of servant leadership."[3]

Congress passed the CARES Act on March 25, 2020, and President Trump signed it into law two days later. The stimulus bill provided $32 billion in direct grants to pay as many as 750,000 airline industry workers, many of them union members, through September 30. Of the total, $25 billion was allocated for passenger airlines, $4 billion for cargo airlines, and $3 billion for contractors, including those who employ caterers and airport workers. Additionally, the law authorized the U.S. Treasury Department to provide up to $46 billion in loans to airlines and other aviation businesses affected by the pandemic. In the end, 35 loans totaling $21.9 billion dollars were executed, according to the General Accounting Office.

The CARES Act was an unprecedented success for airline labor unions, who managed to secure a unique benefit for their members—payroll protections that nobody else got. "After the Gulf War, people got laid off with almost no salary protection," said Joseph Tiberi, then chief of staff for the transportation department of the IAM. He repeated, "After 9/11, people got laid off with almost no salary protection. That's what would be happening right now, if it wasn't for all of the furious lobbying by the labor movement. To have the protection that's in this bill, where airline employees can feel secure in their employment at least through the end of September, is amazing and unprecedented."[4] The protections were unique to the airline industry, the most heavily unionized major industry in the U.S.

It was Nelson who proposed the framework for the payroll support program legislation written by the House Committee on Transportation and Infrastructure. Moreover, throughout the effort to pass the bill and to ensure labor protections, she was the public face of the airline labor movement, appearing regularly on television in addition to lobbying intensely. "The concept was that this would be grants to be used for pay

American Airlines CEO Doug Parker signs an autograph at Dallas Fort Worth International Airport in September 2019 (Ted Reed).

and benefits only," Nelson said at the time. "This is the principle that all of labor agrees on. We wanted to keep people on the payroll, to give money directly to people. This is an unprecedented win for frontline aviation workers and a template all workers can build from. The grants

5. Sara Saves the Airline Industry

we won in this bill will save hundreds of thousands of jobs and will keep working people connected to healthcare."[5] She noted that the bill covered every segment of the airline industry—not just airline employees, but also caterers and airport workers, such as cleaners, janitors, wheelchair providers, and security guards.

Legislators, corporate lobbyists, and labor worked a stretch of 24-hour days in the week preceding the bill's passage, seeking to assure their priorities would be included in the bill. For labor, a series of problems emerged. At times during the week of negotiation on the bill, some suspected that caterers and airport workers might be left out. Eventually they were included. Another issue, which prompted concern just before passage, was that language in the bill would have enabled the Treasury secretary to demand unlimited changes in existing contract agreements if airlines were to receive federal grants. Flight attendant unions managed to eliminate the language.

Throughout the process, Nelson worked with U.S. Rep. Peter DeFazio, a close ally. He represented the Oregon district where Nelson grew up and was chairman of the transportation and infrastructure committee. On March 13, 2020, Nelson presented a proposal to DeFazio, who

Sara Nelson worked closely with former U.S. Rep Peter DeFazio, who represented her hometown in Corvallis, Oregon (courtesy AFA).

told the airlines they should work with her. Five days later, Parker called Nelson to an evening meeting of airline CEOs at the A4A office. The CEOs had come to realize that they needed Nelson's help, partially because airlines are not necessarily popular companies, while labor has friends. Airline executives "couldn't get what they wanted in Washington alone," Nelson said. "We had enough political power to make sure they had to work with us. We essentially negotiated the terms that night and then we went to Congress together."[6]

After Nelson and DeFazio worked out the framework of the relief plan for aviation, DeFazio took the plan to Nancy Pelosi, then Speaker of the House. "She approved it as the foundation of the Democratic plan," Nelson said. "It all happened so fast. It was put together in 24 hours. Our plan was for this to be the blueprint for every other industry, but there was no union push for it in other industries."[7]

In the aftermath of the bill's passage, some in the union movement were not pleased that Nelson received so much of the credit. When the bill language was released on March 25, the draft excluded the requirement for payroll and job protections in the event airlines received loans. In a public statement, IAM District 141, which represents airline workers, criticized Nelson, declaring: "A self-proclaimed labor leader is spiking the ball, claiming victory and credit, but obviously does not understand what's missing in the legislation that she is taking credit for."[8] Nelson countered, noting that "AFA staff found the Senate drafting error and alerted everyone and it got fixed before the Senate voted."[9]

Shortly after the bill passed, IAM General Vice President Sito Pantoja said in an interview, "The IAM's legislative team has been working around the clock, seven days a week since this crisis began, with specific instructions that their priority was to advocate for our members' jobs."[10] Pantoja laid out the changes labor made in the airline industry's original proposal. That included pay protection—which before labor's input was only a loan program—and the concept that grant funds are exclusively for employee wages, salaries and benefits. The APFA President Lori Bassani said at the time, "We worked around the clock over the past 12 days on the stimulus package, [working] closely with our fellow unions at American airlines—IAM, TWU, APA, CWA and IBT—pushing as hard as it is possible for our members and our industry. Also, our union was in daily contact with American's government affairs team. The air carriers would not have gotten the complete package without the support from organized labor. It's that simple."[11]

But it was Nelson who led the fight, and she paid a price in terms of

5. Sara Saves the Airline Industry   49

her own health. On March 13, she began "sipping cough medicine every day after I landed at DCA with a blocked ear." That was the day she had to get a draft of the payroll support program to DeFazio by 2 p.m. By April 14, she was overwhelmed by the medicine's impact on her stomach and the stress of the legislative fight, particularly the effort to resolve the drafting error regarding pay protections. "I ended up in the hospital on the day we won that fight," she said. When Senate Majority Leader Chuck Schumer (D-N.Y.) "called me to make sure I was good with the resolution, they had the EKG running."[12]

As the CARES Act was being enacted, the Democratic presidential primary race was in full swing. Joe Biden, seeking the nomination, said that if he were selected, he would choose a woman to be his

Sen. Bernie Sanders (D–Vermont) has long been a key ally for Sara Nelson and AFA (courtesy AFA).

vice-presidential candidate. Among the names mentioned was Nelson's, more in the context of who might be considered, as opposed to who was likely to be named. On May 1, *Forbes* posted my story, "What About Sara Nelson as Joe Biden's Running Mate?" Portions of that story follow here:

Let's just say upfront that the selection of Sara Nelson to be the Democratic nominee for vice president is a long shot. At the same time, Nelson is not a good person to underestimate. Since 2014, she has been the president of a relatively small labor union, the Association of Flight Attendants, which has just 50,000 members but has punched above its weight for at least three decades. In fact, Nelson has managed to become the voice of the U.S. labor movement, which seemingly is having a resurgence. She is among the best-known labor leaders of the 21st century, and she is among the few who are not white men.

Presumptive Democratic presidential nominee Joe Biden said in March that he will choose a woman as his running mate. Various lists of potential choices emerged. One, posted April 9 in the online site *International Business Times*, was called, "Five Potential Vice President Picks for Joe Biden." It named Tammy Baldwin, Kamala Harris, Amy Klobuchar, Gretchen Whitmer and Nelson. Of Nelson, the *IBT* said, "There is likely no other potential progressive VP pick who checks more boxes for both the left and center of the party."

Asked to comment on her potential candidacy for *Forbes*, Nelson said, "Being mentioned alongside these amazing women is humbling for sure. But my focus is labor organizing. What's exciting is the recognition flight attendants are getting and the force labor can play in our economy and democracy. We are at the table and we're not taking our foot off the gas any time soon."

Among Nelson's advocates is Doug Parker, CEO of American Airlines, who said, "I think Sara would be a great choice. She's smart, she's tough, she's forward thinking and she cares about people. She's very good at bringing together people who have diverse interests in order to get transactions done, and she makes sure she gets work done on behalf of the people she represents." Parker noted that he was not evaluating Nelson in relation to the other potential nominees. Moreover, AFA does not represent American flight attendants, although it does represent the group at three American subsidiaries. "I've known Sara a long time," Parker said. "We spent a lot of time working together on the CARES Act," particularly on the portion that provides $25 billion in grants for airlines to pay employees through September 30. Those grants are "the

5. Sara Saves the Airline Industry

most important part" of the act, Parker said; they ensure that "airlines have the money to keep people employed, to continue to move people around the country and to be ready when demand returns."

Media appreciation for Nelson was clear on MSNBC-TV host Larry O'Donnell's show "The Last Word" on April 11: The CARES Act was the topic. In his introduction, O'Donnell declared, "No Senator knows more about the airline industry than Sara Nelson." She "may be the most effective labor leader working the halls of Congress today," he said, noting she "helped guide the House of Representatives and the Senate to deliver aid to the airlines."

O'Donnell hosted Nelson and U.S. Rep. Katie Porter (D–Mass.), whom he described as "the most formidable pair of guests I have ever introduced on this program at the same time." Porter, he said, "saw Sara Nelson in action and decided 'the Nelson plan' should be the plan to cover workers in other fields." Essentially, "the Nelson plan" provides money for employers to pay workers during the crisis. It keeps workers off unemployment and on the tax rolls, preserves health care benefits, uses existing payroll systems and enables spending.

One of Nelson's strongest labor backers is Cecil Roberts, the president of the United Mine Workers, who said he has long advocated that labor leaders should hold political positions. "Sara Nelson is indeed someone that [deserves] VP consideration," he said. "We should all stand up and applaud that." Roberts said Nelson has gone to bat for mine workers in their struggle to receive federal protection for their pension and health care benefits. Her efforts, he said, have included rallying support from the AFL-CIO; speaking repeatedly at mine worker rallies throughout the Southeast; making a video supporting mine workers, and engaging flight attendants in lobbying Congress on behalf of mine workers. "Here's someone who looked at this as a labor issue and also as a right and wrong issue, and who said 'Something needs to be done,'" Roberts said. "The Bible says we will be judged by how we treat the least of these. Sara realized that a lot of miners gave their lives for this industry, and she took that on."

Nelson is mentioned not only as a potential candidate for U.S. vice president, but as a potential candidate for the presidency of the AFL-CIO, assuming that incumbent Richard Trumka, who is 70, steps down when his term ends in 2021. Were Nelson to run, she would likely face Liz Shuler, AFL-CIO vice president and secretary-treasurer. Shuler tends to stay in the background and rarely gives interviews. "Liz is a solid trade unionist who has demonstrated leadership," said John Samuelsen, president of the TWU, which has 151,000 members including 65,000 in the airline industry, where it is the second largest union. "She doesn't seek accolades." (In 2021, Trumka died and Shuler replaced him.)

Should Sara Nelson be vice president of the United States? "Whether it's Sara Nelson or another labor leader, America would be a better place if trade unionists were in high level government positions," Samuelsen said. "We wouldn't have NAFTA' we wouldn't have normalized trade with China, and the Rust Belt wouldn't have been created. The economic security of our working families would be front and center in our political discourse."

6

Sara Fights Goliath at Amazon

Amazon embodies the capitalist dream of starting a business in your garage and ending up with $120 billion thirty years later. But it has also come to embody something else: an era in which giant corporations fight employee efforts to improve their working conditions by organizing. In 1994, when Amazon founder Jeff Bezos started the company, 15.5 percent of workers were members of U.S. labor unions; by 2023, union membership had declined to 10 percent—the lowest on record, according to the Bureau of Labor Statistics.

Might the trend be reversed in the 21st century? In the early 2020s, Amazon and the union movement were locked in battle in a small Alabama city once distinguished by unionized steel mills. The David vs. Goliath encounter enabled a vision of the past, when labor unions once stormed the automakers and other castles of the manufacturing economy. Today, the moat protecting the castles of the new economy is weak enforcement of the laws that enable union organizing. This is why pro-labor policies of the Biden administration, most importantly its appointments to the National Labor Relations Board, have been important. Often the charge has been led by young people from outside of the organized labor movement. If the low point in the period was when former Starbucks CEO Howard Schultz stepped out of retirement to lead an anti-union campaign, tarnishing his legacy, the high point has been that so many young workers emerged as participants and leaders. That said, they still benefited from the participation of established leaders such as Sara Nelson.

Bessemer, Alabama, a Birmingham suburb of about 25,000 people, was a center of steelmaking from about 1890 into the 20th century. Working class people could make a living, some as members of the

United Mine Workers of America. As the mining jobs left, part of the vast U.S. manufacturing decline that sent blue collar jobs to China and elsewhere, Bessemer's economy deteriorated and Amazon's arrival represented economic revival, despite the irony of an anti-union company coming to save an historic union town.

Of the 11 states that once made up the Confederate States of America, Alabama is the second most unionized, with 8.6 percent of its workers represented by unions, according to BLS statistics. (Mississippi is first with 9.8 percent.) For decades, companies have moved to the South to take advantage of anti-union environments anchored by states' right to work laws, which enable union benefits for workers who do not pay union dues. Alabama's high union membership rate, relative to its peers, reflects the historic presence of manufacturing and coal mining unions as well as public sector union relationships. For instance, IAM Local 2003 includes about 3,500 members who maintain the Army's helicopter fleet at Fort Rucker, about 200 miles south of Bessemer.

In the spring of 2020, at the height of the pandemic, Amazon opened its 850,000-square-foot fulfillment warehouse in Bessemer—a

Sara Nelson rallied workers at the Bessemer Amazon plant in 2020 (courtesy AFA).

building the size of about 15 football fields. Within months, the Retail, Wholesale and Department Store Union (RWDSU) began an organizing drive among the workers, who were 85 percent Black. In November, the union filed with the NLRB for a representation election for 1,500 workers. Amazon, which at the time had about 1.5 million employees, about half in the United States, hired an anti-union law firm to resist the effort. A key tactic was to expand the size of the bargaining unit as an effort to dilute the strength of the initial group; eventually, the unit was expanded to 5,700 workers. "Amazon hired more than 4,000 workers leading up to the election, to pad the rolls," Nelson said. "They treated this as a national political campaign, which of course it was. The entire country was trained on this one union election."[1]

Nelson got involved early. After learning that RWDSU had filed, she said, "I began talking to them right away, asking how I could help." Very quickly, she called Ron Klain, chief of staff for President Biden, who was to take office on January 20, 2021. "This was right out of the gate, our first conversation during the [presidential] transition," she said.[2] In February, in an early indication that he was going to be a pro-union president, Biden posted a video in which he offered support for the organizing drive. "Today and over the next few days and weeks, workers in Alabama and all across America are voting on whether to organize a union in their workplace," he said. "This is vitally important—a vitally important choice, as America grapples with the deadly pandemic, the economic crisis and the reckoning on race. What it reveals is the deep disparities that still exist in our country."[3] Said Nelson, "It was an extraordinary statement of support for labor."[4]

In March 2021, Nelson traveled to Bessemer to support the unionization effort. Later, she recalled the bad weather as she flew in. "I was supposed to go for a rally, but there were tornado warnings and a severe storm," she said. "Amazon closed the warehouse, trying to show that it cares for the workers, so the safest place to be was in the union hall because it had a tornado shelter. We met with workers there."[5] At the union hall, organizers, reporters, workers and supporters gathered to wait out the storm. In an interview with *Jacobin*, a socialist newspaper and web site, Nelson said, "Any traditional assessment would say that there's no possible way these workers could actually be right about how ripe this warehouse is for a union campaign. What I got to see was how nimble the union was down there and what an extraordinary operation was pulled together."[6]

Nelson told *Jacobin* that the organizing drive started because one of the original organizers had previously been a union member and understood the value. He found RWDSU on Google and made a phone call to the small Birmingham office. "That grew into a phenomenon around the world," she said. "People were inspired that these workers who have been treated as disposable were taking on arguably one of the most powerful men in the world."[7]

One event in the Bessemer campaign stands out for its gall: Just before voting started, Amazon placed an unmarked mailbox in front of the plant. The union objected, saying the mailbox created the impression that Amazon had a role in collecting ballots. Ballots were distributed in February; the vote count took place in April. Workers voted against the union 1,798 to 738, while about 500 contested ballots were not counted. Some post-election analysis speculated that the union should have done more to challenge Amazon's dramatic expansion of the bargaining unit, rather than rushing to have an election.

Meanwhile, the NLRB called for a new election, saying Amazon had interfered. The board cited the mailbox as an example of interference. During her visit, Nelson saw the postal box, "inside a big tent, with anti-union literature all around. And there was a big banner on the warehouse that said, 'We pay $15 an hour minimum wage.' They were boasting about this. What was missing was that a non–Amazon employer down the road was paying $17 to $18."[8] In the second vote, counted in March 2023, the union lost by a margin of 993 to 875 among the counted votes.

The second front in the Amazon/union battle was Staten Island in New York City. It's safe to say the odds were different in New York than in Alabama. In fact, workers won an initial victory, although by early 2024 Amazon was still refusing to negotiate. The New York organizing effort was led by two unaffiliated young workers, Christian Smalls and Derrick Palmer, who headed an independent group simply called the Amazon Labor Union. The site was Amazon's Staten Island fulfillment center, known as JFK8. Smalls had started the organizing drive with a walkout over safety conditions in 2020. He benefited from a company misstep: an Amazon attorney described him as "not smart or articulate" in an email that was mistakenly sent to 1,000 people, and then widely circulated. He was fired, with the company rationalizing that he had violated quarantine rules by attending the walkout. On April 1, 2022, workers at JFK8 voted 2,654 to 2,131 to join the union. The warehouse was "the first domino to fall," said Rep. Alexandria Ocasio-Cortez, D-NY.[9]

The next front was an adjacent sorting facility, LDJ5, which employed nearly 1,600 workers, the vast majority of them part-timers. On

Sara Nelson spoke to Amazon workers at a Staten Island rally in 2020 (courtesy AFA).

April 24, 2022, the day before the facility's workers began to vote, two labor rallies took place outside the center. The first involved political figures, led by Ocasio-Cortez and Sen. Bernie Sanders, D–Vt. It was attended primarily by the media because traffic delays due to the Brooklyn marathon delayed many potential participants. The second rally featured various labor leaders, including Nelson. Clad in gray jeans and a red ALU T-shirt, Nelson gave a rousing speech. Of Smalls, she said, "Chris is an incredible leader" who, after he was fired, made an effort to study labor history. "I know what he did preparing for this moment. It was strategic, and he really built a community the way it should be built," she said.[10]

On stage, Nelson and Smalls aligned in declaring, "Eat the rich baby." Said Nelson, "This union's got some serious union drip going on. And I am seriously inspired." The phrase "union drip," which was emerging at the time, is closely associated with Smalls and refers to the stylish clothes, shoes, and jewelry that he wore—tracksuits, sneakers, gold chains, bandanas and sunglasses—with an aura of confidence. The phrase also added cachet to union-branded clothes and accessories. As the crowd cheered, Nelson observed that Amazon workers were following in the path of the labor movement, seeking improvements just as the movement had a century earlier. "Let me tell you something," she said. "There is no fucking labor peace."[11]

Later, reflecting on the rally, she said, "The moment was so exciting. I had been waiting for 25 years for people to wake up to their power, to understand that if they come together they have all the power. There was so much diversity, a whole set of workers who looked like the entire world, and there was a sense of history. It felt like history was meeting the present." Nevertheless, in the Amazon election for the sorting facility, ALU lost with 618 in favor of unionizing and 380 against. "We can't shy away from these fights," Nelson reflected. "The fights make you stronger. You have to exercise your muscles. I said then that there is no labor peace. We have been losing ground ever since we decided there would be labor peace."[12]

In fact, she said, the pandemic created vast new opportunities for the labor movement. It placed immense pressure on blue collar workers who couldn't stay home, while at the same time many white collar workers took advantage of the opportunity to work remotely. "There was so much activity during the pandemic, but we didn't really use the moment like we should have," Nelson said. "Grocery workers in America had more leverage than anyone else in the first few weeks. So did workers in the slaughterhouses. There were horrible stories coming out of meatpacking, and out of Amazon too, like when Chris Smalls was fired. People felt isolated and beaten down. Inequality was going through the roof. The Bessemer workers, taking on one of the richest men in the world, were the first ones to have a public campaign and file for an election. That sparked so much organizing, but I just think there were missed opportunities. Capitalism is always organizing. Labor should be too."[13]

7

She Wanted to Work for Hillary Clinton: Maybe She Did Better

In the summer of 2015, Taylor Garland, a recent Pennsylvania State University grad with an interest in Washington politics, was looking to get a job with the Hillary Clinton campaign. She applied online. No one ever called her. Then an acquaintance suggested she try for a communications post at the Association of Flight Attendants. The job had been open for several months after Corey (Caldwell) Kuhn moved on to become a senior media specialist for the Air Line Pilots Association.

"I applied almost reluctantly," Garland recalled. "On the morning of the interview I was sitting downstairs at the AFA office, waiting to be interviewed, and I realized that on my resume the objective still said: 'Pennsylvania-born girl with Ohio roots looking to elect the first female president.'"[1] The resume also included a reference to a Beyonce song, "Run the World (Girls)." Obviously, Garland was headed down a path that led to working for an inspiring woman leader. But it would not be the one who would lose a presidential campaign to Donald Trump for any number of reasons.

In her first interview, Garland spoke to two AFA staffers, and Sara Nelson stepped in for a few minutes. After the interview, Nelson texted Garland and said, "Great job in there; Let's do an off the record next week." At the second interview, "We talked through things, what I wanted to do long term," Garland said. "I told her I would give her three years." (By 2024, Garland had been on the job for nine years.) A sensitive matter was that while Nelson regularly introduced Sen. Bernie Sanders (I–Vt.) at campaign events, Garland was a Hillary Clinton backer. "She made me justify my support for Hillary," Garland said.

Garland already had a sense of who Nelson was. "My friends told me that she is a leader, that she's going places, that she demands a lot but has a very clear vision, that she is super passionate and motivated. One other thing, she came up through communications, that has always been her baby, and no matter who was in this job, she would work closely with them." In the interview, "Our personalities clicked," Garland said. "Infamously, once she offered me the job, she asked me to start the next day, which I could not do, I needed to give two weeks' notice." Garland started on December 3, 2015. Asked whether she is better off than she would have been working for Clinton, Garland acknowledged that yes, she is, "No offense to Hillary."[2]

Garland grew up in Harrisburg, Pennsylvania. As a teenager, she said, "I was very taken by the election of Barack Obama in 2008. I couldn't vote , but I was involved in the election effort in Harrisburg as Students for Barack Obama president and I went to the inauguration."[3] Although she was accepted to the University of Pittsburgh's pre-med program, she came to realize that her real interest was government and politics. She attended Penn State and double majored in political science and public relations. In 2012, Garland was president of Penn State Students for Barack Obama, which involved encouraging Penn State students to vote

Before she went to work for Sara Nelson, Taylor Garland aspired to work for Hillary Clinton (Michael Theis).

and organizing them to register voters and volunteer for election efforts. She notes that Obama won Centre County.

In her final semester, Garland was accepted into a Penn State mentoring program that matched liberal arts students with graduates working in their desired fields. "I wanted to do something in politics and I was dead set on coming to DC, job or not," she said. She met with various grads, some working on Capitol Hill and some who were consultants. She learned that while the Hill has glamor and proximity to power, it is also an all-consuming job that, at the start, does not pay well. "I figured out that you can make it in DC without working on the Hill," Garland said.

As she approached her 2013 graduation, a mentor offered her a fellowship at Alliance for American Manufacturing, a partnership between the United Steelworkers and manufacturers. The alliance advocates for American manufacturing jobs and suitable trade agreements. "It was the first time I worked with labor," she said. She was involved in a national tour called "Save Our Steel Jobs" that resembled a political campaign, particularly in its emphasis on live events. She enjoyed the job, but "It was hard to get press," she said.[4] Working with Sara Nelson put an end to that problem.

Even before Nelson arrived, AFA was good at media. It engaged with four sets of reporters: those who cover the airline industry; a far larger group that covers Congress; the semi-reporters on social media who track events such as celebrity run-ins with flight attendants, and a fourth group of national reporters and producers who look for stories with national appeal for shows like Good Morning America and cable news. The airline industry functions in a complex environment shaped by the intersection of carriers, unions, airports, regulatory agencies, Congress, media and others. Stories run the gamut from legislative to labor to safety to tales of celebrities who either refuse to turn off their cell phones during takeoff or to give up their first-class seats to wounded vets. Media in cities with hub airports have a particular interest because large airports and airlines employ vast numbers of people locally and many people fly regularly. And of course, social media has vastly amplified awareness of inflight behavior.

"Aviation is a dense union sector and we are recognized within the industry as a key stakeholder, not just as part of a side conversation," Garland said. "In the first few months, I was talking to the 'Today Show' and 'Good Morning America' and to *The New York Times* and other print media. It was super exciting. It was a time when I started to connect my job with my desire, when I wanted to be in politics, that I could better people's lives. I had not intended to work with a union, but I realized that union work is politics. It is politics in the workplace, and you can make a difference in somebody's life every single day."[5]

Garland got an early education in contracts because in 2016, flight attendants from United and Continental were closing in on a joint contract, five years after their carriers merged. The first lesson was that it takes a long time to negotiate an airline labor contract. It takes even longer when two carriers have merged, because both groups want to maintain the best parts of their own contracts in the new one that is under negotiation. If management wants to delay negotiations it's a ripe environment to do that. Moreover, before the 2010 merger, the 25,000 flight attendants at the two airlines had been represented by different unions, AFA and IAM.

In 2011, AFA won 55 percent of the vote in a union election that made it the sole representative of United's flight attendants. The joint contract covered three separate entities—United, Continental and Continental Micronesia. Nelson, elected AFA president in 2014, had to prove herself by securing improvements for everyone. When Garland came on board, "It was the last year of the joint contract negotiations, which had gone on for far too long. For a person with no past aviation experience, it was a lot to take on." Garland credits a two-day AFA review of the contract in June 2016 with helping her to learn the nuances of labor contracts, as well as "the job and the lingo and all that comes with it."[6]

As her awareness increased, her relationship with Nelson evolved. "I can't pinpoint the time, but we came to see that we have a similar work ethic and understanding," she said. "I was young and eager to learn, that helped, and I fell in love with aviation. And over time, my relationship with Sara got closer. We are both workaholics; that can burn us out sometimes. Also, she is very good at communications. She was talking to local and national press during the United bankruptcy, so she has been doing this for twenty years."[7]

Another bond that unites Garland and Nelson is their concern for women's issues and their awareness of AFA's role in advancing them. Its key leaders, Pat Friend and Nelson, have been prominent advocates for women's rights. Nelson's 2014 AFA presidential run boosted that role, and within a year she had Garland by her side. Big sister/little sister seems an appropriate way to describe their relationship. At the 2023 photo session for this book, they brushed lint off one another's outfits and each made sure the other's hair was in place.

7. She Wanted to Work for Hillary Clinton

Many people believe they are experts at working with reporters. But building relationships and understanding what reporters want is not as easy as it appears to be. Not surprisingly, at times, Nelson's media prominence has produced jealousy from unions that fail to achieve the same visibility. Whose fault is that? "We definitely do things differently," Garland said. Among the lessons Nelson taught her are to never say, "No comment."

"Always have something to say to reporters, even if it's not on the record," Garland said. "We want to be a resource, so building and keeping relationships is incredibly important. Also, be strategic about what we are saying and who we are saying it to. We have to realize how much press and public communication can propel policy goals."[8]

The perception that Nelson excessively seeks publicity was especially common when profiles started to appear regularly in 2019. "We never pitched a profile of Sara; we never set out purposely to get them," Garland said. "The requests were all incoming and we worked with them all. Sara is very good at what she does, but it's not without incredible hard work and sacrifice for her and her family and her health. She is not out there to get attention for herself, but she understands she has the power to bring attention to flight attendant issues and worker issues and women's issues and she uses that. People perceive that it's easy, but this is something that she built. She spent 20 years building it."[9]

During an interview in 2023, Garland retraced the key events during her eight years on the job. Nelson became the country's most prominent labor leader in January 2019 as the government shutdown was entering its fourth week. Nelson spoke to the AFL-CIO on January 20 and to reporters at National Airport on January 24. She called for a general strike if the shutdown didn't end soon. It ended January 25. The widely covered speeches and relentless work to define the crisis[4] had obviously played a role. Less than two months later, on March 13, the FAA grounded the Boeing 737 MAX after two fatal crashes involving Lion Air in October 2018 and Ethiopian Airlines on March 10, 2019. "After the shutdown, the high-profile crises in aviation didn't stop," Garland said. The crashes created a crisis for the industry because the public questioned its safety practices and "distrust in the system can spread," she said. After the Ethiopian crash, "We called for the government and Boeing to ground the fleet; they eventually did that."[10]

In 2020, the pandemic reshaped the world. Between the first and last day of March, there was a 93 percent decline in the number of people nationwide who cleared airport security, according to the Transportation

Taylor Garland (left) and Sara Nelson depart Chicago following union day of action in Chicago in 2023 (courtesy AFA).

Security Administration. Just before the sudden realization in early March that the pandemic had arrived in the U.S., flight attendants at Hawaiian Airlines were concluding negotiations on a contract. Asia traffic was already falling, which heavily impacted Hawaiian whose passenger count fell 45 percent in March. In late February, Nelson flew to Honolulu and urged management to get a deal done. The parties reached an agreement in March, which was then ratified by the Flight Attendant AFA members, and the deal was signed in April.

Soon after Nelson returned from Hawaii, AFA was drawn into pandemic response, where it sought to protect the few flight attendants and passengers who flew in those early days as well as to safeguard the jobs of thousands of flight attendants. During the first week Congress spent determining how to respond to Covid, "Sara was writing a plan, making sure this crisis was not going to be put on labor's back the way that 9/11 was," Garland said. "We weren't going to have another 20 years of that, with the layoffs and the bankruptcy contracts. After 9/11, the government didn't respond effectively, and Sara was committed to making sure that those lessons were learned this time. She knew that you can't save enough for a rainy day when demand goes away in two weeks." As Congress considered how to save the economy, Nelson sought to ensure that airlines were included in the solution. Said Garland, "The airlines were up on the Hill for a week before March 18, trying to get a hand from all sides of the aisles. But airlines were not a well-liked industry. Then Doug Parker called and said we need help. Sara said we will help, but you have to agree to our plan. That was the foundation for the payroll support plan."[11]

On March 26, the Senate approved the $2 trillion stimulus package. Throughout the effort to ensure labor protections in the bill, Nelson was, again, the public face of the labor movement, appearing regularly on television and lobbying lawmakers intensely. Throughout the negotiations, Garland said, "I was talking to 10 to 20 reporters a day, some every day all day, especially the ones following operational and Hill relief stuff. We were all trauma bonded. It was an existential year for the country and the industry."[12]

8

In 2024, Flight Attendants Unite, UAW Helps and Sara Looks Ahead

The days around Valentine's Day 2024 were typical for Sara Nelson, a whirlwind of activity that promoted the labor movement but also taxed her health. Early on, the year 2024 was set up to be the year of the flight attendants, with airlines moving to settle open flight attendant contracts after signing off on pilot contracts the previous year. Nelson was in the middle of that effort. At the same time, she had taken on the AFA's long-standing battle to unionize Delta. On February 13 and 14, she was involved in key demonstrations for both: the first at Los Angeles International Airport and the second at Detroit Metropolitan Airport, nearly 2,300 miles away.

In Los Angeles, Nelson led a demonstration of a few hundred flight attendants, then conferred with participants in thirty or so similar events at airports around the country. Then she boarded a red-eye flight to Detroit, sleeping intermittently on the plane. She arrived in Detroit at 6:30 a.m., checked in to the airport Westin, slept for an hour, then began her day. It included a series of Zoom meetings, lunch with UAW President Shawn Fain and then a march through the Delta terminal with Fain and other supporters. After dinner at the airport, she boarded a flight to Washington National and headed home, arriving around 12:15 a.m. on February 15. After a few hours of sleep, she awoke at 6:30 a.m. for a 7:45 a.m. interview on CNBC. Later, she dismissed a question about her health. But in recent years, stress and too much cough syrup triggered a hospital visit during negotiations over the payroll support program;

she has also been sidelined by two hip operations, which resulted in her attending various events on crutches.

The year 2024 began with open contracts at four of the five biggest airlines: American, Alaska, United and Southwest. The three top flight attendant unions—APFA, AFA and TWU—were all engaged, with APFA at American, AFA at Alaska and United and TWU at Southwest. By February 2024, APFA had asked twice to be released from mediation, talks at United and Alaska were moving slowly and Southwest flight attendants had rejected a tentative contract agreement. The leaders of the three unions—Nelson, APFA president Julie Hedrick and Lyn Montgomery, president of TWU Local 556—were working together to generally boost flight attendant compensation. This made 2024 the year of the flight attendant. "I can't think of another time in history when we've been able to take on the entire industry and dramatically raise working conditions and wages for flight attendants," Nelson said in November 2023. "We are going to make historic gains. It will take more strike votes and more actions, but we're all fighting for the same issues—control of our time at work, higher wages, pay for all of our time on the job and better retirement."[1]

Meanwhile, the effort to unionize Delta flight attendants was on a path that so far, after more than two decades, had not led to success. Both of Nelson's predecessors, Pat Friend and Veda Shook, tried to organize flight attendants at Delta. When Friend stepped down in 2010, after four terms and 15 years as AFA president, she said the failure to organize Delta flight attendants was her biggest disappointment.

The first attempt was in 2001, when AFA staged an election at Delta after several years of organizing. At the time, AFA called it the largest organizing campaign in the history of the airline industry. But it was defeated because most flight attendants did not vote. Among the 19,033 eligible voters, only 5,609 flight attendants voted; 5,520 were in favor and 89 against. But because uncounted ballots were counted as no votes, Delta encouraged flight attendants to simply tear up their ballots and not participate. Another problem was that voting began on August 29, 2001. Less than two weeks later, the September 11 terrorist attacks combined with a weakening economy to put the brakes on air travel, reducing support for the union. "Delta's entire campaign focused on creating fear and uncertainty in flight attendants' minds," Pat Friend told *The Washington Post*.[2] The headline in the publication Labor Notes read, "Delta Flight Attendants Vote 98% for Union—And Lose."[3]

In 2008, AFA sought again to organize Delta before its merger with

Northwest. The merger was announced April 15 and the votes were tabulated in May. About 40 percent of Delta's flight attendants, or 5,232 people, voted in favor of membership, while only 89 voted against. However, since the bargaining unit had 13,389 members, the union fell far off the 50 percent voter participation required. The vote was viewed as an indicator that once the integration with Northwest was completed, AFA would easily win at Delta. After all, Northwest was 80 percent unionized. "A successful vote would have made integration of the two flight attendants' groups more seamless, as Northwest's flight attendants already are represented by the AFA," *The Pioneer Press*, of St. Paul, Minnesota, reported. Pat Friend told the newspaper, "A larger portion of the Delta workforce than ever before voted for union representation. Those supporters, combined with strong union support at Northwest, will clearly be enough for the flight attendants to win union representation after the merger with Northwest is finalized."[4]

But in the 2010 union elections following the merger, organized labor suffered surprising defeats. In the flight attendant election, the vote was 9,544 to 9,216 against unionization. "It's not for me that I am disappointed," Friend said afterwards. "It's really for the flight attendants, and the destruction of their 63 years of collective bargaining, and for the core group at Delta, who have been fighting for this since 1996." Friend was reminded at the time that the union would appeal the result, but said the potential loss at Delta "is not the way I thought my career would end."[5] Not only did AFA fail to organize flight attendants, but the IAM also lost elections to organize fleet service workers, as Delta staged an aggressive anti-union campaign. About 51 percent of flight attendants turned down the AFA, while 53 percent of fleet service workers and rejected IAM representation.

These failures were followed by another one five years later, when the IAM tried to organize Delta's 20,000 flight attendants in 2015. The union said it submitted nearly 12,000 signed cards to the National Mediation Board calling for an election. Somehow, thousands of the cards had fraudulent signatures. The union and the airline each blamed the other side for the fraud and applauded the call for a Department of Justice investigation. No results were ever announced.

In 2022, the unions announced they would try again in a three-union effort. The AFA sought to organize flight attendants, the Teamsters sought to organize mechanics and the IAM sought to organize fleet service. The following account of the airport walk is revised slightly from my *Forbes* story entitled, "Labor Dream Team Calls on Delta's Detroit Hub."[6]

8. Flight Attendants Unite, UAW Helps, Sara Looks Ahead 69

UAW President Shawn Fain and Sara Nelson strolled through Delta's hub at Detroit Metro Airport in 2024 (courtesy UAW).

Nelson enlisted Shawn Fain, president of the United Auto Workers, to join her in the effort to boost visibility as the union seeks signatures on union cards. "This walk is cutting through the fear cloud," said Nelson, as the two top labor leaders walked the Delta hub, accompanied by about 20 supporters. "This is about visibility and pushing through the intimidation management tries to create." The group circled the Delta terminal, taking a ride on the airport monorail. At one point, Nelson led in singing "Solidarity Forever" outside a Delta club.

Fain is a Detroit hero. Following a successful six-week strike against the big three automakers, he was termed "hero of the year" by *New Republic* writer Timothy Noah and "labor leader of the year" by CNN Business. Fain can't go anywhere in Detroit without people greeting him and asking him to pose for a photo. This happened several times during the airport walk, as he wore an "AFA Supporter" button and even gave one to a Detroit-Austin, Texas, passenger. Afterwards, the soft-spoken leader spent 90 minutes eating dinner at an airport restaurant with about 10 flight attendants, listening more than talking as they discussed Delta working conditions and organizing efforts.

"This is what we do as unions: We support each other," Fain said. "We support organized labor. We support other workers who want their fair share of the fruits of their labor." When Fain was elected UAW president in March 2023, Nelson "reached out right away" to offer support, he said. "I knew her reputation, her fight and her militancy to do what's right for working people. We share a lot of that." Nelson has "been a real good resource to me as a newly elected president," Fain said. "She's been in that role for 10 years. She has a lot of experience as a sitting president. She's been a great source of information and a good friend."

Besides flight attendants and UAW members, the airport walk included the top two leaders of the Delta Detroit chapter of the Air Line Pilots Association. "We're here to support unionization for flight attendants and other employee groups at Delta," said Ryan Breznau, chapter chairman. "Our flight attendants, mechanics, and other employee groups deserve industry leading compensation and work rules, and the only way they'll achieve this is by organizing." Breznau, who previously flew for Northwest regional carrier Compass, noted, "You have a lot of ex–Northwest people here in Detroit who are strong union supporters."

The walk included not only Northwest veterans but also more recent hires. A theory is that people new to the airline are less likely to support unionization. Nelson said Delta has several thousand recent hires. Also, with about 28,000 flight attendants, more than any other airline, Delta has many flight attendants on reserve. Many of them don't fly much, creating fewer opportunities for union supporters to engage with them, Nelson said.

Delta declined to comment for this story. An irony in airline labor is that Delta has set contract terms. In 2023, Delta signed the first contract with its pilots and the other airlines all responded by saying they would generally match. As for flight attendants, Delta announced in June 2022 that it would become the first U.S. carrier to pay flight attendants not just for flying time, but also for boarding time. Now the four big airlines with open contracts say they will generally match Delta rates and boarding pay policy. On Valentine's Day, Delta's non-union employees received profit-sharing checks for 10.4 percent of their eligible earnings. Delta said that since 2007 it has distributed $11 billion in profit sharing. Nelson said the money should be part of contracts, not subject to executive whim.

At the airport dinner, Fain heard that rapper Ludacris and ex-football player Tom Brady had appeared before Delta workers in Atlanta and Tampa as the company announced the bonuses. "We're not Ludacris

8. Flight Attendants Unite, UAW Helps, Sara Looks Ahead

and Tom Brady," he joked, speaking of himself and Nelson. But in labor circles, perhaps they are.

What does the future hold for Sara Nelson? In November 2023, Nelson and her son Jack were in Hawaii, during her first vacation since the pandemic began three and a half years earlier. Nelson said later. "At the coffee shop in Honolulu, I was red-faced from my morning walk up to Diamond Head. I was not publicly presentable, I was waiting for my order and two women stepped up. One of them asked, 'Are you Sara Nelson? OMG! We're your biggest fans. We love you. When are you going to run for president of the United States?' To which Jack replied instantly, 'Let's just say 2028 is going to be a big year.'"[7] Could Nelson run for public office? She is generally coy when I ask her.

9

Child of Brooklyn

New York City has long been a center of the U.S. labor movement, especially for garment workers, teachers, longshoremen and public transportation workers. But it had not been central to the airline labor movement, and it didn't help that New York City–based Pan American World Airways shut down in 1991. That changed in 2017, when John Samuelsen, a one-time New York subway worker, was elected international president of the Transport Workers Union.

Samuelsen is very obviously a New Yorker. His accent is recognizable, he might use his hands to make a point while talking, and his loyalty to the city is a point of pride. He is not troubled by the occasional disparagement of New Yorkers by residents of other regions. Rather, it enhances his loyalty and deepens his awareness of his uniquely New York City career trajectory. One minute, he was a guard at the city's largest jail on Rikers Island; the next he was a subway track inspector. Then he was leading TWU Local 100, the historic home of New York's bus and subway workers, a local founded by a New York labor hero whom he has always respected and sought to emulate. And then he was in charge of the biggest labor union at two Texas-based airlines, American and Southwest.

"I think being from New York helps me," Samuelsen said. "It contributes to a healthy perception by the bosses on the airline side, that the days of bending over backwards to cooperate with the company are over. As for workers, I think I have a direct interaction style. I talk to everybody, everywhere. I do tons of face-to-face conversations. If there is a pre-existing bias about guys from New York, I think I have disarmed a lot of that by just being out there and talking."[1] In fact, Samuelsen recalls that in 2010, after he was first elected Local 100 president, a consultant told him that if he wanted to advance, he would have to moderate his

9. Child of Brooklyn 73

Brooklyn accent. "I think she honestly believed it made me seem unsophisticated," he said. "Consultants only think about what is the reaction of the broader public, but I don't give a rat's ass. I would never change my accent, which is God given. My usefulness would be done."[2]

Samuelsen recalls one incident when his city of origin was used against him. It came during a failed effort by a renegade mechanics' labor union, the Aircraft Mechanics Fraternal Association, or AMFA, to raid American Airlines mechanics in the early 2020s. The raid followed a widely-publicized 2019 confrontation with American Airlines President Robert Isom at LaGuardia Airport, "There was a guy in Tulsa who thought that it was disrespectful for me to challenge the president of American Airlines about jobs in Tulsa," Samuelsen said. "There was probably some anti–New York bias involved in that. There were snooty references on Facebook to me as a New York bus operator. But I've experienced very little of that."[3]

Samuelsen has lived his entire life in the same house in Gerritsen Beach, a self-contained peninsula in southern Brooklyn. The neighborhood of about 5,000 people has been largely Irish-Catholic since the early 1920s, when former residents of downtown Brooklyn's Irish shantytowns arrived after they were forced out because they lived in the proposed path of the Gowanus Expressway. Gerritsen Beach largely maintained its character until it was reshaped by Hurricane Sandy, which struck on October 29, 2012. Sea water poured in, reaching a foot high in some areas.

"When I was growing up, it was a seriously gritty, working-class Irish neighborhood, one of the grittiest parts of Brooklyn," Samuelsen said. "There's still an element of that, but the demographics have changed a bit. The place is right on the water. After Hurricane Sandy, there were some rich people who came in and bought waterfront houses. A lot of the beach house shanties are redone now, and the neighborhood has less of a gritty feel to it. For a lot of us, the only way we can afford a house there is because our parents handed down their houses to their children." For New York, the neighborhood is politically conservative. "Right now, in Southern Brooklyn, there are still Trump flags on some of the houses," Samuelsen said in September 2023.[4]

Samuelsen's family was among the early arrivals in Gerritsen Beach. His grandmother on his mother's side, Mary McMahon, came from Derry, a city in Northern Ireland. She married a Scotchman of Irish lineage and bought the house where the couple raised a family. On Samuelsen's father's side, both grandparents were born in the U.S to immigrant

John Samuelsen lives today in Gerritsen Beach in the same house he grew up in (Michael Theis).

Irish parents. In the house, "Ireland was a subject of constant conversation [about] its beauty, the heartache of the troubles in the north, and the constant discrimination that Catholics faced, which drove so many of them here." One of Samuelsen's the uncles was a strong supporter of the Irish Republican Army, the paramilitary force that sought to end British rule in Northern Island. Young John became "well versed on the issues around the British occupation." Today, he says, "It's a big part of my life. I may have an American passport but the blood going through my veins is Irish. I'm an Irish citizen in the diaspora."[5]

Samuelsen's father, Warren Christian Samuelsen, was known as "Bunky" after a character in a cartoon strip. Born in Brooklyn, Bunky Samuelsen spent 40 years in the meat business, generally in a job known as "lugger." In the 1906 novel *The Jungle*, Upton Sinclair writes about the job: "There were the beef luggers, who carried two-hundred-pound quarters into the refrigerator cars, a fearful kind of work, that began at four o'clock in the morning, and that wore out the most powerful men in two years."[6] Samuelsen said his father "was fiercely strong; he would carry 180-pound hindquarters from the tractor trailer into the wholesale market for butchers to fabricate them."[7] (In the meat business, to fabricate is to cut, bone and portion large cuts of meat to menu specifications.)

9. Child of Brooklyn

Bunky worked various jobs, sometimes as a lugger, sometimes as a driver—either for himself or for other men's companies. Typically, slaughterhouses delivered meat from Pennsylvania to the meat market in the West Village, and Bunky transported it to restaurants and hotels in the area. "From a hind quarter you get a short loin that gives you porterhouse steaks or top rounds for roast beef," his son recalled. "I used to go with him when I was on breaks from school; I loved it." For a time, Bunky Samuelsen operated a butcher shop on Gerritsen Avenue. "I worked there in my teens and early 20s, and I learned how to cut meat, but it went under," John Samuelsen said.[8]

"My father was a 100% man's man, the alpha male of the house," he said. "I was always surrounded by incredible role models in fatherhood and in what it means to be a husband and in how to carry yourself with honor and how to intervene against bullies. Now, almost all of the men that were in my realm when I was a kid have passed away, including my uncles. They were the last of Brooklyn's hard men, hard men with this gentle side. They were nearly all Irish. They worked their fingers to the bone to take care of their families. They carried themselves with a code of conduct that is remarkable. You can stay up all night drinking, but you have to fulfill your obligations, to get your ass out of bed and go to work. If you don't feel good, if you feel ill, you're not feeling your best, that made no difference. My father would always say, 'Get your ass out of bed and get to work.' That was his mantra. I don't see myself as nearly as hard as these men, but from them I learned to be fair, to have humility, to defend the weak, to never back down from a bully, and to go to work. I've tried to do that with my life. I haven't always been perfect, but those lessons have served me well. Now I tell my kids the same things."[9]

Bunky Samuelsen was a member of Amalgamated Meat Cutters and Butcher Workmen of North America, which merged into the United Food and Commercial Workers in 1979. "He was a union man, but he wasn't an activist," his son said. "He was just a guy who went to work every day to take care of his family."[10] The more engaged union parent was Theresa Foy Samuelsen, John's mother. She was a homemaker until the 1970s, when she went to work as a claims administrator for an International Association of Machinists local in Manhattan. She eventually became lead administrator. When the IAM privatized fund management, she went to work for the Teamsters Bakery Drivers and Industry Pension Fund, where she worked for 30 years. "For my mother, the union was her life," Samuelsen said. "She always had interactions with workers over benefits and pension claims and she had tremendous respect for the union movement."[11] Sometimes John would visit Theresa in her Union Square office in Manhattan and they would have lunch at the original Ray's Pizza in nearby Little Italy.

John Samuelsen was born in September 1967, the fifth of five children, including four boys. Their work histories include an alphabet soup of union membership. Oldest brother Joe worked in printing machine manufacturing, then for Brooklyn Union Gas and was in both the IAM and the TWU. Brother Warren worked as a technician and then a salesman in telecommunications. He was in three unions: Communications Workers of America, International Brotherhood of Electrical Workers, and International Brotherhood of Teamsters. Sister Theresa was a stockbroker, and brother Billy was a telephone repairman, a CWA member who retired from Verizon after participating in several strikes.

John Samuelsen is not the sort of person whom you would imagine as the youngest of five children: He lacks the reticence, or the sense that he has been coddled, that is often associated with being the baby of the family. "Being the youngest is the reason why I think he became successful," said Joe Samuelsen, his oldest brother. "He got a lot of attention from everybody, and he developed very good social skills. Our parents treated us all the same, but I think he was their favorite." John was born with unusual strength, said his brother, who recalls that "When John was very young, still in diapers, I took my father's bowling ball out of the bag. It weighed 16 pounds. I put it on the floor and I went to the bathroom. When I came out, John was lifting the ball off the floor with both hands."[12]

The brothers spent their childhoods engaged in fishing in nearby Jamaica Bay, playing baseball and following the New York Mets. Joe Samuelsen,

John Samuelsen's dad taught him: "Get your ass out of bed and go to work." Undated photograph (courtesy TWU Local 100).

born in 1957, said he was an original fan of the team, which began play in 1962. John followed his lead. "I took him to games," he said.[13] In 1973, when John was six,: the Mets won the National League pennant and played in the World Series. The loss provides one of his earliest memories. "I have a vivid childhood memory of the Mets losing," he said. "I remember the heartache, but it was beautiful in a way. My brothers and father were plopped in the living room watching that Series intently. A lot of my early memories are baseball related."[14]

While the Mets have had their high points, the team's disappointing 2022 season triggered memories of the low points for the Samuelsen brothers. The Mets had 101 regular season wins, the second most in their history, but were eliminated in the second round of the playoffs. "It's a heartache," Samuelsen said, a few weeks later. "I'm not watching baseball right now. The life of a Mets fan is misery and betrayal. All of the frustration that my brothers and father felt then, the feeling that we were good but we didn't really do enough, it's all come back to me now."[15] Joe Samuelsen said he gave up his season tickets at the end of the 2022 season, after holding them since 2005.

Samuelsen's favorite Mets player, catcher John Stearns, joined the team in 1975. "He was a beast when I was a kid," said Samuelsen, who recalled a violent 1978 collision between Stearns and Pirates star Dave Parker. Parker, who was 6–5 and 230 pounds plowed into Stearns who was holding the ball at home plate.[16] Stearns played for the Mets from 1975 to 1984 and was known for being a tough guy who played through injuries. Joe Samuelsen recalls that the collision with Parker "made a big impression on John." Once, Stearns tackled a pitcher who had thrown at another Mets player. "John thought that was amazing," Joe Samuelsen said.[17]

Perhaps the biggest game the brothers attended was in April 1983, when Tom Seaver pitched on opening day, marking his return after a 1977 trade that many Mets fans consider the worst decision the team's front office ever made. "Seaver pitched well, yielding just three hits to the Phillies in six innings. I took him to that game; he still talks about it," Joe Samuelsen said. When Seaver came out to start the game, he declined the customary ride from the bullpen in a cart. Instead, "He walked down the right field line, and the ovation was second to none. It is something you never forget."[18]

10

Rock Bottom at Rikers

Gerritsen Beach is a rough neighborhood. One thing Samuelsen vividly recalls from his youth is being hit by people. It wasn't just other kids. It was also teachers and nuns in the Resurrection Roman Catholic Church school system, where all of the Samuelsen siblings were educated. "If I didn't come in with my homework done, I got my ass kicked," John Samuelsen said. He was hit on his rear end, on his upper legs, and across the backs of his hands with a ruler. Once, he said, a lay teacher hit him in the back of his head with a brass keychain. "I later made amends with her," he said. "I realized that I was a very mouthy kid."[1]

In retrospect, "I have no problem with any of it," he said. "I was a mischievous kid. It got me to where I am in life. I learned to read, I developed a love for history and politics and I learned about consequences. The lay teachers were very physical, even more than the nuns. I learned to be stealthier with my mischief and I learned about having adversaries whom I couldn't overtake in conventional ways. I admit, I provoked a lot of what happened. If I was teaching eighth grade, I wouldn't have wanted a little smart ass Irish kid cracking jokes all day. I was probably a teachers' nightmare. But most of what I have learned in life, I learned there."[2]

Following grammar school, Samuelsen attended Nazareth Regional High School in East Flatbush. There, he said, "I learned how to write and how to communicate, to put sentences together and to be creative. I had teachers who saw something in me and worked with me, and that launched me into my campaigns for office with confidence." Samuelsen concedes that he was not a dedicated student. "There were days in seventh and eighth grade when I missed school and faked notes from my mother," he said. "But at Nazareth, I could not get away with that. If you missed school there, your father had to come and re-enroll you, and to call in sick, your parents had to make the phone call."[3]

Although Samuelsen today stands 5'10" and weighs about 250, he was small as a youth. He was "one of the shortest guys on the field"[4] when he played little league baseball and just 5'7" when he graduated from high school. "The public school kids picked on us Catholic school kids," his brother Joe Samuelsen said. "They would say, 'He's a Ressy, let's get him.' The public school kids by and large did not play any sports. Some of them were little thugs. They were like stray dogs. You had to fight back or get picked on. They tried to beat me up and take my collection plate money when I was twelve."[5] He referred to a quote from actor and comedian Chris Rock, who was bussed to high school in Gerritsen Beach and once said, "Ain't nothing scarier than poor white people."[6]

John Samuelsen remembers the regular threat of muggings as he walked several hundred yards from school to the bus. "Brooklyn in the early 1980s was the roughest place one could imagine," he said. "It was a free-for-all. I would get chased running full speed to the bus, hoping the bus would be there. There were literally eight or ten attempts at mugging me, sometimes me alone and sometimes with the other Irish kids. It was not a matter of race; it was a free for all. Everybody was fair game—Black, Irish, Latinos. I had friends of every nationality one could imagine and I had fights with other Irish kids. But the strong went after the weak."[7] Said Joe Samuelsen, "Basically, Irish kids picked on other Irish kids."[8]

It is striking to hear John Samuelsen say that, in the end, his most lasting impression of the attempted muggings near the bus stop was "the utmost respect for the bus operators." He rode the B78 bus to and from school. It was not a school bus, but a city bus with a TWU driver. "Long before I ever represented them, the bus operators had my eternal respect," he said. "They were the heroes. They saved me from being flat-out mugged. Once in 1981, when I was 14, I had a kid with a knife out flailing in my face. The bus operator got out of his seat and protected me. He was a big, soft, gentle Black man, at least until he didn't want to be gentle any more. Years later, I went back to look for him and thank him, but I couldn't find him."[9]

Samuelsen graduated from high school in 1985 and headed for Southampton College (now Stony Brook Southampton) on Long Island, about 90 miles from home. Awarded a nearly full academic scholarship, he originally intended to study in the school's marine sciences program, which seemingly represented a natural progression from his childhood interest in fishing. But the requirement to study organic chemistry was a deterrent. "Organic chemistry was the most difficult thing I ever laid eyes on in my life," he said. "I had selected it for all the wrong reasons. I

John Samuelsen, Local 100 acting vice president of maintenance of way, walks the tracks during the August 2003 blackout (courtesy TWU Local 100).

was just a kid. I viewed college as a four-year party. and I actually had no idea what I wanted to do in life. After three months, I switched to political science and I did well, but I didn't last. I left college after two years. Then I came home. I worked a bit in the butcher shop with my brother, and then I got a job working as a shift manager at the deli counter in The Food Emporium in Manhattan. I took the tests for the Corrections Department and for transit worker. And Corrections called."[10]

In 1990, three months before he turned 22, Samuelsen went to work as a corrections officer at Rikers Island prison. In Samuelson's experience—he spent three years as a corrections officer—Rikers' terrible reputation was fully deserved. "It was the most depressing atmosphere one could imagine, and the toughest place to work," he said. "You're locked up in a room with the prisoners. On any given day, you're locked up with rapists and murderers. An inmate might spit in your face, but you can't respond physically, because you're under so much scrutiny in terms of use of force, and a lot of the time it works on the presumption that the corrections officer is the guilty one. One time, I was assaulted by a prisoner. I was locking him in his cell at the end of the day. He didn't want to be locked in, and he punched me. I fell, landed on my right wrist, and tore some nerves. I had to have surgery. It still hurts and I still have a scar. That kind of thing is common. It happens all the time. People don't go to prison because they're choir boys."[11]

One compensating factor was that Rikers Island corrections officers—the term "prison guards" is always avoided because it is considered derogatory—were unionized. "It helped," Samuelsen said. "I worked the rotating shift called 'the wheel.' That means one week 7 a.m. to 3 p.m., then one week 3 p.m. to 11, then one week 11 to 7 a.m. I would call in sick a lot. I had some interaction with the union. They helped me when I got disciplined for not showing up. But the corrections department would force you to work overtime. Sometimes, I would work 3 to 11 at night, and they wouldn't let you leave. Rikers is a series of jail cells. A cell block could have cells two through 20. You could be in two working 3 to 11 and another person on a p.m. tour doesn't come to work, so you are locked in until relief comes. Sometimes you get locked in for 16 hours. One Friday night I had a wedding to go to, and I got stuck on overtime. They didn't want to hear it. They said, 'You're working. That's it, kid.' The pay wasn't bad, especially with overtime."[12] In 1990, his first year, Samuelsen made $39,000. He still felt it wasn't worth it.

Joe Samuelsen said his brother was traumatized by working at Rikers. "The prisoners were vicious. So many people threatened him with harm; he felt like he was in prison with them." On shopping trips to Kings Plaza Mall in Brooklyn, John "felt like he was going to see one of those guys who had gotten out and wanted to hurt him. He kept looking around. This happened a lot. It was a happy day for all of us when he got out of there. Guys with regular jobs don't have any idea what it's like. John wasn't the same John then. Usually, he is easy going, and he's still the exact same John he was as a teenager. He's kind of a celebrity here now, but he does not act like he's above anybody. There are no airs about him."[13]

After three years at Rikers, Samuelsen put his name back on the active list for a transit job, which he had not pursued after taking the test in 1990. In March 1993, he started as a track worker. "It was a life changing moment," he said. "It was like I had total freedom. I was in a massive depression, the worst depression of my life, after Rikers. Suddenly I had no more jail, no more darkness, just from taking that track worker job. It was a new lease on life."[14]

Although John Samuelsen's years as a corrections officer were far from enjoyable, a redeeming feature was that late in 1992, he met Lisa

John Samuelsen met Lisa Pemberton in 1992. Here they attend the victory party after his 2009 election as Local 100 president (courtesy TWU Local 100).

Pemberton at an Irish fair at Coney Island. Pemberton is a mix of English, German and Welsh, but "It was love at first sight for me," Samuelsen said. "I don't think that was really the case for her."[15] Pemberton was a bookkeeper for Brooklyn-based Superior Transcribing Service, started by her mother in 1957 and now the country's oldest medical transcription service. The courtship took time: the couple was not married until July 22, 2000.

"There was a long time in between, mostly due to carousing on my part and to an unwillingness to become a marriable person until I hit thirty and started to get myself together,"[16] Samuelsen said. Pemberton had a daughter, Alexandria, born in 1991, and later the couple had two sons. Alexandria has worked as staff coordinator at an orthopedic surgery firm. Older son John Henry, born in 2001, graduated from St. Francis College in Boston with a major in political science and works in Dublin, organizing for Sinn Féin, the ruling political party. Meanwhile, Jack Duggan, born in 2002, is an engineer and a member of the International Union of Operating Engineers Local 30, which maintains heating and cooling systems in New York skyscrapers. The two boys seem to represent different elements of their father's makeup. John "is very cerebral," while Jack is "viscerally blue collar [with] an edgy blue collar Brooklyn attitude," Samuelsen said. "Put them together and you'd have me as a kid, but a lot more mature than I was."[17]

11

"The transit authority did not give a rat's ass"

In March 1993, his first day as a transit worker, John Samuelsen signed a union card. This occurred at the transit system's training center in Bensonhurst after union representatives handed out cards and a union leader delivered a compelling speech that triggered Samuelsen's interest in track safety. Track safety would become a key issue in his ascension through the TWU ranks. The speaker "talked about how the transit authority did not give a rat's ass when you got out on the tracks," Samuelsen said. "I was glued to everything he said, although once I was out in the subway working, I found that everything he said did not translate into practice, because the union did not always fight back on safety. But it was an eye-opening experience to see how incredibly dangerous it was. The transit authority bosses were very indifferent, very nonchalant, about putting men and women in harm's way in order to get another 15 minutes of production. It has always been shocking to me how blasé some of them are about human life."[1]

Although he was pleased to join the TWU, Samuelsen at first did not fully grasp the implication of membership in a storied New York union. "It wasn't like I was frothing at the mouth to be a union activist when I was 18, but when I signed that card, I was super excited," he said. "When I was a kid, there was something special about TWU: You could tell by the cars my friends' fathers drove if they were members. They got new cars every few years and they had the ability to go to the Poconos and the Jersey shore on vacation. These are things that weren't common when I was growing up. I didn't know nearly what I would come to know about the early history and the union's connection with Ireland, but it was a great moment. And then I learned very quickly that on the tracks, TWU was the only thing between life and death.

I was put into numerous unsafe situations when I was a young track worker."²

In the New York City subway system, crews work constantly on the 248 miles of track. Passengers rarely see these crews; their awareness of track work is limited largely to instances where a train slows due to work ahead of it. Unfortunately, sometimes trains don't slow and workers are injured or killed. "It still happens, even though the union has put a ton of effort into making it safer," Samuelsen said.³ For instance, in November 2023, a subway worker was killed when he was struck by a train near the Herald Square station while he was alerting train operators that there were workers on nearby tracks.

Subway trains normally travel at speeds up to 35 miles an hour. They are supposed to slow down when they approach working track crews, informed first by lights placed on the track about 600 feet out from the crews, and then by flags held by crew members. Typically, the setup in a subway tunnel includes two tracks running in opposite directions. Each track has three rails, including the electrified third rail—its current high enough to kill anyone who touches it. Between the two tracks is a small clearance area, nothing more than that. On the outer side of each set of tracks is a cement walkway.

"If a train is bearing down on you, we have a flagger out there, he signals when a train is coming, and the train operator is supposed to slow down and stop before he gets to the work area, but there are occasions when that doesn't happen," Samuelsen said. "Sometimes, the flagging lights get knocked over; sometimes train operators have medical conditions; sometimes a train is making a reverse move and coming from the wrong direction. All three of these things have happened many times over the last 30 years, and we've had fatalities." When he began working on the tracks, Samuelsen said, "The biggest problems were that the Transit Authority did not want to slow the trains down, or the supervisors didn't follow all the rules, so that they could maintain the on-time performance."⁴

Track workers build, maintain and inspect tracks. In his first month on the job, Samuelsen built tracks at the transit agency's Coney Island Yard. There, piles of rails, ties, clips, and spikes are fabricated into tracks. Then the tracks, in 39-foot sections, are loaded onto trucks and delivered to sites where cranes lift them onto the sites where they are needed. Some sites are underground, some elevated, and some are in open cuts in the ground. Samuelsen's first impression was positive; it was a far cry from Rikers.

John Samuelsen speaks at his first press conference as Local 100 president in 2010. Far left is transit advocate Gene Russianoff; at front right is Councilman James Vacca (courtesy TWU Local 100).

"I loved swinging a hammer, and I liked the communal aspect of working in a track gang," he said. "The camaraderie is unbelievable." Track work has clear advantages over working in a subway cab or as a conductor, who is subject to being spit on or punched. Additionally, with overtime, a trackman can earn $150,000 a year. But bad supervisors can diminish the enjoyment. "Maybe a third of the bosses are decent," Samuelsen said. "Others are whip crackers. The laziest track workers can become the worst whip-cracking bosses, demeaning to workers. I ran into some penny ante track bosses, but after leaving Rikers, I had no trouble dealing with them. That was nothing compared to the misery of those three years in jail."[5]

In the summer of 1993, Samuelsen began to form his perception of workplace dynamics, of the tension between workers and bosses, as well as the potential role of collective action. "I walked into a situation by a fluke," he said. "It was the greatest thing that happened to me in my early union life."[6] The site was the welding plant in the transit authority's Linden shop in Brownsville, Brooklyn, Samuelsen's first post after training. The plant's role is to make rail sections that are "continuously welded,"

11. "The transit authority did not give a rat's ass"   87

which means that the usual 39-foot sections are welded together. The advantage of longer rail sections is that they are safer than sections that are patched together. But installation is more difficult. Several work trains are equipped to move the 500- to 600-foot sections.

When Samuelsen entered the welding plant, he found a longstanding dispute between union members and managers who were dedicated to speeding up production, despite the safety diminution. "When I was just two or three months into the job, I watched firsthand the organization of worker resistance," he said. "I saw debates among the rank-and-file track workers, about two dozen of them. Some were militant, hardline workers who fought back, some were neutral and some sided with the employer. I became involved in discussions, sitting around a lunch table. I learned that track workers standing together against the bosses could move mountains. But I also learned that a union fight-back is only as strong as its weakest link. I tried to talk to some of the fellows who weren't involved or seemed to side with bosses. The key was to try to get through to them."[7]

"A big concern was that there were different job functions at the welding plant. If somebody had an easy task for the day, they didn't want to screw that up. But I saw it as a moment to make things better for everybody by spreading out the easy work. And I learned that communication is the key to organizing, that every union action begins with a conversation, and that being irrationally hostile to track workers who don't agree with your position doesn't make sense. Disagreement doesn't make them bad. They aren't necessarily pro-company. Track workers all have their own opinions and we have to work our way through that. It takes a quest to find commonality at all costs, rather than just being dismissive of those who disagree." At the struggle's conclusion, some militant workers were rehired after being fired, and workers gained more control over the pace of the welding work. "The production going forward was done at a safe pace, and the bosses knew that if they were disrespectful of the work force the workers would work more slowly," Samuelsen said.[8] He noted that the settlement was reached by rank-and-file workers, without the involvement of union leadership.

Early in 1994, Samuelsen became involved in a conflict with a specific supervisor. His gang was based at the Fourth Avenue and 45th Street station in Sunset Park, Brooklyn. The supervisor, Samuelsen recalled, seemed to thrive on shows of physical strength. Some involved carrying protective "third rail mats," which weigh about 140 pounds and are used to cover the electrified third rail so that workers didn't accidentally

John Samuelsen speaks at a 2011 rally, with New York State Senator Martin Golden (right) and Brooklyn bus rep Willie Rivera (second from left). A "lock box" would keep mass transit funds from other uses (courtesy TWU Local 100).

touch them. "I could carry them on my shoulder without any problem, especially when I was 25," Samuelsen said. "I liked carrying a mat. It was made of rubber; it didn't dig into my neck; it was easy for me. But this guy, who was Italian, would carry two mats on his shoulder. I had to giggle at this, it was so bizarre. Also, he would never lay the signal lights out right. He was always trying to intimidate people to work without protections, because his way of speeding things up was to not take the time for safety measures."[9]

Over the weekend of July 4, 1994, the problems between Samuelsen and his unlikable supervisor erupted at the Sunset Park station at 36th Street. "We had driven a truck there for a maintenance job," Samuelsen said. "We were walking down the stairs to the subway, where the passengers entered. We were carrying tools and the third rail mats. But when I got to the top of the stairs, this supervisor told me to bounce it down the stairs to the bottom. I said I wouldn't do it and he started screaming at me. Then he threatened to fire me. He thought I was on probation, which would give him the right to fire me right there, but the truth was that I had already been on the job more than a year, so he didn't have that right any more. I started in March 1993 and here it was July 4th in 1994.[10]

"So I said, 'Go ahead. You're a moron, trying to get me to throw a mat down the stairs with riders all over, walking up and down the stairs.' I said, 'This is great; it will be in *The Daily News* tomorrow.' Then I smiled and said, 'You can't fire me, you imbecile, I'm not on probation.' And he cursed at me, he said, 'You lazy Irish c—.' So then I put the mat down on the ground and I took a memo book out of my pocket and I said, 'Can you repeat that?' and I wrote down what he said. I had a bunch of witnesses there too. Then I told him, 'You can't call me that. I will meet you on Fourth Avenue. I'm going to beat the shite out of you.' But he never showed up.[11]

"Later, I filed charges against him. There had also been a guy with me, a guy who looked like a model, a pretty boy, and this Italian supervisor called him an Irish queer. This supervisor abused everybody; we had a ton of letters from witnesses and his victims. And I was able to harness all this anger and outrage, and we got him busted down from level two to entry level supervisor. The funny thing is that I went on to have a working relationship with this guy. He kept moving up the ranks, became a bigger boss, and I had contact with him after 2000, when I won my first election to take over the chairmanship of the track workers."[12]

Leadership in confronting bad bosses and advocating for track safety enabled Samuelsen to win a 1994 election to be shop steward of his track gang of about 15 workers. Shop stewards represent workers in dealing with management. "People were getting hurt on the tracks, so it wasn't a celebratory election," Samuelsen said. "It was about the fight against unsafe working conditions. I cut my teeth in that job, learning to organize workers, doing collective fight-backs in pursuit of a safe workspace." Eventually, in 1997, Samuelsen moved to another job classification: track inspector. "Inspectors make $3 an hour more, but it comes with a ton of responsibility and it's dangerous when the trains come," he said.[13]

Late in 1997, Samuelsen was elected one of three vice chairmen of the TWU's track division, which included about 1,700 workers at the time. (It has since increased to about 2,000 workers.) As vice chairman, he could do unannounced track safety inspections, conducted when crews were working. The inspections "became the foundation for everything I did going forward," said Samuelsen, who remained an inspector until 2009, as he moved up the ranks in union leadership. "I came to see that the tracks were a super dangerous place, with lots of problems, centered around oncoming train traffic and third rail safety." He made hundreds of unannounced inspections and shut down dozens of sites. The transit authority was not pleased. "I kept stopping jobs," he said. "The company said it was obstruction of government administration. They tried to fire me. I kept getting called for drug tests at the last minute. If you get called for a drug test and you don't show up, that is considered a positive test result."[14] Between 1997 and 2000, Samuelsen was called for about a dozen drug tests. However, over time his inspections led to improvements.

As vice chairman, besides inspecting track, Samuelsen oversaw hundreds of grievances. He became familiar with the many nuances of the contract and of track safety protocol. "Nobody knew the safety protocols better than I did," he said. "That's how I was able to shut down unsafe work."[15] Samuelsen found an ally in Roger Toussaint, whom he met at the welding plant in Linden, where he was assigned to Toussaint's gang. He ran for track division vice chairman on Toussaint's ticket in 1997, and in 2000 he ran for track chairman on a ticket where Toussaint ran for Local 100 president. It won decisively. For the first time, Samuelsen's was in a job where his salary was paid by the union rather than the transit authority. He earned about $65,000 annually, up from about $55,000 as a track worker.

John Samuelsen speaks against workplace sexual harassment. This photograph, taken at the new MTA headquarters, was used on the cover of the *TWU Bulletin* for Summer 2012 (courtesy TWU Local 100).

Again his role expanded, and he engaged in workplace issues such as seniority and days off. For example, he wanted workers with high seniority to be able to specifically select the jobs they would work. One case involved the overseeing of the fuel pumps in the Linden shop. "It was very light work where you weren't humping rails or walking around in the dark with the third rail close by," he said. "The bosses had been putting their ass kissers in those jobs, but we made an argument they should go on the seniority list." Another case involved favoritism in awarding overtime pay. When supervisors inspect track work sites, they are joined by a person who sets up the signal flags. The jobs are often assigned as overtime, which could add up to several thousand dollars a year. "The supervisors would bring their ass kissers or their nephews," Samuelsen said. "We made the argument that these jobs should be seniority pick work."[16] After TWU won the case, the precedent was set that high-overtime jobs should be awarded by seniority.

Another issue for the track chairman was days off awards. The transit authority preferred that track work be done on weekends, when fewer people rode the subway and fewer trains were scheduled. That meant weekend work for many track workers, with days off during the week. In the late 1990s and early 2000s, Samuelsen said, the transit authority sought to expand the amount of weekend work. It mandated that all Bronx track work would be done on weekends. The union protested strongly, mounting work stoppages.

Tensions peaked during a 2001 demonstration at a Bay Ridge 50th Street construction project, when the transit authority used a crane that the TWU found unsafe. "Four other guys and I climbed on top to a 39-foot panel section and we wouldn't get off," Samuelsen recalled. "The standoff lasted all day. They called out hundreds of cops: they called out horse cops too. Some of the track workers threw track fasteners at the supervisors. The cops were trying to get us off the panel. Finally, they brought in the borough commander for Brooklyn, and he negotiated a settlement that led to the transit agency putting the track back together. The settlement was that no TWU Local 100 members would work near the crane. The bosses had to go up there."[17] The incident, covered in *The Daily News*, enhanced Samuelsen's profile in the union, which perhaps contributed to a falling out with Toussaint.

12

Mike Quill and the Strike Culture of TWU Local 100

The TWU Local 100 has a long tradition of striking the transit system, a tradition that began with a fiery Irish leader named Mike Quill. Samuelsen has many commonalities with Quill, whom he calls a hero. They share fearlessness, a knack for interacting with the media, a staunch advocacy for workers, a refusal to be dull and their Irish identity. Both made the climb from subway worker to leader of a union that has long embodied New York toughness.

"John used to work track on the subway. He shows that you can do that and have the innate core set of skills to go from laying track to becoming president of the union and negotiating with governors and legislators," said Roberto Ramirez, a New York political consultant with a storied background that includes five terms as state assemblyman representing the Bronx and 40 days in prison after he protested U.S. test bombing at Vieques in Puerto Rico in 2003. At one time, Ramirez was the TWU's attorney. "John is an equal opportunity challenger, whether you are the MTA or an airline or another union," he said. "He is a rare combination, because most people can have a good idea, but only a smaller group of people can take those ideas and shape them into a process. Few have the ability to take their ideas and alter reality. That is what a real leader does."[1]

The same applies to Quill, a founder of Local 100 who is best known for leading a 1966 strike that shut down the subway system for 12 days. Quill was a familiar figure in New York, someone who engaged regularly with reporters when the city's nine daily newspapers were its principal source of information. Samuelsen first heard of Mike Quill long before

12. Mike Quill and the Strike Culture of TWU Local 100 93

he ever thought of himself as a union leader. "My father liked him," he said. "My father watched television and read *The Daily News* and had a lot of respect for the guy. He was like a far-off legend to me."[2]

Over the years, however, Quill became a touchstone in Samuelsen's life, providing inspiration as a loyal Irishman who fought first for his country and then for transportation laborers. Quill fought for the Irish Republican Army, immigrated to New York in 1926 and went to work as a night gate security man for the IRT, then an independent subway line. In 1934, he co-founded the TWU. Quill battled antisemitism and the infamous U.S. Senator Joe McCarthy. He also backed the Civil Rights movement from its early days. When Quill died, Martin Luther King, Jr., called him a man who "spent his life ripping the chains of bondage off his fellow man."[3]

The strike that Quill led began January 1, 1966; A judge issued an injunction that day. On January 2, the union reduced its demands, but the transit authority obtained a judge's order for the arrest of Quill and eight other union officials. On January 4, immediately before his arrest, Quill told reporters, "The judge can drop dead in his black robes. I don't care if I rot in jail. I will not call off the strike."[4] Taken to jail, Quill—who was already in poor health and was obviously under stress—suffered a heart attack after two hours in a holding cell in a West 37th Street precinct building. An ambulance took him to Bellevue Hospital; later he was transferred to Mount Sinai Medical Hospital. Negotiations continued until January 13, when they concluded with a settlement that provided significant wage increases. Quill was released from the hospital January 25; he died at home three days later. Ultimately, despite the wage gains, the strike also had a negative outcome: the New York State Legislature approved the Taylor Law, which prohibits public employees in the state from striking.

Samuelsen was born the year after Quill died. When he took over as TWU international president on May 1, 2017, at age 49, he became the youngest president since Quill took the office in 1937. Like Quill, he believes that "trade unions are the vehicle for economic security and the government has to create an environment where trade unions can flourish." Samuelsen's downtown Brooklyn office houses Quill's desk as well as some of the early contracts Quill signed. "Mike Quill was a founder of this union that I love," Samuelsen said. "To think I would be running Local 100, like he did, never crossed my mind. To sit in the chair Mike Quill sat in is surreal."[5]

In a book entitled *The Man Who Ran the Subways: The Story of*

Mike Quill greets Martin Luther King, Jr., before the civil rights leader addressed the TWU convention in 1961 (courtesy TWU Local 100).

Mike Quill, published in 1968, a young reporter named Hank Whittemore wrote Quill's story. (Whittemore's publisher preferred to use the name L.H. Whittemore as the author's name.) Quill was " a poor man's version of James Bond, Charles de Gaulle and Casey Stengel, all in one," Whittemore wrote. "A pumpkin shaped elf, he haunted the subway tunnels of New York and transit systems around the world, wooing his fellow workers to a radical vision. The slave of an impish humor, he stood in the center of the storm he created and thoroughly enjoyed himself."[6] Quill obviously enjoyed the attention, and did not seem to mind that he

12. Mike Quill and the Strike Culture of TWU Local 100   95

was blamed and hated for the 1966 strike. Quill "was bad news, and for that reason he was on the front page as often as the weather," the book said, noting that he "barely concealed his amusement as his listeners took in the blarney, the tough wit, and the outrageous pyramid of illogic from this amiable rouge."[7]

Whittemore was 26 when he started on the book. He was hampered because Quill died at 60, soon after he began his research, eliminating the chance for interviews with his subject. "Quill led a very colorful life," Whittemore said. "As a writer, I've always written about eccentrics or underdogs," and Quill was both. "At age 15 or 16, he is in the South of Ireland, helping the IRA," Whittemore continued. "Then he comes to New York, works in the subway, and rails against the conditions and wages, which were terrible. The subways were private companies then; they had spies and guys who would break strikes. Later, Quill joins the Communists, which was a good thing during the fervency of the 1930s. They came here to start unions. He learned all about civil rights and social equity through them. People started to call him 'Red Mike.'" He was far advanced in thinking about civil rights and an early supporter of Martin Luther King, Jr."[8]

The Communists in the 1930s were considered a viable political force with thousands of supporters in New York. "They organized the TWU and set up an Irishman to head it," Whittemore said. "Quill elbowed him out. They thought Quill was a puppet, but he understood the Communists and he used them."[9] The alliance with Quill lasted for a dozen years, ending in 1948, near the start of the Red Scare, when Quill broke with the party. Roger Toussaint, who preceded Samuelsen as Local 100 president, admires Quill for his ability to mobilize membership, but notes that "He participated in purging the TWU of most of its leftist leaders during the McCarthy era." Toussaint said in an interview that Samuelsen followed a similar path by red-baiting him. "I am a radical revolutionary," he said. "I am a foreigner, an immigrant, and I don't bow to any national flag."[10]

Quill was deeply involved in New York City politics, and had varying relations with the city's mayors of New York City. He was friendly with Robert F. Wagner, Jr., who served from 1954 to 1966. But he had nothing in common with John Lindsay, Wagner's debonair, patrician successor, who served until 1973. The famous New York columnist Jimmy Breslin once wrote, "John Lindsay looked at Quill and saw the past, and Mike Quill looked at Lindsay and saw the Church of England."[11] By contrast, Wagner "knew how to deal with Quill; they understood each other,"

Whittemore said. "In public Quill would rail against the city, threaten a strike, make demands. The *New York Times* and most of the papers would say that Quill crushed the city, and dealt the city a financial blow. But Wagner would give Quill credit and let everyone think Quill won. The thing was if you couldn't give Quill cash, then give him credit.

"When Lindsay came in, he wouldn't even talk to Quill. He looked down on him. He didn't understand the history; he didn't understand what Quill was fighting for, what he meant, what the collective bargaining system was. Quill had been a part of developing that and he believed in it. In collective bargaining, you could go in and talk to each other. Quill wanted back and forth in dialogue. That's what unions are about. But Lindsay wouldn't play the game; he sent other people in to talk. Unlike Wagner, Lindsay wanted to give little cash and take all the credit. He ended up giving twice as much cash as Wagner did."[12] Whittemore, a graduate of Notre Dame who was then a reporter for *The White Plains Reporter Dispatch*, recalled watching news about the 1966 strike on television. "Quill would be talking; he had that twinkle in his eye and he said outrageous things. My wife and I were both fascinated. I said 'I am going to write a book about him; that came right out of my mouth. I didn't even know that I could get a book published; my goal was just to write a book, to have it on the mantelpiece."[13] (I felt similarly about Samuelsen, although I had published three books when I first spoke to him.)

Whittemore became even more fascinated when he read Quill's *New York Times* obituary, which stretched over a page. He began researching newspaper stories in the White Plains Library and in the New York Public Library, where he plowed through issues of *The Daily Worker* and the *TWU Express*. He read transcripts of the House Un-American Activities Committee, where the Communist role in the creation of the TWU was fully explored.

"It wasn't fiction, although it almost sounds like a cartoon," Whittemore said. In doing interviews, Whittemore found that many of the people close to Quill "were suspicious of journalists; they didn't think journalists understood." He reached out to Paul O'Dwyer, an Irish-born civil rights and labor lawyer whose brother, William O'Dwyer, was mayor from 1946 to 1950. Whittemore said Paul O'Dwyer told him, "I don't think you have the memory of Michael in a good light." Nevertheless, O'Dwyer agreed to several interviews. Wagner, mayor from 1954 to 1966, was particularly helpful. "Wagner ended up with a law office in the Empire State Building," Whittemore said. "I interviewed him there.[14]

"I was a young man with a young wife and a small child, living in an apartment, working six or seven days a week on a newspaper as city hall reporter, and on the radio in White Plains, and also trying to research a book in the hours I could do it. I was amazed it could happen." Somehow, he found a receptive contact at publisher Holt, Rinehart and Winston, which agreed to publish the book and gave him a contract for $1,500, half in advance and half on delivery. "I took the money and quit my jobs," he said. He went to Ireland and spent ten days interviewing Quill's relatives and digging into public records.

After the book was written, he decided he might have a career as a writer. He went on to write several books, including *The Super Cops*, a bestseller that was made into a movie; 100 cover stories for *Parade Magazine* and scripts for the TV cop show Baretta. Then he had a second career as a Shakespearean actor. "It was Quill that started it all for me," he said. "I learned about doing something without being assured of an end result, just doing it to do it as well as I could, and it led to all these other things."[15]

Following Quill's death, it was 14 years until New York's next subway strike, which came on April 1, 1980, and lasted 11 days. Local 100 struck even after the MTA got a court order prohibiting a strike. Under the Taylor Law, the union was forced to pay a $1.25 million fine and give up dues checkoff for four months. But it won substantial wage increases: 9 percent in the first year and 8 percent in the second, plus a cost-of-living adjustment. For New Yorkers, perhaps the chief memory of the strike is that Mayor Ed Koch stood on the Brooklyn Bridge, cheering for the commuters who walked across it to get to work.

In 2020, Local 100

Local 100 Founder Mike Quill is shown in an undated photograph (courtesy TWU Local 100).

posted a 40th anniversary tribute with a headline that proclaimed, "It was April Fool's Day 1980, but the TWU Local 100 membership was not joking." The story noted that Koch "did more harm than good during the strike [when he] lamented to the press: 'The unthinkable has happened and now we have to figure out how to live with the unthinkable and we will.'" As for the Taylor Law, the post said, "The courts came down hard on the union, fining all strikers two days pay for each day on strike under the onerous Taylor Law. The union was fined $1 million, a stunning sum for 1980, and as well, dues checkoff was lost for a period of time."[16]

At the time, the leader of Local 100 was John Edward Lawe, "a rugged Irish immigrant who had labored in a road repair crew and in Ireland's peat bogs before arriving in America in 1949 at the age of 30."[17] Samuelsen remembers that he was 12 years old during the strike and that Lawe, "was the last off-the-boat Irishman to be president."[18]

Compared with the 1966 strike, the 1980 strike had less intense membership support. Roger Toussaint said that in 1966, "Quill always had an emphasis on a mobilized membership. The way to judge leadership and strikes is whether they take place in the context of a mobilized membership." But in 1980, "Lawe voted to end the strike [and] the strike took place despite him," Toussaint said.[19]

13

Who If Anybody Won the 2005 New York Subway Strike?

In December 2005, Local 100 struck the subway system, shutting the city down for three days. Two decades later, John Samuelsen questions whether the strike was worthwhile, while then–Local 100 President Roger Toussaint defends it. Obviously, the strike's effectiveness is debatable. What's not debatable is the rift between Samuelsen and Toussaint, a one-time ally who became a bitter foe. Toussaint, who took office as president of Local 100 in 2001, retired in 2009 after serving two terms. Today, he is largely retired, living in Kennesaw, Georgia, an Atlanta suburb where his son and five grandchildren also live. Meanwhile, when Samuelsen looks back on the 2005 strike, he sees an instance where he learned the hard way that a strike may create more problems than it solves.

Born in 1956 in Port of Spain, Trinidad, Toussaint came to the United States at age 17. He went to work for the MTA in 1984, first as a car cleaner and then as a track worker. He quickly developed a strong interest in the union, becoming a leader of a group of dissident members who opposed an old guard union leadership. At the time, the 33,000-member union was majority Black and Hispanic, but much of the leadership remained "old guard" Irish. "I was the first guy who was not handpicked by the old guard," Toussaint said. "I was part of a rank-and-file movement that had been organizing since the late 1980s."[1] In 1995, he was elected chairman of the 1,900-member track division. He served two terms before he was elected president of Local 100, a job he took over on January 1, 2001, when he became the local's second Black president.

Like Samuelsen, Toussaint was troubled by MTA's adversarial

relationship with its employees. "When we took over the union, the universal perception among transit workers was that the MTA had no respect whatsoever for the workforce and was complicit with management," he said. "From the beginning, we embarked upon a project to turn that around, to win respect for workers and to fight the disciplinary machine they had put on transit workers' backs." In particular, Toussaint said, MTA historically had a harsh policy regarding absences and sick time. Employees were required to inform the agency two hours before they called in sick. Once they did so, they also had to call in every time they left their homes or changed location, even if it was just to go to the supermarket. Under this strict policy, MTA issued thousands of disciplinary write-ups annually, mostly for sick time and attendance violations. In any three-year period, Toussaint said, half of all members had some type of charge leveled against them. "You would end up getting tripped up, and each violation would be recorded separately," he said. "Everybody would have charges or multiple charges."[2] Also, the agency would send transit police and sometimes a doctor to check up on sick employees.

In 2002, Toussaint successfully negotiated a contract, but it was not a contract he loved. The problem was that the previous contract expired in October. That month, Congress approved a resolution authorizing the use of military force against Iraq. "We knew that a war with Iraq was coming and that there would be a disadvantage to being on a transit strike in the middle of a war," Toussaint said. Still, the union got wage increases and a major change in the sick leave policy, protecting the 70 percent of employees with the best attendance records from sick leave surveillance. "They were freed of the at home requirement," Toussaint said.[3] However, to resolve a larger deficit in the union health plan, Toussaint agreed to a concession in health plan administration, replacing a trust with three officers from the union and three from the agency. The contract was overwhelmingly approved.

The 2005 negotiations were far more complex. At 12:01 a.m. on Friday, December 16, the contract expired. The two sides had talked for weeks, but, "in the last few hours before the deadline, the MTA suddenly insisted on major changes in the pension plan," Toussaint said. "They wanted to triple the employee contribution to 6% from 2%. They were offering a wage increase, but with a tripling of the pension contribution. Under New York State law, pensions are under the purview of the state legislature, but they were still insisting on it." The proposed changes included an increased contribution, an increase in the retirement age to

62 from 55, and reduced pension payments. As for pay, the two sides were close, with the MTA offering a bit more than half of the 6 percent annual raises sought by TWU. The pay might have been negotiable, but Toussaint saw the pension changes as unacceptable. He did not want to work without a contract. "We had always operated under the mantra that our strike deadline was a real deadline—no contract, no work—and that had to be taken seriously," he said. "All of the other unions in New York had worked without a contract for several years and we weren't going to do that."[4]

Timing became a factor. "We didn't want to go on strike on a Thursday and Friday because we would lose weekend pay; a good share of the workers had Friday and Saturday off," Toussaint said. "So we came up with a strategy to give MTA until Monday to change their position. When they didn't, we began a strike on two properties that Monday, and we extended the strike to all properties on Tuesday."[5]

The subway shut down at 3 a.m. Tuesday. Unfortunately for the TWU, the strike was illegal under the Taylor Law. Hours after it started, the case went to court before State Supreme Court Justice Theodore T. Jones in Brooklyn. Jones ordered Local 100 not to strike and imposed a fine of $1 million per strike day. Meanwhile, talks continued—and made progress.

By Thursday, December 22, the union agreed to go back to work. Although there was not yet a signed contract, Toussaint had a tentative agreement. By late Friday morning, service was back to normal, in time for Christmas Eve. Two days after Christmas, Toussaint announced the settlement terms: TWU accepted the MTA salary proposal and the pension policy was unchanged. However, MTA agreed to contribute 1.5 percent of salary to help defray health care costs, and Martin Luther King, Jr. Day became a paid holiday. But three weeks later, members rejected the new contract by seven votes, with 11,234 opposed and 11,227 in favor. In a second vote, in April, more people voted and a slightly altered contract was approved. The vote was 14,716 to 5,877 in favor. Toussaint said the seven-vote defeat reflected opposition by Samuelsen and his allies, who "misrepresented what was in the contract."[6]

The drama didn't end with the contract's approval. On April 10, Judge Jones sentenced Toussaint to 10 days in jail for contempt of court. In announcing the sentence, Jones said, he was "confounded by the tortured tale of these negotiations," and noted, "It is unfortunate that it came down to an illegal strike, but it was nonetheless illegal."[7] Besides the jail sentence, he fined the union $2.5 million and eliminated dues checkoff. On April 24, Toussaint reported to The Tombs, a city jail on the lower West Side of Manhattan. As the New York Post reported the following day, "Ever-defiant transit-union chief Roger Toussaint yesterday staged an over-the-top surrender to authorities to begin his brief jail stint at The Tombs—walking across the Brooklyn Bridge surrounded by hundreds of supporters screaming, 'No Toussaint, no peace!'"[8]

About 500 supporters accompanied Toussaint, who wore a red union T-shirt and a black TWU jacket, the Post said. In the jail's civil ward, his fellow inmates included a deadbeat dad and a "rogue landlord" who declined to make court-ordered repairs to his property. Sentenced to ten days, Toussaint was released after 86 hours, taking advantage of one law that provided time off for good behavior and another that ensured he was released before the weekend. "Being in jail was inconvenient, but the main thing was the removal of dues checkoff," he said.[9] After being re-elected president in 2005, Toussaint got dues checkoff restored as he negotiated the 2008 contract. When his term ended in 2009, he chose not to run, and he moved on to a post as a TWU international vice president and director of strategic planning. In 2012, he retired with 28 years in the union. Besides being a grandfather, he gives occasional

Roger Toussaint said, "Mayor Bloomberg should shut up" after the city said it would fine subway workers if they walked out in December 2002 (courtesy TWU Local 100).

13. Who Won the 2005 New York Subway Strike?

speeches and sometimes offers union leadership training. Between 2016 and 2019, he consulted for the Amalgamated Transit Union.

The runup to the strike marked the end of the last vestige of a working relationship between Samuelsen and Toussaint. They even disagreed on whether they had once been friends. Samuelsen said Toussaint "was a very good union rep in the 1990s and in the early years of his presidency. He was very effective—a good organizer, audacious, and a unifier. He had a good first term but then, at a certain point in time, something in him changed and he lost support. By 2005, the union was in a state of civil war."[10] Toussaint, he said, became self-absorbed and had conflicts with his staff. One area of conflict was a Toussaint effort to sell the union headquarters.

"As we were organizing picket lines and picket captains, Toussaint was trying to sell the building," Samuelsen said. "There was no focus on the strike. The 14 members of the 'maintenance of way' executive board wrote a letter urging him to delay discussion of the sale until after the contract was settled, because that was interfering with our ability to organize workers for a fight. But when we put the letter out, he fired everyone who signed it."[11] Toussaint said he had appointed Samuelsen to be vice president of maintenance of way, replacing an elected leader whom he appointed to strike preparation duty. But he fired Samuelsen from that job two weeks before the strike because "I had reports about him undermining our prestrike mobilization, not carrying out general instructions and discouraging people from participating. He could not be credited for any mobilization at all."[12]

Samuelsen said Toussaint negotiated a contract with good health care in 2002, but the 2005 negotiations fell short. "The strike wasn't a good tactical move," Samuelsen said. "There was no point to striking over proposed pension plan changes, since the state legislature—not the transit authority—oversees the pension plan. We struck, and I supported the strike, and I built picket lines all over the four boroughs. I even worked with the guys he fired to build those picket lines, and they held up wonderfully. Nobody crossed the picket lines—nobody."[13]

Still, the lesson, Samuelsen said, was that "you can win contracts in New York City without going on strike. I am philosophically in support of striking, but I learned that sometimes, when you set a strike deadline, you put a gun to your own head. You can't say 'We won't work an hour without a contract.' If you go on strike just to hold to the deadline, you can end up with no contract and no work." Additionally, in New York, the Taylor Law presents a problem, although not an unsolvable one. "In

New York, workers don't have to be told to strike," he said. "They can engage in organic job actions, not run out of the president's office. We have the ability to control the pace on the bus, on the subway and on maintenance, and that's incredibly impactful. I don't understand why somebody would choose a full-blown strike action."[14]

In today's labor climate, when support for labor is widespread, at least theoretically, the notion of a strike has a romantic appeal. But it is not always the case that strikes benefit the workers who must endure them. "There is a fetishized romanticization of striking," Samuelsen said. "I am looking at Starbucks, Amazon and all of those romanticized job actions that haven't led to a contract. This whole stuff around striking is driving me nuts. Strikes aren't a weapon in themselves. They are part of a sequence of events to win a contract. I'm 100% in favor of striking as long as it's used tactically, as part of a strategic campaign. But I'm not in favor of striking so that workers can say we struck."[15]

14

Battling New York's Organic Green Tea–Drinking, Neo-Liberal Hipsters

After the 2005 strike, John Samuelsen was demoted from Toussaint's leadership team and sent back to the track gang, based at 45th Street and Fourth Avenue in Sunset Park, where he had first worked on a track gang in 1994. Tough blow to take? Not really. Samuelsen relished the opportunity to return.

"I went back to my tools, back to my gang," Samuelsen said. "I still held my elected job as chairman of track, but Toussaint stripped me of all my other duties. I had mixed emotions about that, but mainly I was extremely happy to get back to my gang quarters where I was welcomed back into a congratulatory environment. The work atmosphere, the locker room atmosphere, the camaraderie of a track gang is incredible. There's all kinds of people; it's like the United Nations: Irish, Italians, Dominicans, Puerto Rican, Caribbean, African American. I was very comfortable in that location; I had roots there."[1] At the time, Samuelsen acknowledged, no women were part of the gang of about two dozen people, although the local had bargained for favorable accommodations for women. Any woman track worker would be paid for travel time to the nearest station with a women's locker room. If the nearest locker room was a half hour away, the worker would get paid for an extra hour of work each day.

In any case, for Samuelsen, the opportunity to work 20 minutes from home by car was extremely favorable. He worked nights, enabling him to join his wife in their commitment to homeschool their three children. In fact, Lisa Samuelsen did most of the teaching; her husband said he "provided logistical support," by cooking and grocery shopping.

Homeschooling enabled the couple to offer "a Christian worldview," that reflected Lisa's "non-denominational Christianity" rather than John's Catholicism, Samuelsen said. The teaching emphasized the wealth/power distribution embodied in the trade union movement. "We were determined to raise our children as Christians, and we certainly did that," Samuelsen said. "The whole context for me is the North of Ireland, where it's not a Catholic fight, it's a Republican fight not tied to Catholicism."[2] Rather, both Catholics and Protestants advocate for an independent country.

Similarly, in the Samuelsen homeschool curriculum, the focus was not on political parties but on the spirit of trade unionism. "We wanted them to have a blue-collar Christian worldview," Samuelsen said. "I don't embrace the mainstream politics of Democrats or Republicans, and we put a massive emphasis on thinking about trade unionism, understanding that trade unionism is the pathway to success for working kids, rather than having faith in a single political party, the Democrats," Samuelsen said. Asked to identify a political figure whose beliefs were taught, Samuelsen named Franklin D. Roosevelt, whose economic policies "pulled the U.S. out of a worldwide Depression."[3]

Despite living a comfortable life in Brooklyn, Samuelsen remained enmeshed in union politics. In 2006, he ran for secretary-treasurer of Local 100, narrowly losing in a five-person race. "If I had run for president I would have won," he said, but instead he agreed to run for secretary-treasurer as part of an anti–Toussaint ticket. "I didn't run for president because I wanted to hold the anti–Toussaint coalition together," he said. "But it was not a strong enough coalition. It was a group that was more interested in a civil war in the union." After his defeat, Samuelsen continued to work as a gang shop steward. In 2009, he mounted a strong campaign for president and defeated a Toussaint loyalist. "The desire to do that work never left me, and I had a huge amount of encouragement,"[4] Samuelsen said. He took office in January 2010 and won two elections, staying in the job until 2017.

When Samuelsen first became Local 100 president in 2009, MTA CEO Jay Walder told him the agency was broke and "threw a ton of concessions at me," he said. They included forgoing promised wage increases in 2010 and 2011 and restructuring the medical package. "He threatened me with layoffs if I didn't open the contract, but we refused," Samuelsen said. It doesn't seem that Walder's two years as CEO went particularly well. He raised fares, laid off nearly 1,000 workers before rehiring them the next year, cut back service and maintenance and then left suddenly

14. Battling New York's Neo-Liberal Hipsters

John Samuelsen speaks at a rally outside MTA Headquarters at 2 Broadway in October 2016 (courtesy TWU Local 100).

to run the transit agency in Hong Kong. Perhaps his departure was related to the TWU's nightly pickets at the Upper West Side condo he bought in 2010 for $1.6 million. The incident exemplifies the TWU's hardball approach. Today, Samuelsen says that Walder "engaged in the right-wing bean counter's dream," and maintains that Walder "stretched out maintenance cycles, which led to a near implosion in the state of repair in 2016."[5]

As president of Local 100 and later of the TWU, Samuelsen had a spot in the upper echelon of New York labor leaders. During this time, New York's leading politicians were three mayors: Mike Bloomberg, Bill de Blasio and Eric Adams and three governors: David Patterson, Andrew Cuomo and Kathy Hochul. Samuelsen's leadership has been colored, particularly in the public perception, by his relationship with these politicians, particularly de Blasio and Cuomo. For de Blasio, Samuelsen has long harbored contempt; his relationship with Cuomo has changed over time.

De Blasio defines Samuelsen's vision of a certain type of Democrat—"white collar, neo-liberal elitists who scorn blue collar working people while pretending to have concern for them."[6] The situation is epitomized by a 2015 incident when de Blasio backed the arrest of a veteran bus driver after a traffic accident. The bus struck a 15-year-old girl who had been crossing the street with a walk signal on her way to school in Williamsburg, Brooklyn. She was pinned under the front of the bus, and her leg was severely injured.[7] The bus driver, one of about 10,000 drivers who are Local 100 members, was charged with failure to yield. He was at least the third New York City bus driver arrested under a right-of-way law that had taken effect the previous year.

"In the first year of his first term, de Blasio had a bus driver arrested and humiliated for an accident," Samuelsen said. "This driver was African-American, a longtime driver, and he was making a left hand turn on his route, around dusk, in the manner he was required to do, not speeding or doing anything wrong. Buses have blind spots. He hit somebody who was sent to the hospital. At the hospital, he was crying. His wife and children and grandchildren showed up, they were all praying for the person he hit."[8] But de Blasio had instituted a plan called Vision Zero, intended to reduce pedestrian fatalities. Its centerpiece was a new law that made failure to yield a misdemeanor if a driver, even including a bus driver, kills or injures a pedestrian. Convicted drivers faced fines of up to $250 or 30 days in jail. "Vision Zero proponents say that bus drivers should set the standard for other drivers, and that the punishment under the law is not excessive," The New York Times reported.[9]

Samuelsen called de Blasio "an alleged lefty with a turncoat, sell-out, anti–blue collar mentality, especially towards high wage blue collar workers." The mayor sent Brooklyn borough highway police to the hospital. They "hauled out the bus driver in a perp walk like he was a thug or mugger, and they arrested him," he said. De Blasio "did it to win respect among the progressive left proponents of pedestrian right-of-way, all the granola-eating wimps in Williamsburg and Park Slope. "There's a whole segment of yuppified gentrifiers who hate blue collar New Yorkers," Samuelsen said. A lot of them are interlopers, like de Blasio, who come from somewhere else and think they run the place."[10]

In response to the arrest, the TWU placed an ad in *The Daily News*, featuring a drawing of de Blasio wearing a sash that reads "Mr. Progressive" and putting handcuffs on a bus driver. The ad headline proclaimed "Uncuff 'em, Mayor De Blasio!"[11] The union also sought to exempt bus drivers from the law as long as they were not engaged in other activities such as speeding or texting. "Many of the lefties, many of the Democrats on the city council, fought us tooth and nail," Samuelsen said. "That was the turning point for me. The Democratic party institutionally doesn't give a rat's ass about working people."[12] The TWU sued the city and reached a court settlement that prevents the arrest and charging of bus drivers for striking a pedestrian as long as they are not guilty of any other offense.

Samuelsen initially forged alliances with Gov. Kathy Hochul and Mayor Eric Adams. Of Hochul, he said, "After looking at Cuomo and De Blasio, she does not seem nearly diabolic enough to be a high elected official." Samuelsen's engagement with New York officials diminished when he became international president. However, he was angered when a Hochul appointee opposed giving Metropolitan Transportation Authority mechanics and cleaners the same raises that subway workers received in their 2019 contract. "It is now abundantly clear that Gov. Kathy Hochul is complicit in the shameful ripping off of unionized MTA railroad workers," Samuelsen said in 2024.[13]

As for Adams, New York City's mayor since 2022, Samuelsen noted, "He grew up in Brooklyn and has a blue-collar Brooklyn mentality, [unlike] hipsters who walk around like they own the streets, pushing fancy baby carriages, then stop and have a cup of organic green tea at a Vietnamese restaurant." The hipsters, mainly out-of-state white people, are gentrifying neighborhoods like Greenpoint, Park Slope and Williamsburg, he said. "They oppose Eric because he's not one of them. There's this whole philosophical battle between average New Yorkers and social progressives obsessed with policing and every social liberal cause."[14]

Samuelsen was initially a Cuomo supporter. "Cuomo built stuff and, to his credit, he compelled the Second Avenue subway to completion," Samuelsen said. Cuomo was known to be an extremely difficult person, but he and Samuelsen initially had a good relationship. That was important, Samuelsen said, "because I was leader of a major public sector trade union that bargained contracts in New York State. It was not like this was Camelot the whole time, but there was an uneasy alliance with Cuomo, and that was beneficial for Local 100."[15] In 2011, Cuomo made contract deals with the two largest state-employee unions, the Civil Service Employees Association and the Public Employees Federation, that froze their members' pay for three years. In return, the unions got two-year no-layoff provisions.

Afterwards, Cuomo said the three-years of zero pay wage freezes should set a pattern for all state unions. During Local 100 contract talks in 2014, Samuelsen said he confronted Cuomo at a midtown rally. "I told Cuomo on TV to take his three zeros and shove them up his ass," Samuelsen said. "I got a phone call from him the next day. He said, 'Who the hell do you think you are, saying that to the governor of New York State?'

I got in an argument with him. He said he came from the same place as me, and I said, 'Get a grip governor. We don't come from the same place. You were raised with comfort; your father was governor. I was raised in grit.'"[16] Later, as negotiations dragged on, Samuelsen threatened to bring a few thousand TWU members to Albany to demonstrate against the governor.

The tactics worked, Samuelsen said. In the December 2014 edition of the Transport Workers Bulletin, he wrote that members "are starting the New Year off right with a two percent across-the-board wage increase courtesy of the five-year contract we negotiated with the MTA in April 2014. The contract was our most important victory of 2014, not only because of the excellent wage and benefit increases contained in it, but because we achieved it through negotiation, and not arbitration or strike. Negotiation appears to be a bit of a lost art, especially in the public sector, with most unions relying on binding arbitration to get a contract."[17]

In the years after the contract deal was reached, Cuomo and Samuelsen had a cordial relationship. "I could call him and he would answer or call me back, which was extremely helpful," Samuelsen said. "He understood what was occurring with the MTA."[18] On December 31, 2016, Samuelsen was among the well-known New Yorkers who joined the governor for a celebratory New Year's Eve party at the new 72nd Street station and for the inaugural ride, which traveled to three stations. In March 2018, Cuomo publicly backed a TWU effort to organize flight attendants at JetBlue. Cuomo tweeted: "JetBlue Inflight Crewmembers deserve the protection of a trade union. Good luck with the vote."[19] The tweet linked to a *Daily News* story about the TWU's organizing drive for JetBlue's 5,000 flight attendants. In an interview at the time, Samuelsen said the tweet showed that "Governor Cuomo is doing exactly what the trade union movement needs from our elected officials: he is backing workers." Cuomo "recognizes that the trade union movement is a vital force in America for the economic security of working people," he said.[20]

As Cuomo prepared to run for his third term, Samuelsen—after attending a Cuomo fundraiser—said in a 2019 *New York Times* story about the governor's fundraising that Cuomo "has been the best governor for the trade union movement ever."[21] He added that the union had happily contributed to Cuomo. But later in 2019, the relationship began to fray. Samuelsen and Cuomo split over the governor's selections to the MTA board and over his backing of an investigation into the high overtime pay some MTA workers had accumulated. In an interview with *The New*

York Times, Samuelsen compared Cuomo to Trump, saying the governor was circulating lies about workers. "There's no evidence at all of widespread criminality. It's a big lie," Mr. Samuelsen said. "This is what Donald Trump does."[22]

When reports of Cuomo's harassment of women emerged in 2021, Samuelsen became the first major union leader to break with the governor. "My sense was, how can the trade union movement stand with him if, as a result of that report, it becomes clear that he engaged in workplace criminality or misbehavior?" Samuelsen said. On the day Samuelsen spoke out, Cuomo tried to call him three dozen times, seeking a retraction that never came, Samuelsen said. "I have people on the progressive social left in New York that still criticize me and say I was a Cuomo ass kisser," he said. "What I say is 'We brought home contracts that blew every other union out of the water.'"[23]

15

Transit Union Brings Tough Tactics to the Airline Industry

Strikes are rare in the airline industry. That doesn't mean airline labor unions lack influence. They can slow work or threaten to strike: The threat of a strike alone can deter passengers from booking. And even though the Railway Labor Act diminishes their ability to strike, the threat remains. No one who saw the confrontation between John Samuelsen and American Airlines President Robert Isom during a meeting at LaGuardia Airport on May 21, 2019, was left with that impression that airline unions lack power.

The face-off between the former New York City subway worker and the soon-to-be CEO of the world's biggest airline occurred towards the end of a difficult four-year negotiation for about 31,000 mechanics and fleet service workers following the 2013 American/U.S. Airways merger. The creation of the world's biggest airline required that the two biggest transportation unions determine whether they wanted to co-exist or fight one another in a representation election that would replace one of them. While IAM represented mechanics and fleet service workers at U.S. Airways, the TWU represented both groups at American. In 2014, the two unions chose to create a joint association to negotiate for their combined membership. That process took time, as did the negotiations that followed. Merging labor contracts is always one of the toughest pieces of an airline merger.

Preceding the encounter, Isom had come to LaGuardia airport to speak to employees. As recently as January 2024, the moment was preserved on YouTube and on the TWU Internet site as "TWU President Samuelsen Takes Contract Fight to AA President Isom's Face." During

15. Transit Union Brings Tough Tactics to Airline Industry

the conversation, Samuelsen spoke passionately about ongoing contract talks and about an American proposal, later dropped, to move some maintenance work offshore. He also raised the issue of class difference, telling Isom "You're not the first Ivy League guy that we've dealt with and we've beaten." But he also credited Isom because he had " the chutzpah to stand up here."[1]

As he addressed Isom, Samuelsen was surrounded by union members. He began by laying out the history of the existing contract. In 2003, American had become the last of the major airlines—Southwest not included—to declare bankruptcy after travel fell off after the September 11 attacks. In every bankruptcy, labor contracts were renegotiated to the airline's advantage. Said Samuelsen, "The fact of the matter is that you have a business plan; you're trying to implement that business plan off a 2003 concessionary deal in the aftermath of the 9/11 attacks [where] you were given broad management prerogatives by a bankruptcy judge." Then, Samuelsen referred to the American's full-year 2018 results, when the carrier reported a full-year, pre-tax profit of nearly $3 billion. "You intend to execute work rules, scope changes, that would allow you to increase dramatically the $3 billion you're making off the backs of your unionized workers," Samuelsen said. "And that's not going to happen. You're not going to get what you want. [And] If this erupts into the bloodiest ugliest battle that the United States labor movement ever saw, that's what's going to happen."[2]

Samuelsen spoke powerfully, referring to his subway background as he raised the threat of a strike. In the process governing negotiations under the Railway Labor Act, "self-help," which refers to the right to strike, is the final step. "If we ever get to a point where there's self-help, we are going in engage in absolutely vicious strike action against American Airlines, to the likes of what you've never seen, not organized by airline people but organized by a guy that came out of the New York City subway system that's well inclined to strike power and who understands that the only way to challenge power is to aggressively take it to them," he said.[3]

"I hope we get to the point of release," he said. "I doubt that would ever happen, but if we do, we're going to shut this place down because we're going to defend our members, we are going to defend future generations of workers that want to be employed—our children, our grandchildren. Not all of us go to college, not all of us become CEOs in the airline industry, not all of us become CFOS or CSOs whatever you are. We are going to preserve these jobs." Then, toward the end of his talk, Samuelsen spoke more personally to Isom, saying, "We've been in fights with powerful people before, perhaps more powerful than you. You don't really look that powerful, you look like a nice guy, but your business plan betrays that." He added, "I will say the one thing, the fact that you already have the chutzpah, a New York word, to stand up here, is impressive because I don't see a whole of people doing that."[4]

In response, Isom says he is willing to negotiate, but unwilling to tolerate ugly strike tactics. "The concern that all of us here have, I speak for everybody in the room, I know that we want American Airlines, above all, to succeed now and into the future," he says. "We have 90-some-odd years of history and I want another 90 years of history. I want the people of American airlines to be able to recommend this company—to their relatives, to their children—to come here to work. [But] I will tell you this, that anybody that seeks to destroy American Airlines, that is not going to be productive. It just won't. We have to be able to work together, to see the views of both sides. Believe me, I will send people back to the table. There is no problem with that. I will tell you what, the rhetoric that says 'We are going to go to battle,' we can't win this way."[5]

In a 2022 interview with *Forbes*, Samuelsen said, "It wasn't about Isom personally, but rather about American's efforts to offshore work, to betray American workers. That was at the heart of the debate, and we prevailed in the contract. Isom arrogantly believed that once they set the plan in motion, they wouldn't be derailed, but [the unions] derailed them. My impression of that day is that Isom is a super smart guy who will ruthlessly pursue profit, and he believed he could steamroll the union. He was wary about being in a roomful of workers—airline executives are not used to being challenged—and I was in his face. I think he handled himself okay. He didn't lose his temper. He was probably seething, but he remained steady."[6]

Roberto Ramirez, a former TWU attorney, said the airline industry represents a different, larger challenge for Samuelsen. "The greater the industry, the higher the likelihood there will be abuses," he said. "You have a world today that is globalized, and you have John, who stands between that and the well-being of membership, which is still very much a United States workforce."[7]

As Samuelsen spoke, American mechanics had already engaged in a slowdown that had impacted the carrier's summer 2018 operational performance. Initially, given that it was illegal, union officers couldn't talk about the slowdown, so news of the action could only be reported "according to sources"—a term journalists use when the people providing them with information need to remain anonymous. Under the headline,

15. Transit Union Brings Tough Tactics to Airline Industry

John Samuelsen speaks to an MTA worker in 2018. "We're fighting for the restoration of the Democratic party," he said at the time. "The party shifted to emphasize white elite liberals" (courtesy TWU Local 100).

"American Airlines Encounters Labor Slowdowns Due to Slow Pace of Contract Talks," a July 14, 2018, story in *Forbes* reported that "American Airlines' summer operational performance is being impacted by work slowdowns by mechanics and fleet service workers angered by the slow pace of contract negotiations, sources say."[8]

Out of a total of 6,329 daily American flights, the slowdowns were impacting as many as several dozen flights a day. They were sufficient to make American an industry leader in flight delays over the previous 30 days. As usual, mostly all of the delays were caused by weather. These slowdowns had occurred periodically over several months in various cities—particularly Chicago and Dallas, both major American hubs with maintenance bases. "Everybody's pissed, everybody's angry, because American should have settled this contract a long time ago," a worker who asked not to be identified told *Forbes*. In the story, Dennis Tajer, spokesman for the Allied Pilots Association, spoke ambiguously about the slowdown. Asked whether one was occurring, he said "Right now there are a lot of distractions. We have a bunch of clothes on the floor and people are trying to get dressed with the lights out."[9]

In the *Forbes* story, union officials declined to comment and an American spokesman said the carrier had no indication that a work slowdown was occurring. Instead, American spokesman Ross Feinstein said, "The summer is an incredibly busy travel season and it is normal for operations to be challenging from time to time. Our maintenance team is incredibly professional and fantastic at taking care of our customers. We appreciate all they do. It's part of why we are proud to do more of our own maintenance work than any other airline."[10] At the time, American didn't know that a slowdown was taking place, and the airline chose to ignore the exclusive reporting.

However, the slowdown continued. In 2019, American hired an economic consulting firm, to analyze maintenance data, which showed that an unusually high number of aircraft were out of service every morning. In May 2019, American went to the U.S. District Court in Fort Worth, Texas and asked for a temporary restraining order to end the work slowdown, saying flights were being delayed. In June, Judge John McBryde agreed with the carrier, saying the restraining order was warranted because American would likely win on its claim that the two unions were violating federal labor law. In August, McBryde ruled that the slowdown was illegal and ordered the unions to tell workers to avoid interfering with American's operations. McBryde wrote that the only reasonable explanation for the delays was "concerted action on the part of plaintiff's mechanics and related employees" deliberate to gain leverage in contract negotiations."[11]

Additionally, American management complained to McBryde that Samuelsen; Sito Pantoja, IAM general vice president for transportation, and Alex Garcia, TWU international executive vice president, had failed to satisfy a requirement in his earlier temporary restraining order that they tell their members to stop their slowdown. American accused the three union leaders of making it clear in their statements to their members that they didn't agree with the order. Said Pantoja, "The day after McBryde imposed the temporary injunction on us, the work went from slow to a crawl, mainly in Charlotte and Philadelphia. Then the judge banged us in the head again. He said, 'If you don't cut this out, I will impose a $200,000 a day fine.' But we didn't pay any money. We got an agreement a year later, after we refused to negotiate with the company unless they postponed the hearing with the judge. We kept postponing until we finally got a deal."[12]

On September 6 an unfortunate event came to light. An American Airlines mechanic appeared in federal court in Miami, charged with disabling a navigation system on a flight of 150 people in July, *The Miami Herald* reported. No one was hurt because the tampering triggered an error alert, which the pilots recognized.. The mechanic, who had tampered with the air data module, said he was upset over stalled contract negotiations. Pantoja and Garcia quickly issued a statement disavowing the mechanic's act. Both leaders had begun their careers as airline employees—Pantoja at TWA and Garcia at American. They did not want to endanger safety.

In a joint statement, they said "The TWU/IAM Association condemns, in the strongest possible terms, any conduct by any individual that jeopardizes the safe operation of an aircraft. Safety is the number one priority for our IAM and TWU members involved in the maintenance and operation of aircraft. These members are the most highly-trained safety professionals in the airline industry. As a result, the US air transportation system is the safest in the world. Any conduct that jeopardizes that safety is not tolerated or condoned by the leadership or members of our organizations."[13] Ironically, the mechanic's court hearing occurred as the two sides were making progress in negotiations. On September 11, 2019, a *Forbes* headline proclaimed "Is American Airlines Nearing a Deal with Mechanics and Fleet Workers?"

Samuelsen threatened a strike in his confrontation with Isom. But, again, airline industry strikes are exceedingly rare. In the first two decades of the 21st century, there were two strikes: One by Spirit Airlines pilots, who walked off their jobs and shut down the airline for six days in 2010, and another by Northwest Airlines mechanics, who were out for 15 months in 2005 and 2006. The 2010 strike brought Spirit pilots' pay closer to industry standard rates, their union said. But the strike by Northwest mechanics, staged by the renegade AMFA union, was widely considered a failure. It did not have support from other unions and most strikers lost their jobs.

16

Jason Ambrosi Moves to the Left Seat

When Jason Ambrosi took over as the twelfth president of ALPA, in January 2023, it was not unreasonable to say that it was both the best of times and the worst of times for the union. On the plus side, his election came at a time when pilots at every major airline were in negotiations that would lead to vastly improved contracts. But at the same time, the airline industry was facing unprecedented threats to its vaunted safety standards, including a growing acceptance that perhaps—in a radical shift—commercial aircraft could be flown by one pilot instead of two. Congress also was set to consider the reauthorization of the Federal Aviation Administration, which occurs every five years and which typically is the framework for changes to the legislation that governs the industry.

At the time of the ALPA election, Ambrosi was 49 and had been president of the Delta ALPA chapter for two years. The national presidency, he said, "was not something I was looking for; it was not on the radar." But as the leader of Delta's pilots, Ambrosi was a natural candidate to oppose Todd Insler, president of United ALPA. The two airlines have historically represented the largest ALPA locals. As an early backer of coronavirus vaccines, Insler had accumulated some very committed critics. Additionally, United pilots saw an early tentative agreement on their contract as inadequate; it would ultimately be rejected by 94 percent of United pilots. "I had various people from airlines other than my own asking me to get involved and run, and I figured I had a reasonable chance to beat the other guy," Ambrosi said. The October 2022 election among the union's 200-member board of directors, which represented 40 airlines, resulted in an overwhelming victory for Ambrosi, who received more than three-quarters of the votes. "Frankly, the outpouring of support was surprising," he said.[1]

16. Jason Ambrosi Moves to the Left Seat

While ALPA has generally been an effective and powerful lobbying group in Washington, it had not always seemed to be the foremost leader of airline labor in the years preceding Ambrosi's election. Both Ambrosi and Insler, who were visible leaders at their airlines, said during the campaign that they wanted to expand ALPA's visibility. At the time, Sara Nelson was the most prominent airline labor leader in Washington, while Dennis Tajer was often called on to represent pilots on TV and cable news shows. "I respect all labor leaders," Ambrosi said, "But when it comes to aviation and aviation safety, pilots are front and center. Part of my campaign was to get ALPA out there more and to make sure our voices are heard."[2]

Even after he was elected as national president in October, Ambosi continued to oversee the negotiations that led to a tentative agreement at Delta. The two sides reached an agreement in principle in December 2022. The leader of an airline's ALPA chapter "is a quarterback who works with the negotiating committee and the subject matter experts," Ambrosi said. "I was very proud to get that across the line in December."[3] Approved in March, the Delta contract immediately became the standard for the U.S. airline industry.

Ambrosi was born in Chicago in November 1972, the grandson of

Jason Ambrosi took over as the 12th president of ALPA in January 2023 (Michael Theis).

a Pan Am mechanic. His father was a Navy photographer during the Vietnam war and later ran a graphic arts firm that worked on the Sears catalogue. He was also a private pilot. The family moved to Libertyville, north of the city, so that Ambrosi and his sister could attend Libertyville High School. "I didn't know what I wanted to be when I was a kid," Ambrosi said. However, he said, he was sufficiently pushed by his father and his grandfather to pursue aviation "when you have to pick something" in high school.[4] At Embry-Riddle Aeronautical University in Daytona Beach, Florida, Ambrosi found that he enjoyed flying. He graduated in May 1994.

Afterwards, to accumulate hours of flight time, Ambrosi worked as a flight instructor and a helicopter pilot in the Daytona Beach area. In 1996, he went to work for Atlantic Southeast Airlines, a College Park, Georgia-based regional carrier that flew for Delta Air Lines. Initially, he flew the Embraer EMB-120 Brasilia, which seated 30 passengers. He quickly gravitated to union work, joining a committee and also participating in a demonstration during Atlantic Southeast Airlines negotiations. "As a Chicago native, I understood unions and I was generally supportive," he said. "I walked my first picket line in my 20s when I was making $16.25 an hour. We were picketing, trying to get a decent contract. I wore a sandwich board sign. It was cool with my buddies; we were all like a family then."[5]

His Chicago roots meant that Ambrosi envisioned working for American or United. However, when America and Delta offered him jobs, he chose Delta. He started in February 2000 as a Boeing 727 flight engineer, or "second officer," then moved to first officer after a year. First officer on a 727 was a great job, he said, because "the captain had all the responsibility and the engineer did all the work."[6] Again, he got involved in union work; in 2001 he was elected Atlanta second officer representative. But everything changed after the September 11 terrorist attacks, which triggered a severe slowdown for the airline industry. Delta, which once had as many as 129 B-727s and was the last major U.S. carrier to operate the aircraft, decided to retire them all. The last flight was in April 2003, as the Iraq War was starting. Ambrosi was furloughed after three years on the job. He gained the distinction of being one of the few pilots ever furloughed from a position on the Delta ALPA master executive council.

The furloughs raised questions. While ALPA agreed to furloughs for 300 pilots, immediately after the attacks, it protested the same fate for 1,100 more. An arbitrator largely backed that protest. Had the furloughs been a response to the war, they would have been permitted under the force majeure stipulation in their contract. But the arbitrator determined that they were a response to economic conditions and were not permitted. Ambrosi said he lost faith in ALPA and the carrier, which furloughed the 300 young pilots and then brought back retired pilots to fly in their place. It was a dark period for Delta, he said and "it was ridiculous that the union would agree."[7] He wondered whether ALPA had lost touch with its members.

During his furlough, Ambrosi did not sit still. He headed for Las Vegas to interview for a startup charter carrier called Primaris Airlines. He hoped to fly one of the Boeing 757s the airline planned to operate, but instead he was offered a job working on the team that wrote the carrier's operating certificate and sought FAA approval to fly. "I had just left union work, so it was a change to be part of the certificate team," he said. "But I did that and then I flew 757s for them. My furlough only lasted seven or eight months, but I didn't trust Delta not to furlough us again, so I stayed off the property for five years."[8]

Returning to Delta in 2008, Ambrosi flew as a Boeing 767 international first officer. More importantly, in 2008 he also married his wife Heather; the couple has two children and lives in Griffin, Georgia, south of Atlanta. In 2015, Delta pilots voted down a tentative contract agreement for the first time. "It was as if pilots woke up and were active like a union again," he said. "I got involved after that."[9] He worked on new hire briefs and became membership committee chair in Atlanta. In 2019, he was elected to be MEC secretary and in 2021 he was elected to be MEC chairman. Two years later, he was ALPA president.

In 2024, after many older pilots retired and younger ones took their place, ALPA looks far different than it did a decade earlier. "Some parts of ALPA have gotten stale," Ambrosi said. "We are here to embrace generational change. We have a lot of new people. We need to be better than, 'Get off my lawn.' We need to challenge ourselves. I want to make ALPA ready for the next generation."[10] In particular, ALPA has backed younger pilots is in its advocacy for maintaining mandatory retirement at age 65.

Also in 2023, ALPA engaged in multiple contract negotiations, helping pilots to reach deals at Alaska, Delta, JetBlue, United and Spirit. After an initial tentative agreement at United was rejected by pilots, ALPA helped to craft an improved deal. "We supported United to get them where they are," Ambrosi said, noting that an initial tentative agreement did not work out. "I'm proud to say that ALPA carriers have

Captain Jason Ambrosi (left) and First Officer Jason Lounsbury share an MD-88 cockpit (courtesy Jason Ambrosi).

bargained up. We're not here to tell them what they need to do, but we're here to give them support for whatever is right for their pilots."[11]

Another early success during Ambrosi's first year was the decision by Air Canada pilots to join ALPA in March. "We brought Air Canada in, something that was tried three or four times, and we merged in record time," Ambrosi said. "That was a proud moment. We said 'Let's focus on what we can do, not what we can't do, and let's figure out the small details along the way. In a few short months they were in." The merger added 4,500 Air Canada pilots, bringing ALPA membership to 73,000. The addition meant that 95 percent of all commercial aviation pilots in Canada are represented by ALPA. Canada's second largest carrier, WestJet, joined ALPA in 2017. In January 2023, its 1,800 pilots signed a contract that merged its low-cost airline, Swoop, into its bargaining unit. "Now they can't whipsaw one another," Ambrosi said. "They raised the bar in Canada."[12]

17

How the Allied Pilots Association Made the World Safer

Pilot unions, known for seeking contract improvements, also have an additional role—one to which they can be equally or more committed: They advocate for safety. U.S. commercial aviation provides what many consider to be the safest transportation system in the history of the world. ALPA and APA have played major roles. both as forces in Washington, where legislation and regulations are written, as well as in daily practice and oversight. One compelling dynamic is that if pilots perceive unsafe conditions, their unions will back them up if they decide not to fly. Another is that today, these unions lead the fight to ensure that commercial flights are piloted by two people, despite the push to reduce costs by shaving the safety margin that is ensured by having two pilots in the cockpit.

Additionally, however, in recent years APA took extraordinary steps following two fatal Boeing 737 Max crashes in 2018 and 2019 that killed a total of 346 people. The relatively small union, representing 15,000 American Airlines pilots, challenged one of the most important and powerful companies in the aviation establishment. In 2018, Boeing had about 153,000 employees and $153 billion in revenue. It also has a strong Washington presence because it is not only one of the world's two primary commercial aircraft manufacturers but also a major defense contractor. Nevertheless, APA worked to expose Boeing's choice to prioritize cost savings over safety during development of the Max, which was first delivered to an airline in 2017.

Boeing paid a heavy price for its dishonorable conduct. Its market share and stock price declined, the company shed its CEO in a management shakeup and regulators around the world grounded the aircraft. Boeing also faced increased regulatory scrutiny.

APA's pivotal move came in May 2019, when the union provided *The Dallas Morning News* with an audio recording of a November 2018 meeting with Boeing officials. The meeting took place after a Lion Air Max crashed, but before the March crash of an Ethiopian Airlines Max. Pilots were angry that they had not been told that Boeing added new software to the Max, a new 737 model. The secrecy enabled Boeing to tell airlines that pilots would not require additional simulator training, which takes pilots out of service for days at a time and increases costs. Also at the meeting, APA officials urged the Boeing officials to take emergency action, which likely would have resulted in the aircraft being grounded before the second crash. But Boeing declined.

One month before the meeting, on October 29, 2018, Lion Air Flight 610 crashed, killing all 189 passengers and crew aboard. The crash was attributed to flight control problems resulting from a failed angle of attack sensor, which measures the angle of oncoming air. Its failure triggered an anti-stall software system known as MCAS, an acronym for maneuvering characteristics augmentation system, supposed to prevent stalls by minimizing upward pitch at certain angles of oncoming air.

In November, Boeing reached out to American to seek a meeting with the carrier and APA. The APA President Dan Carey responded that the union wanted to meet without American executives. The meeting took place a week after Thanksgiving, at APA's office in Dallas. It included seven officials from APA and four from Boeing. Privately, Carey asked an associate to record the meeting. "The recording was meant for us and for our protection," said APA spokesman and American pilot Dennis Tajer. "The meeting was very heated, professional but intense. We asked the same question we had been asking, 'Why did you put something on the airplane that can kill us and not tell us about it?' They said they were sorry and told us what we could do to combat it when it occurred. They said do the runaway stabilizer checklist and depower the stabilizer trim, which would take away the stabilizer trim from MCAS. We took that at face value, and we briefed our pilots: If it happened again, run a checklist, turn off the trim. Boeing said that they expected a software fix within six weeks and that the odds of this happening again were remote, and we felt confident enough to continue to fly the aircraft."[1] At the time, the recording of the meeting had not yet been made public.

At the meeting, speaking of the Lion Air pilots, pilot Michael Michaelis, APA safety chairman, declared, "These guys didn't even know

17. How the APA Made the World Safer

the damn system was on the airplane—nor did anybody else." He also told the Boeing executives to issue an additional emergency airworthiness directive to update the software. "My question to you, as Boeing, is why wouldn't you say this is the smartest thing to do?" Michaelis asked. "Say we're going to do everything we can to protect the traveling public in accordance with what our pilots unions are telling us."[2] Todd Wissing, another American pilot, said the MCAS system was not noted in the Max training manual. "I would think that there would be a priority of putting explanations of things that could kill you," in the manual, Wissing told Boeing executives.[3]

In a 2023 interview, Tajer recounted the events that led up to the pivotal meeting. At the time of the Lion Air crash, American had taken about two dozen Max aircraft—the first delivery was in September 2017—and had put 14 into operation. "We were flying the airplane and the crash got our attention," he said.[4] Within a few days, an FAA bulletin emphasized to pilots that MCAS could improperly activate the stabilizer trim settings, pushing the nose of the airplane downward. The pilot, FAA said, should counter the erroneous MCAS nose down input by turning off the electronic trim system.

"When we asked the American flight safety team if this was for all

Dennis Tajer: "We came out early with the outrage and the world listened" (courtesy Dennis Tajer).

737s, we were told that it was just the Max, that the Max was different, " Tajer said. "Asking that question, we felt, broke down the doors of why the crash happened. A few days later, we received another bulletin from the airline which said that according to Boeing, the Max had a system called MCAS that would run the nose down if it thought that the airplane was approaching stall. They had to admit that the Max was different, because you had to disconnect the trim or bad things would happen.[5]

"This was unknown until then. Boeing hid it from all of us, including American Airlines," Tajer said. "We learned that MCAS had no limit. In trim, it will take the nose down in ten seconds, and you can't pull back on the stick to get the nose back up before MCAS kicks in again; it runs in bursts. When you intercept, it stops for five seconds, then it starts up again. The Lion Air guys pulled back, but then it started up again. They put this on the airplane and hid it from us. They engineered it to take over the airplane in seconds and kill us."[6]

Tajer's first reaction when he read the first FAA bulletin was to call Michaelis. "I asked Mike, 'What is this thing called MCAS?,'" he said, "I don't know any more than what's in the bulletin." Tajer proceeded to open the Max flight manual. He entered MCAS in the search function, and found that it was listed as an abbreviation, but nowhere else. He suggested to Michaelis that perhaps Boeing had included MCAS in the list, then forgotten to take it out. "That was a joke I made at the time," Tajer said. "But it turned out that's what happened. We later learned, to our great shock, that Boeing tried to convince pilots that MCAS should make no difference to the pilot, so that rather than inundate the pilot with information they did not believe was necessary to fly the airplane, they left it out of the book. Boeing was worried that if the airplane required something vastly different, it would require training beyond an iPad course—simulator training, which is in person and time-consuming."[7]

For the aircraft that remained in service, Boeing provided a procedure to address the activation of MCAS, "but it didn't address how powerful and relentless MCAS was," Tajer said. "In the media, I was saying that we were shocked and angered that Boeing withheld information that something that was hidden from us could have killed us. As soon as the crash happened, it was covered by world news. We came out early with the outrage and the world listened and wanted to learn more. A huge corporation had made a horrid engineering mistake, an outrageous moral decision, and a pilots' union was telling the story. It sounded like a screenplay for a bad movie."[8]

17. How the APA Made the World Safer 127

Then a second crash occurred. On March 10, 2019, Ethiopian Airlines Flight 302, scheduled to fly from Addis Ababa to Nairobi, Keyna, crashed minutes after takeoff, killing all 157 people aboard. Again, MCAS was implicated. The system had activated two minutes into flight, pitching the plane into a dive. The pilots initially disabled the trim tab, which disabled MCAS. But when the dive continued, they turned the trim back on. Unfortunately, that reactivated MCAS, and the plane crashed. Most of the world's aviation regulators quickly grounded the aircraft, although Boeing continued to maintain that it was safe. But by March 18, all of the 387 Max aircraft including those in the U.S. in the world had been grounded.

At American, Tajer noted, APA was prepared to say pilots would cease flying the aircraft when the FAA grounded it. "We were not in conflict with American, but we were going to say to them, "Please stop flying this," he said. "When an immediate threat to passenger safety happens, we make decisions. They are not made with bravado, they are made with great hesitation, when the cost of not doing something is extraordinary. It is a call that cannot be made by an individual pilot, but only by a group that has a union behind it. There are two reasons why pilot unions started in the U.S.: One is to protect lives, and the other is to improve the profession. Often they overlap."[9] Around the world, it was two years before the Max would fly again. During that time, Congress investigated the FAA approval process and concluded that Boeing had too much influence over it.

After the second crash, Tajer again fielded dozens of media calls about the Max. "The question of our credibility became the most important thing," he said. "The world was asking why was this airplane flying after the first crash without a fix. As one of the pilot unions flying it, we had to detail why we felt comfortable flying it after the first crash."[10] Carey wanted the union's story to be told. In May 2019, he dispatched Tajer to talk with reporters from *The New York Times*, to say that APA had a recording of a meeting between the union and Boeing and to let them listen to it. While Tajer was in the meeting with two reporters, someone interrupted to say that *The Dallas Morning News* had the recording and had published a story. "I felt embarrassed then," Tajer said. "They were looking at me contemptuously; it was stressful. I said 'Let me make a call.'"[11]

Tajer stepped out of the meeting and called Carey, who said that he had let the *Morning News* reporter listen to portions of the tape. Tajer asked why, and Carey said that he didn't want the responsibility for leaking the tape to be on Tajer alone. "He realized how serious this was and so he stood in front of me to stop the bullet," Tajer said. "That moved me. Then I went back up and finished the interview."[12]

Boeing suffered consequences, including the diminishment of a reputation it had built since its founding in 1916. After testifying before Senate and House committees in October 2019, Boeing CEO Dennis Muilenburg was fired. Additionally, a 2020 Senate committee report concluded that the FAA's certification process for the aircraft had given Boeing too much authority. In December 2020, the FAA said it would reform how it certifies new airplanes in line with legislation passed by Congress. In the same month, various carriers flew the Max for the first time since it was grounded; American operated a Miami–LaGuardia flight on December 29. The FAA also required that Boeing install new software in the aircraft and provide special simulator training for pilots. In 2024, the FAA grounded 171 Max aircraft following a mid-flight blowout of a plug filling an unused emergency exit on an Alaska Airlines flight.

In January 2021, Boeing agreed to pay a $2.5 billion settlement, resolving a Department of Justice charge that it had conspired to defraud the FAA's Aircraft Evaluation Group. The sum included $1.8 billion to airlines, hampered by the 20-month grounding of the Max, as well as $500 million for a fund for families of crash victims and $244 million to pay a fine. In March 2021, Southwest ordered 100 Max planes, the largest order since the aircraft's ban.

The recording's release was not the only stressful moment of the crisis for the APA and Tajer. The union challenged not only Boeing, but also a narrative that pilots at foreign airlines were not as well-trained as their U.S. peers. "We interrupted that narrative," Tajer said. "It starts to suggest that the pilots were to blame." Tajer said that Carey told him, "Make sure we continue to say how these pilots tried to save lives. Everybody is trying to blame these pilots. I will not have that. I will not blame dead foreign pilots for these crashes.' "As for Boeing, it obviously was not pleased. "They were annoyed we were telling a story that was different from theirs," Tajer said. At meetings that included leaders of APA and Boeing, Boeing "would say 'It's difficult when Tajer is out there saying what he's saying," Tajer said. "Our officials all said he was speaking on behalf of APA. " Tajer said he takes comfort in knowing that "everybody, especially the families, who spoke at the hearings, was on this noble cause to ensure this never happens again. In part, the reason the story got out was because a pilots' union decided to tell the world the story, with the risk that we might be wrong."[13]

17. How the APA Made the World Safer

Tajer said one night after the first crash his daughters saw him sitting at the kitchen table and said, "Dad, you looked tired in those interviews." I said, "I'm exhausted, but we have to do this." When they asked me if I was worried I might get fired, I said that we don't have a choice, we have to tell the story." He repeatedly thought of Michaelis, the APA safety chairman, who did multiple interviews while battling cancer. One day, when both Tajer and Michaelis were working late at APA's office, Tajer noticed a bulge under Michaelis' shirt, and asked, "Are you packing?"[14] Michaelis lifted his shirt and showed tubes running underneath it, and requested that no one be told of his cancer. He died at 58 in July 2019 of pancreatic cancer and complications from gallbladder surgery. In his final months, Michaelis had simultaneously battled against cancer and for aviation safety.

Another inspiring moment came early in 2019, following the Ethiopian Airlines crash, when FOX News sent a limo to pick Tajer up for an interview. In a conversation with the limo driver, Tajer revealed he was headed for the interview, and the driver said he would go to a coffee shop to watch. Afterwards, the driver texted him to say, "I watched it, thank you." Then the driver said, "I am Ethiopian, thank you for telling that story," and Tajer thought, "This happened in another land. This will always stick with me, his gratitude that we made a difference for something that happened across the globe."[15]

18

How ALPA Fights for Airline Safety

In February 2023, six weeks after taking office as ALPA president, Jason Ambrosi was on the road to Buffalo, N.Y, for a ceremony that commemorated the victims of the crash of Colgan Air Flight 3407. The crash, in icy weather on February 12, 2009, was a signature event in the history of U.S. commercial aviation safety regulation. Fifty people, including one on the ground, were killed when the Bombardier Q-400 stalled and crashed into a house. The Buffalo commemoration came as Congress was starting work to work on FAA reauthorization. Ambrosi's participation was a statement that made clear his commitment to being engaged in preserving the toughened safety standards that were implemented following the crash. As of early 2024, Colgan 3407 was the last fatal crash in U.S. commercial aviation.

In the aftermath, the families of the victims became influential lobbyists for airline safety, which is not unusual after fatal crashes, and ALPA allied with them. The Airline Safety Act of 2010 raised the minimum number of flying hours for a first officer from 250 hours to 1,500, with exceptions for military-trained aviators. The change was controversial because it raised the barrier to becoming a commercial pilot, at a time when demand for pilots was high, while not addressing the cause of the crash. Both Colgan 3407 pilots already had more than 1,500 hours. The 1,500-hour requirement became a burden for smaller airlines, which were having trouble hiring pilots, and for young pilots who historically have taken low-paying jobs in order to accumulate sufficient hours to fly commercially.

Flight 3407 was operated by Continental Express. The National Transportation Safety Board found a key cause to be the pilots' inadequate response to stall warnings. The captain jerked the control column back, raising the nose too high, when he should have lowered it, the board found. The board also found that the captain had failed three check rides at other airlines, and that neither he nor the first officer had sufficient rest before taking off from Newark, New Jersey. In fact, the first officer had commuted from Seattle to Newark the night before the early morning flight. In response, Congress required the FAA to record training failures, disciplinary failures and other pilot records in a database available to airlines. Additionally, in 2011, the FAA announced new rules to address pilot fatigue, including limiting daily duty time to a maximum of 14 hours, and requiring ten hours of rest, up from a minimum of eight. But the new rules did not apply to cargo pilots and did not fully address the pre-flight situations of the two Colgan pilots.

In Buffalo, speaking to an audience composed largely of the families of the crash victims, Ambrosi emphasized their role in advocating for tougher standards and his own commitment to making sure those standards survived. "Together, each person here today—and countless others—has contributed to ensuring those we lost in the Flight 3407 accident leave a legacy of saving lives in the air and on the ground—a legacy of making sure our country sets an example for the world," he said. "Because of first officer qualification and training requirements and other improvements, U.S. airline passengers are dramatically safer today."[1] After the ceremony, he flew back to Washington, where work on FAA reauthorization would be one of his principal tasks in his first year on the job. "It was a tough time to take over a job," he acknowledged. "But a lot of the legislation is for safety. US air travel is the safest in the world and we're committed to keeping it that way."[2]

Congress' arcane method of doing business is a puzzle to many; fortunately for pilots, ALPA is embedded in the legislative process and Ambrosi stepped in quickly. "I've attended multiple hearings and multiple safety summits," he said in October 2023. " We've done a lot of Hill visits, trying to bring our issues front and center, and I've been out there in the media, trying to get in front of this stuff, and it's been working. Since the beginning of the year, we've built and improved our relationship with the FAA and the DOT; we've engaged with them, and I've appreciated their willingness to engage."[3]

Despite ALPA's success in lobbying on reauthorization, the battle for aviation safety is continual. During 2023, a dispute over the installation of 5G cell phone towers near airports made clear that not everyone shares the airline industry's commitment to safety. Rather, in January, 5G tower deployment by telecommunications companies suddenly became

Jason Ambrosi: "The best safety device on an aircraft is to have two well-trained rested pilots" (Michael Theis).

an issue, as Verizon and AT&T sought to install towers too close to airports. The 5G signals could potentially interfere with aircraft altimeters, which use radio waves to measure distance above the ground. Altimeters are critical when planes land in low visibility, and they were impacted in a few hundred older commercial aircraft. The dispute shocked the airline industry, which had not envisioned that anyone would so blatantly place financial concerns ahead of safety concerns. The solution was to wait until July so airlines could retrofit altimeters with filters. That cost millions of dollars. It turned out that the Federal Communications Commission, which had approved the new towers, did not coordinate with the FAA.

Ambrosi said "5G is a perfect example of where government branches weren't talking with each other. There should have been better collaboration. Unfortunately, it took a lot of arm-twisting to get the cell networks not to turn up the power per se. This was all about big money and business. The cell phone carriers couldn't have cared less what happened to the airlines, and the airlines were caught off guard. Everybody had to scramble."[4] He noted that the threat hasn't fully dissipated. The cell phone companies have agreed to extend voluntary mitigation measures that limit the power of 5G transmissions at 188 U.S. airports until January 1, 2028. "The underlying safety and economic issues around 5G

C-band deployments by telecommunications services providers (telcos) have only been kicked down the road," the International Air Transport Association said in May 2023.[5]

An even more frightening threat looms. Two European aircraft manufacturers, Airbus and Dassault, have advocated for single-pilot operations during long-haul flights. No U.S. passenger carrier has backed the effort, but cargo carrier FedEx has been an advocate. In 2023, ALPA joined with two European pilot unions in a joint campaign against single-pilot operations, which already has an acronym: SPO. Theoretically, acquiring an acronym may be viewed as an early step towards gaining acceptance. Given the influence of Airbus, it is likely that such acceptance would come first in Europe. The European Union Aviation Safety Agency—the European Union's equivalent to the FAA, known as EASA—has said that nothing will change before 2027; SPO, if it comes to fruition, is even further off.

Nevertheless, a proposal exists for longer transatlantic flights to be operated with just one crew member and, at times, one pilot. Such flights currently use two crews—one can take over when the other reaches its maximum flight time. Under the proposal, during part of the flight, just one pilot would be in the cockpit, while the other sleeps in the aircraft's rest area. "This raises safety concerns, not to mention security," Ambrosi said. "If something bad happens, you need to be able to have crew resource management. The best safety device on an aircraft is to have two well-trained rested pilots. Single pilot is a threat and Europeans are trying to blaze a trail on it. It will become our problem if something happens elsewhere in the world, because that would put pressure on us and our airlines. So we're working to make sure we fight this at a global level."[6]

Aviation safety has a third formidable advocate for safety besides ALPA and APA. It is Capt. C.B. "Sully" Sullenberger, who landed U.S. Airways Flight 1549 on the Hudson River on January 15, 2009. The Charlotte-bound flight took off from LaGuardia, but lost power in both engines when the plane struck a flock birds. The incident brought national recognition to Sullenberger, First Officer Jeff Skiles, and three flight attendants as professionals committed to aviation safety. Sullenberger became a hero, his status reinforced by the 2016 release of the film "Sully," which starred Tom Hanks as Sullenberger. The movie was directed by Clint Eastwood and based on Sullenberger's autobiography Highest Duty, published in 2009. It grossed $241 million worldwide, against a production budget of $60 million. Arguably, as much of a hero as Sullenberger was in the minutes following the bird strike, he has been just as much of a hero in his role as an airline safety advocate since the event. A January 2023 story in *Forbes* was entitled "Hero Pilot from 2009 Remains a Hero Today, Fighting Threats to Airline Safety."

The *Forbes* story followed Sullenberger's visit to Charlotte, where the Sullenberger Aviation Museum was under construction. The museum not only commemorates a historic event in airline safety but also seeks to expand opportunities for members of underserved communities to participate in aviation, which Sullenberger called "one of the most transformative industries in the world."[7] The visit occurred three days before the fourteenth anniversary of the crash. Sullenberger retired from U.S. Airways in 2010; he started his career at its predecessor, Pacific Southwest Airlines, in 1970. Since he and Skiles landed Flight 1549, he has spent much of his time advocating for airline safety, often as a keynote speaker. Like Ambrosi, he has spoken out against the push for single pilot cockpits and the effort to build 5G towers near airports.

The idea that commercial aircraft could fly with a single pilot "has been floated primarily for economic reasons," Sullenberger said. "It's a dumb, dangerous, and ironically unnecessary risk. Some people say we have a terrible pilot shortage and this is the way to fix it, but that's looking at the problem in the wrong way," he said. "If we were having a hard time attracting primary care physicians to rural mountain areas, would we reduce medical school from four years to two? No, we'd say that's crazy, because it is crazy. Rather than lower standards to meet an imagined crisis, we should be finding ways to attract and retain people." Perhaps the Sullenberger museum can help, he noted: "Part of the reason for the museum is not just to inspire and elevate people but also to provide a well-defined pathway to get people to a professional aviation career."[8]

Regarding the cell phone controversy, Sullenberger called it not only a "crazy and unnecessary indication of the absolute hubris of the telecoms, uncaring about real serious safety issues on the part of aviation, " but also a government failure, because "you have gray areas of independent federal agencies in different domains" that don't collaborate or even communicate about a critical safety issue." He said the Federal Communications Commission "should never have auctioned the spectrum they did when, for 60 years, radio altimeters were built to use a spectrum that did not have adjacent interference. There was no adult in the room to force the FAA and the FCC to show each other real data and have a real conversation."[9]

As for Boeing's calamitous cost-saving effort to reduce pilot training for the 737 Max, Sullenberger said the outcome shows what happens when companies don't take seriously the importance of quality, safety and good governance. Rather, at many U.S. companies, "we find that the people running our major corporations are almost never subject matter experts; they are all corporate experts," he said. Boeing's 1997 merger with McDonnell Douglas exacerbated negative trends, he said, which increased in 2001 when the company moved its headquarters Chicago from Seattle, where most of the manufacturing took place. In 2022, Boeing moved its headquarters to Arlington, Virginia. "I give a lot of talks about leadership and governance and corporate culture," Sullenberger said. "But I have not found a business school that teaches the subject of safety, even though there is a strong and compelling case for safety because if you get it right up front, the improvements always pay for themselves."[10]

On the fourteenth anniversary of Flight 1549, Ambrosi praised Sullenberger and Skiles, noting that they worked together to make an emergency landing that saved the lives of 155 passengers and crew. "Two highly qualified and fully experienced professional pilots are the foundation upon which our aviation system is built," Ambrosi said in a prepared statement. "There is no automated or remotely operated replacement for the collaboration, communication, and airplane feel made possible by having at least two pilots on the flight deck."[11]

It's not that pilots are anti-technology, Ambrosi said. It's more that technology has limits. "As labor, we get labeled as being anti-technology," he said. "In fact, we embrace technology when that technology improves safety. But we also know that every single day, technology doesn't always do what it is supposed to do in aviation, pilots fix it, and no one's the wiser. Pilots are there to make sure automation is doing what it is supposed to do."[12]

19

U.S. Airways Leads the Parade to Bankruptcy

The 21st century brought a series of traumas for the airline industry. The impact of the September 11 terrorist attacks was heightened by an eight-month recession that started months earlier in March 2001. Travel was diminished by both events. An even deeper recession, triggered by a housing market crash, lasted a year and a half from December 2007 to June 2009. Then, in the spring of 2020, a global pandemic struck, slowing air travel to a trickle. The industry recovered each time, but it always seemed to put employees on the defensive. The number of airline employees stood at 731,072 in December 1999. It fell to 587,299 in December 2008. By October 2023, it had climbed to 812,381.[1] One way to follow the industry's course during the 21st century is to examine the path taken by U.S. Airways, its eventual merger partner, American Airlines and by Jerry Glass, who played key roles at both carriers. He was the key architect of management's labor strategy, first as a U.S. Airways executive and then as an independent contractor for American.

By the start of the century, Crystal City, Virginia-based U.S. Airways was already the most consolidated member of a consolidation-oriented industry. The first of its four mergers came in 1968, when Pittsburgh-based Allegheny merged with Indianapolis-based Lake Central. Still, it remained a regional East Coast airline, partially because an attempt to merge with Pacific Southwest Airlines in 1987 failed to make it into a national carrier—despite name changes to U.S. Air in 1987 and U.S. Airways in 1996. "The route structure expanded but remained focused on short routes between East Coast cities, where revenue per available seat mile was relatively high due to a lack of competition."

When lower-cost competitors, led by Southwest, moved into the region, U.S. Airways' revenue advantage collapsed, leading to an increasingly difficult existence for a carrier that had its major presence at four airports all within a few hundred miles of each other: Charlotte, Philadelphia, Pittsburgh and Washington National. Very quickly after the terrorist attacks, it became clear that the U.S. Airways model— which involved major carrier labor rates and a regional carrier route system—was unsustainable. This was the world Glass stepped into when he started at U.S. Airways in 2002.

Glass entered the airline industry by chance, after being laid off from his second post-college job. Born in New York City in June 1954, he attended lower East Side public schools and graduated from Stuyvesant, long considered one of New York's most prestigious public high schools. He went on to Boston University, earning a bachelor's degree in political science in 1976. The following year, planning a public sector career, he earned a master's degree in public administration from George Washington University and found a job with the Veterans Administration, working on long term care for veterans. "In the '70s the VA decided that they were going to get rid of the community care facilities where they placed psychiatric patients who couldn't be placed anywhere else," he said. "They wanted to get out of the psychiatric care business and to use long-term care facilities. I went all over the country assessing the facilities; I visited five or six of them. It was a very tough assignment. After four months, I said, 'I can't do this; the VA system is a mess.'"[2]

Glass moved to another field, higher education, to work as an economic analyst for the American Association of University Professors, a professional association and, increasingly, a union for some members. He worked on an annual report on college professor salaries and benefits. After 18 months, he was laid off. Then he saw an ad for a job as director of research at the Airline Industrial Relations Conference (AIRCon), which at the time was the labor policy organization for the scheduled U.S. airline industry. It was 1980 and Glass, by chance, entered the airline business. The conference eventually disbanded, but Glass has remained in the airline industry for nearly 45 years.

The conference reflected the airlines' belief that they could engage in coordinated bargaining, where one carrier would sign a contract with a labor group, and then the other carriers would sign similar contracts. It wasn't a great plan. The carriers' labor executives "would have a handshake agreement that no one would exceed X percent," Glass said. "But then the first airline settled with the flight attendants and the next airline busted through the agreement and that was the end of coordinated bargaining." (Glass could not recall whether it was United or TWA who exceeded the other's agreement.) The organization then evolved into one that exchanged contract information. "My job was to develop a negotiator's handbook, where negotiators would be able to see every provision of every other contract," he said.[3] He stayed for nine years, rising to become executive director. Then he went out on his own, forming J. Glass and Associates in September 1989.

Meanwhile, things were changing in the airline business. The Eastern Air Lines strike began in March 1989, as three unions simultaneously walked out to protest the labor policies of its chairman, Frank Lorenzo. Lorenzo, it may be said, was an industry visionary who shaped the modern airline industry as no one else has, introducing low fares, presiding over key consolidations, building the Houston and Newark hubs that became cornerstones for United and originating the strategy of using bankruptcy court to reorganize failing carriers. But he did not excel in labor relations.

The Eastern bankruptcy represented a war between Lorenzo and the carrier's unions. When Eastern shut down in January 1991, it was clear that nobody won. Subsequently, three other leading postwar airlines—Braniff, Pan Am and TWA—also failed because, like Eastern, they failed to adapt to the hub system that had come to dominate the U.S. airline industry in the 1980s. Although Eastern faced many insurmountable hurdles during the 21-month strike, the key conclusion was that no airline could survive a long strike. In that environment, Glass has negotiated about 300 airline labor contracts, 30 railroad contracts, and more than 100 in other industries. Not a single one ended in a strike.

In starting his own firm, Glass believed that "You could take what AirCon was doing, create negotiating handbooks and customize them for every airline negotiating with a particular work group. The comparative studies I had done were the genesis for the idea. That evolved into developing labor strategies for particular airlines, which eventually evolved into actually being at the table, negotiating."[4] His first client was Phoenix-based regional carrier America West Airlines. There, Glass came to know the management team that would go on to reshape the airline industry. That team included Bill Franke, attorney Steve Johnson, and executives Scott Kirby and Doug Parker. Over the next three decades, Glass repeatedly represented the airlines they ran.

In one of his earliest negotiations, Glass represented United, which purchased Air Wisconsin in 1990 so that it could acquire the carrier's slots at O'Hare Airport. United outbid American, and then broke up Air Wisconsin, selling off its turbojet Dulles operation to Atlantic Coast

Airlines, its Chicago turbojet operations to Trans State Airlines and its O'Hare jet operation to private investors. (This became the current Air Wisconsin, which is still headed by the same investor group.) "United was buying assets and airport slots, not the airline," said Glass. His job was to negotiate the separation of several thousand employees from Air Wisconsin. Some were offered jobs with the acquiring carriers. He negotiated with AFA, ALPA, IAM and the TWU, essentially the same parties he would negotiate with over the next four decades. He was later hired to represent both Atlantic Coast and Air Wisconsin in their labor negotiations. "My reputation grew by word of mouth," Glass recalled. "I started getting business from other airlines."[5] For America West, he negotiated a pilot contract in 1995 and a flight attendant contract in 1997.

Management labor and employment firm Ford Harrison purchased Glass' company in 1994, making him a consultant. Over the next eight years, Glass negotiated airline contracts, consulted on labor matters for airlines, and even branched out into the railroad business. "I was known purely as an airline guy," he said, although in 1994 he started a trade association for the labor relations departments of commuter railroads.[6] Its members included Amtrak, the Long Island Railroad, the Massachusetts

Unidentified American Airlines flight attendants protest the slow pace of raises at the Charlotte airport in February 2017. The 2013 merger had brought a promise of industry leading wages (Ted Reed).

Bay Transportation Authority, New Jersey Transit and the Southeastern Pennsylvania Transportation Authority. Between 1996 and 2002, Glass's company produced revenues between $1 million and $2 million annually.

In 2002, Glass got a call from U.S. Airways CEO Dave Siegel, who offered him a job as senior vice president in charge of labor. "I had been traveling a ton, on the road constantly, and I wanted to be home more," Glass said. Home was the Washington, D.C., area; he arrived in 1976 to attend George Washington University, where he met his wife Karen, and never left. The couple married in 1980 and went to Bermuda for their honeymoon. At the time, Glass still worked for the American Association of University Professors. As they were leaving, Glass recalls, "The executive director of AAUP told me, 'There's a lot going on here, but don't worry.' This is a weird thing, but whenever somebody says 'Don't worry,' I start worrying.' And the first day back, I got laid off."[7]

The marriage survived and the couple had two daughters. By 2002, the girls were teenagers. One was at college and one was a high school athlete in Burke, Virginia, and Glass wanted to see more of her games. He started at U.S. Airways in April 2002. When he arrived, the carrier was in bad shape. It was as if the terrorist attacks had ripped the cover off the gradual ongoing deterioration of its financial model. The most immediate problem was National Airport, which was closed for three weeks in the aftermath of the attacks. After the closure, traffic returned very slowly, over a period of years, just as it did throughout the Northeast, where U.S. Airways was focused.

"We were in a new revenue environment," Glass said. "No matter what projections were made, revenue came in lower. And we had bloated costs." In 1996, CEO Stephen Wolf had agreed to a pilot contract that offered parity plus 1 percent pay—a rich offer for a regional carrier that competed with the global U.S. carriers whose longer routes enabled them to distribute costs over more miles. U.S. Airways had high revenue per available seat mile, a common industry metric known as RASM, but it also had higher cost per available seat mile, or CASM. Low-cost competitors moved in and so did Delta. "Delta decided to try to put us out of business by starting a lot of overlapping routes," Glass said.[8]

On August 11, 2002, four months after Glass' arrival, U.S. Airways filed for Chapter 11 bankruptcy protection. The day marked a turning point for the major carriers, triggering trips to bankruptcy court for every one of them except for Southwest, as well as a final round of consolidation. However, for U.S. Airways, the first bankruptcy turned out to be insufficient in its cost reduction. Said Glass, "The plan was for a very quick bankruptcy. We were going to be in and out in five months." On emergence eight months later, in March 2003, the problems remained: high costs and overly optimistic revenue projections. "It was nobody's fault," Glass said. "We had some of the best minds in the industry, but we were in uncharted space. We entered a recession and revenue did not come back."[9]

In fact, the unions were generally willing to go along with the airline's plan, but the plan turned out to be insufficient to enable survival in the declining airline economy. "What we did was we said, 'Let's build a business model patterned after JetBlue and America West, kind of a hybrid with hubs but also some point to point,' but in order to survive we had to have their costs," Glass said. "Rather than take the approach that everybody would take a 10% pay cut, we tried looking at America West and JetBlue labor rates and conditions." Glass focused on pilot costs because pilots are by far the highest paid work group. The unions each had their own reasons for cooperating. The ALPA thought if it accepted pay cuts, it could save its defined benefit pension plan. AFA President Pat Friend "was a fantastic leader in understanding that going into bankruptcy you wanted to have a contract, so she took the lead in getting local AFA leadership to get a deal." The IAM, the largest union at U.S. Airways, was traditionally difficult for Glass to work with, "but the good news was that they had a long relationship with US Airways and you could make a deal with Robert Roach," head of the airline division.[10] Meanwhile the Communications Workers of America, which represented agents, came around slowly, but made a deal after the bankruptcy was filed.

"This is not to say it wasn't difficult and hard to get done," said Glass, who left the carrier in 2005 after it merged with America West. "But as it turned out, we didn't ask the unions for enough cost reduction. We asked for what we thought was just enough to get us by, which in hindsight turned out to be not the right decision. We should have gone deeper." A barrier was that U.S. Airways couldn't work out a deal with the Pension Benefit Guaranty Corporation, which oversaw the pension plans. "You had this perfect storm of a recession and high interest rates and we were using outdated mortality data," Glass said. The high interest rates upped the value required to be set aside to pay the pensions. Also, the airline wanted to terminate the pilot pension plan but keep the others. It was all too much. "We had so many battles to fight," said Glass. "It was whack-a-mole. Every time we thought that we had beaten one crisis, another one popped up. We were first. We didn't have a playbook. We had nobody to look at to say we could learn from somebody else's mistakes."[11]

20

Saying No Is Easy; the Hardest Thing Is Getting to Yes

While the first U.S. Airways bankruptcy failed, the second one changed the airline industry. Not only did labor costs fall, but also it triggered a wave of mergers that is viewed, two decades later, as the last major round of industry consolidation. "If the competitors allowed US Airways to have significantly lower labor costs, that would have given US Airways a huge competitive advantage," Glass said. "United and Delta and American were suffering from the same problems that US Airways had: an inability to predict revenue because revenue was coming in much lower than projected."[1] The low-cost carriers—Frontier, JetBlue, Spirit and Southwest—were expanding into the Northeast and had more than 400 aircraft on order at the time. Meanwhile, the big three carriers—American, Delta and United—had large fortress hubs with substantial numbers of business travelers. But U.S. Airways had high costs and lesser hubs.

U.S. Airways emerged from its first bankruptcy on March 30, 2003, just seven and a half months after filing. It had secured $1.9 billion in annual cost savings, including a $1 billion reduction in labor costs, $500 million in aircraft lease reductions and $400 million in supplier, management and operating cost cuts. It had also secured a federally-backed $1 billion loan, primarily financed by loan guarantees from the Air Transportation Stabilization Board (ATSB) that was set up by Congress to provide relief for the airline industry after the 9/11 attacks. Its new principal owner was the Retirement Systems of Alabama, which made a $240 million equity investment in the airline and got a 37 percent stake. It sounds good. But it wasn't.

20. Saying No Is Easy; the Hardest Thing Is Getting to Yes 143

"Almost immediately after emerging from bankruptcy we realized we didn't get enough from labor," Glass said. "So we started developing plans for how we were going to further lower costs, initially outside of bankruptcy. Nobody wanted to go into bankruptcy a second time; that seemed almost like the kiss of death. Nevertheless, we internally developed a new set of concessions we were going to seek from the labor unions. Not surprisingly it didn't go well." During the first round of negotiations, Glass recalled, he sat at the table with ALPA negotiators and one of them said, " 'We don't want to do this again; we want this to be the one and only time.' " Glass responded, "The world is so unpredictable I don't know how many times we will have to come back until we get it right."[2] But he had not expected to return so soon.

U.S. Airways' second bankruptcy filing occurred on Sunday, September 12, 2004. "It was a really bad day, very depressing, and honestly there were days where we thought we were not going to get out of it,"[3] Glass said. This time, the ATSB agreed to allow the airline to spend the $718 million in remaining cash collateral from its guaranteed loan—a major boost. The carrier developed a plan to merge with America West Airlines, bringing in the Phoenix carrier's young management team. The merger was referred to as "Project Barbell," because the carrier that it would create was big on the East Coast and West Coast but had nothing in the middle of the country, a problem that was addressed later when a 2013 merger with American Airlines added hubs in Chicago and Dallas.

The second time, Bill Pollock, president of the U.S. Airways ALPA chapter, was willing to work with management. Pollock was a longtime U.S. Airways pilot who valued the carrier's survival. He once said he felt that if he could ensure that people who wanted to stay could stay and the people who wanted to leave could leave. If the airline failed, he said, nobody would have any choice. "Bill obviously had a duty to represent his members, but he also had a relationship with US Airways CEO Bruce Lakefield" Glass said.[4] Pollock and Lakefield were both Navy veterans; the former had been a Navy pilot and the latter had been a submarine commander. "During the second bankruptcy, survival was not assured, and no clear path through bankruptcy existed because US Airways, even the second time, went before other carriers," said a story I wrote for *TheStreet* in 2012. "Pilots made very significant pay and pension concessions, more than any other pilots have made. Needless to say, Pollock was ousted as union president soon after he saved US Airways, and he returned to flying. Sometimes, I hear of US Airways pilots who refuse to fly as first officer on Pollock's flights. And I think, if it wasn't for Bill Pollock, they probably would not be flying at all."[5]

As for the IAM's role in the second bankruptcy, "IAM was extremely difficult," Glass said. "They refused to negotiate with us. For six weeks they would go into a back conference room in our office and read the newspaper all day." Once the IAM contract was rejected by the bankruptcy court judge, Glass said, Robert Roach, the union's general vice president for transportation, approached him. "Robert Roach came to me and said, 'Give us 24 hours to negotiate before you reject our contract.' I said, 'I will give you 24 hours, but at the end of that 24 hours, you have to take whatever we say we can do out for ratification.' He agreed and it ratified."[6]

Glass generally has been able to forge positive relationships with labor. Of Sara Nelson, he said, "Sara is one of the best at what she does. She represents her people fervently but she also knows how to make an agreement. I have incredible respect for people that can do that because not every labor leader can." Similarly, Roach and Sito Pantoja, his successor as IAM vice president for transportation, could close a deal. "When they said something, you could bank on it," he said. Glass recalled several instances where he negotiated with Pantoja. The first was in 1991, when Los Angeles investor Kirk Kerkorian was considering whether to acquire TWA. Kerkorian hired Glass to work on the labor contracts. "That was an experience, dealing with Kirk Kerkorian and his group," Glass said. "I remember going to his office and, this is no exaggeration: His conference table seemed as long as a football field."[7]

Jerry Glass has negotiated more than 300 labor contracts and never had a strike (courtesy Jerry Glass).

Glass reached a deal with the unions, but the deal died because cash-strapped TWA sold its London routes to American, and Kerkorian didn't want the carrier without the London routes. Later, America West CEO Bill Franke considered merging America West with TWA, with the condition that the IAM had to negotiate a deal within a 72-hour timeframe. "It was all done in my office," Glass said. "We knocked out an agreement in time, but then Bill decided not to go through with it; he concluded that it wasn't doable." In any case, Glass said that Pantoja is "an honorable man who can absolutely close a deal. When he says he will do something, it will happen, but when he says he can't, then he can't."[8]

Years later, after the U.S. Airways–American merger, IAM and TWU formed a joint bargaining association, and Glass negotiated with both Pantoja and John Samuelsen. Of Samuelsen, he said, "John is very open; he gets very upset about things that management does." Glass did not approve when Samuelsen confronted American President Robert Isom in a meeting room at LaGuardia Airport in 2019. "That was totally inappropriate, for him to have done that, to the same company that voluntarily gave the TWU and the IAM an average 25% increase right in the middle of negotiation," Glass said. "The whole thing was very unfortunate and patently unfair. But I've met John a couple of times, and he's always been very pleasant."[9]

Glass said he has always taken the approach that he needs to understand what the other side can and can't do. "My philosophy on negotiations is to try and be as transparent and truthful to the union as possible, even when it will result in offending them if there is something I can't do or something I view as ridiculous," he said. "I think it's important not to lie to the union and to tell them the truth, even when it's going to hurt their feelings. I also believe that the easiest thing in the world to do is to say no; the hardest thing is getting to yes, to help solve the union's problem. I've always taken the approach that I put myself in their shoes and try to make a deal." By the end of 2023, Glass had negotiated more than 300 labor contracts and never had a single strike. "That's one of the things I'm proudest of," he said. "What labor generally says about me—they say it to my face—is 'He can be an asshole to negotiate with but, boy, does he know how to close a deal.'"[10]

Glass cites two sets of negotiations as his toughest in the airline industry. The closest he ever came to a strike, he said, was in 1998, when he was negotiating with AFA at America West Airlines. Negotiations were in a cooling-off period, the final 30-day stage before the parties are released with the option to engage in "self-help," which enables workers to strike or employers to lock workers out. In this case, "we got to midnight on the thirtieth day of the cooling-off period and still did not have a deal," Glass recalled. "Rather than strike, the union agreed to extend the end of the cooling-off period by a few hours since we were making progress on finalizing a deal. Bill Franke and Doug Parker had flown into DC to advise me on getting the deal closed. They stayed at my office while I was at the table and about 2:30 a.m., after the cooling-off period expired, we reached a tentative agreement, which was ultimately ratified."

If there had been a strike, Glass said, the airline was prepared: It had flight attendants on standby and it had prepared for court challenges if the union were to implement its CHAOS (Create Havoc Around Our System) strategy—which involves intermittent strikes at select sites. "We had a legal theory at the time that argued that CHAOS was an illegal job action," Glass said. "Who's to say whether we would have prevailed in court, but it was a countermeasure we deployed in case a strike had occurred."[11]

Another tough negotiation, he said, involved former U.S. Airways pilots after the airline merged with America West in 2005. The group was disadvantaged by a controversial seniority ruling by arbitrator George Nicolau, who seemed to favor the America West pilots in awarding seniority at the post-merger airline. In the seniority negotiations, Glass recalled, "George told both parties, especially the US Airways pilots, how he was going to rule and what they needed to do to get to a different ruling, and the east pilots blew him off. It was very difficult for them to swallow." For years following the merger, the former U.S. Airways was referred to as "the east" and America West was referred to as "the west." The award "made the job even more difficult when we were in negotiations for a transition agreement to merge the contract," Glass said. "We had been making great progress, but the Nicolau ruling blew everything up. It took seven and a half years to get an agreement."[12]

At one point, the former U.S. Airways pilots formed their own union. It was called USAPA, for U.S. Airways Airline Pilot Association. Negotiations with USAPA, Glass said, were "hands down, the toughest. No one was close. They were very true believers. One of their negotiators once proposed costs they knew we couldn't afford; it would have put us in bankruptcy. I said, 'How can you make a proposal like this?' and he said, 'This is what we deserve. You're a smart management team. You will figure out how to make it happen.'"[13]

21

How Labor Enabled the American–U.S. Airways Merger

Labor unions staged a coup in the bankruptcy court where American Airlines filed in 2011. Historically, airline bankruptcies enable reductions in employee compensation and other costs. But in American's case, the outcome differed substantially from what American management had intended. Rather, a potential acquirer courted the carrier's unions and, with their support, was able to seize control. Doug Parker headed the acquirer's management team which, by this time, was experienced in the art of bankruptcy. In 2005, when it ran America West, it gained control of U.S. Airways. Small and Phoenix-based, America West was neither financially stronger nor better located than U.S. Airways. Its advantage was an aggressive young management team, which turned out to contain three future global carrier CEOs: Parker, Scott Kirby and Robert Isom.

Between 2002 and 2011, about a dozen other U.S. airlines filed for Chapter 11 bankruptcy, including Delta, Northwest and United. While Chapter 7 of the bankruptcy code establishes a method for a company to liquidate by using assets to pay debtors, Chapter 11 allows a company to reduce its costs and debt so that it can emerge as a stronger company. Following their emergence from bankruptcy, Delta and Northwest merged into what would become the strongest U.S. carrier; United merged with Continental and American merged with U.S. Airways. In every case, unions were part of the bankruptcy creditors committee, and they exercised influence in determining the outcome. But they were generally limited to arguing against the reductions in their pay and benefits and perhaps avoiding the very worst possible outcomes. The precedent made what happened in the American bankruptcy seem all the more remarkable. American filed in November 2011. Five months later, in April

2012, U.S. Airways said it had gathered support from American's three major unions for its effort to merge with American. The unions, led by APFA President Laura Glading, helped to convince the creditors committee to support the U.S. Airways bid.

Parker, Kirby, Isom and Derek Kerr came together as a team at America West Airlines. They were always merger minded. At America West, they considered a merger with TWA. They tried unsuccessfully to take over bankrupt American Trans Air in 2004. And in 2005, they successfully took over U.S. Airways. In 2006, when they pursued a merger with Delta. it failed dramatically, and some said it appeared they were in over their heads. But they learned that they needed support from the workforce of the company being acquired to make a merger work. Subsequent efforts to merge with United also failed. It was said then that United used U.S. Airways to enable its merger with Continental. Probably so. But Parker said United's merger benefited all airlines because it reduced the industry's capacity. When American filed for bankruptcy, his team was ready.

The key was that they assiduously courted the three largest American labor unions: APA, APFA and TWU. Kirby was put in charge of the effort, which was seen as a long shot; he went to work in February 2012. On February 24, a day after she was re-elected to a second term as APFA president, Laura Glading's advisor told her that Kirby wanted to meet with her in New York. Meanwhile, by late February, APA President Dave Bates was also preparing to initiate contact with U.S. Airways. "They knew support from labor was critical," Bates said. "They had learned that from their Delta and United [merger efforts]. I suspected they would eventually reach out to us, but I wasn't sure when, and for my part I wasn't going to sit around and wait."[1]

Instead, Bates asked Jonathan Ornstein, president of Mesa Airlines and a friend of Kirby's, to set up a meeting. The APA's early thinking, said Dennis Tajer, the union's longtime spokesman, was that in 2003 pilots had taken a 23 percent pay cut as part of a grand bargain intended to keep the airline out of bankruptcy. "We watched the other airlines get napalmed by the bankruptcy process," he said. "So when Kirby and Parker came to us, it was like coming to someone under siege in a bomb shelter and saying, 'I've got a way out for you.' You're excited to hear it, but you're wary."[2] Meanwhile, TWA president Jim Little learned that U.S. Airways was seeking a merger, so he called Parker, whom he knew because TWU represented dispatchers and fleet service workers at America West. Meetings followed all the initial contacts.

21. The American–U.S. Airways Merger

A critical session came on March 12, 2012, in a room beside the kitchen in the Oceana Restaurant on West 49th Street between Sixth and Seventh avenues. There, Bates, Kirby and Tajer discussed the synergies between the two airlines' networks, the possibility for a better contract than American was offering, and the key point that U.S. Airways would make repeatedly throughout its push for a merger: The combined carriers could move from domestic weakness on their own to combined domestic strength.

The meeting, over dinner, was cordial. It seemed likely, if not inevitable, that a merger between American and U.S. Airways would occur, given that Delta had merged with Northwest and United had merged with Continental. Kirby "talked about consolidation continuing, and there were only two dancers left on the floor," Tajer said.[3] It was not lost on the parties that in 2006 Delta had fought off U.S. Airways' clumsy bid to merge, partially due to a "Keep Delta My Delta" campaign mounted by the Delta ALPA chapter. Part of Delta's advantage, Kirby said, was that U.S. Airways stepped in too late.

"Kirby said 'We waited too long, but we're not going to let that happen this time,'" Tajer said. At the end of the dinner, Bates and Kirby began discussions on the framework for a collective bargaining agreement—one that was far better than what American had been seeking. Kirby said U.S. Airways would add $400 million to whatever contract American management was offering, and Bates responded, "Why not $800 million?" Tajer recalled. In fact, the final deal was worth $1.3 billion more than American originally offered. "Unions usually go through the carwash in bankruptcy, but we came out with a pay raise," Tajer said.[4]

After the dinner, Bates and Kirby began exchanging text messages. At a follow-up meeting in Phoenix on March 22, Parker and Kirby joined Bates and APA vice president Tony Chapman. By then, Parker and Kirby had talked with all three of the key American unions, who were working in concert to make the merger happen. The day after the Phoenix meeting, Kirby spoke at a J.P. Morgan investment conference. Asked what lessons U.S. Airways had learned from its failed 2006 effort to acquire Delta, he responded that if you want to do a merger in the airline business, "it's important to have allies," particularly labor allies. "One thing we learned is that you can't do it alone," he said. "In an ideal world, it's important to have the constituents of bankruptcy, particularly labor, on your side. An outright hostile transaction won't work."[5]

Evidently, Kirby liked the food at Oceana. On March 19, a week after he had met with Bates and Tajer, he met there with Glading and her

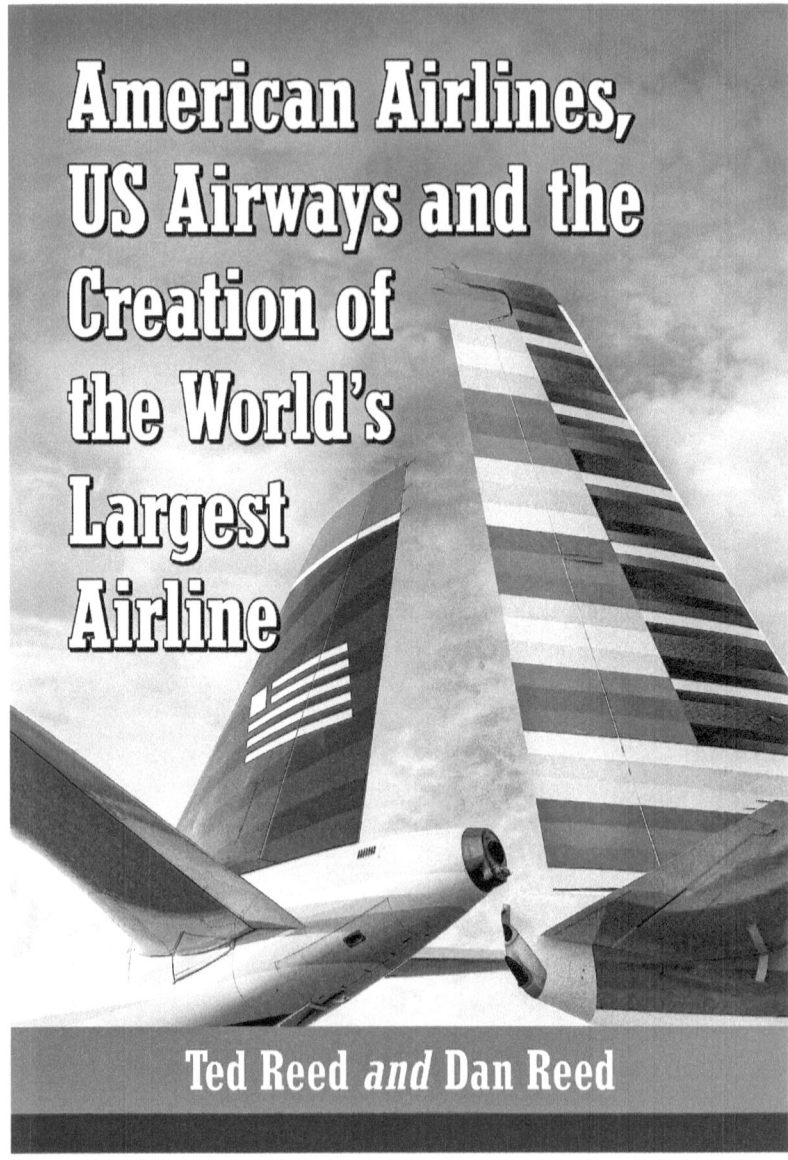

U.S. Airways management worked with American Airlines labor unions to enable a 2013 merger.

advisor, Dan Aiken. Kirby laid out his hopes for a merger, just as he had with the pilots. Glading was interested but wouldn't commit to anything more than a trip to Phoenix on March 31. There she had dinner with Parker, Kirby, two of her advisors and Tom Weir, the airline's treasurer, who is also her cousin. "I sat next to Doug," she said. "He said, 'I want a deal. I want you to do this, but I don't want you to just use our agreement to get more in negotiations. I want you to decide that you really want it.' He didn't want us to play both sides, and I made the commitment that if I was really going to do it, I would be all in." After dinner, Glading called her union's U.S. Airways negotiating team and asked them to fly to Phoenix to discuss the U.S. Airways proposal. "I knew that if I signed that deal, it was not just a possible contract," she said. "It was a commitment to do whatever I could to bring about a merger."[6] She was fortunate, she said, that despite a close election for the union presidency, her entire board backed the merger.

As for TWU, during the week of March 12, Jim Little was at the AFL-CIO annual meeting in Orlando when the union's bankruptcy attorney called to say that U.S. Airways was actively pursuing American. "I already knew Doug Parker from America West, where we had the fleet service workers and the dispatchers," Little said. "I thought he was a pretty sincere CEO. He was always upfront with us. He didn't come across as a stuffed shirt; he came across as a guy you could have a beer with. So I went to a hotel room and called Doug Parker and he called back. I asked, 'Are you making a run at American? Is this for real or are you just a spoiler?' He said it was real but he didn't want to talk about it on the phone."

On March 22, Little was in Phoenix to meet with U.S. Airways executives. "We talked about the structure and [Parker] went into details and finances and what he thought the business plan would look like, and I was very impressed," Little said. "When I got back to New York, I called Dave Bates and Laura Glading. I told them I had been to Phoenix. I said it looks like this could be very serious."[7] The three unions were all on the same page. They were put off by American's restructuring plan and willing to consider putting aside doubts and aligning with the America West team.

Of the trio, Glading played the biggest role. She became a major player on the creditors' committee, which took the lead in advocating for a merger that American strongly opposed. Glading was the only union leader to attend every meeting, and she forged relationships while there. "I spoke with others who had been through bankruptcy, asking them what worked and what didn't work, and everybody talked about getting a seat on the creditors' committee, having a vote, and having a say," she said. "After that, I went to every meeting, and I never shut up."[8]

Glading worked to develop relationships with other creditors. "You can go in there all principled and saying, 'This is outrageous and obscene; the labor unions make sacrifices and the lawyers get rich,' or you can go in and try to work with people," she said. "And I bonded with everybody, because I went in there thinking I have to know what their interests are too." Another step she took was to convince her board that it needed a blue-chip firm to represent flight attendants. "I noticed that all of these advisers and lawyers and investment bankers knew each other," she said. "They all worked at the same firms and they would move from firm to firm and they had all worked on bankruptcies together. So I said I want us to have one of these guys too. I want somebody who has lunch with these guys." The APFA hired investment banking firm Jefferies as its financial advisor. It was expensive, Glading said, but "it was one of the best moves I made."[9]

Even though their strategies varied, the unions stuck together. "The interaction and coordination between APFA, APA and TWU were extraordinary," Bates said. "We were all in favor of the merger, and we were all going the same direction. There were never any significant bumps in the road between us."[10]

A decade after the pilots' restaurant meeting, Tajer recalled he was impressed that Kirby came alone. "I always thought that was a gutsy move," Tajer said. In fact, Tajer mentioned this impression to Kirby a few years after the meeting, and, he recalled, "Kirby said, 'Yeah, nobody else believed we could do this with labor.' The rest of his team didn't believe. They just said, 'Good luck with that.'"[11]

22

From a Freedom Flight to the Airline of the Stars

In the first two decades of the 21st century, Sito Pantoja negotiated about two dozen airline contracts for the IAM. His best deal, he said, came in 2020, when he and Alex Garcia, TWU international executive vice president, negotiated contracts for 31,000 workers at American Airlines. Ironically, it was the last one. "My last deal was my greatest deal," he said. "I'm proud that we have mechanics making well over $130,000 at American Airlines. That contract was unheard of. It set the tone in the industry for ramp wages to go from $20 or $25 an hour to $30, up to $38, and for annual salaries to reach the $80,000 to $90,000 range. If you make that and your retirement is secure because you have a 401K and a [defined benefit pension], you're going to be just fine when you retire. That was always my goal, to try and create the three-legged stool of a pension plan and private savings and social security. You combine all those things and you can retire with 80% of the check you got when you were working. That's not bad for an airline worker. It meant people could go from middle class to upper middle class."[1]

Despite the American deal, and a 2016 deal with United that set the stage for expanding IAM jurisdiction to about 30,000 workers at United and other carriers, Pantoja's departure from the union was unpleasant. He was forced out in a battle over an incident that he perceived as corruption by other senior union officials; he chose to speak out instead of keeping his mouth shut. Being ousted was a blow: Pantoja had spent 44 years in the IAM after starting out as a TWA mechanic at John F. Kennedy International Airport in 1977. In his last job, as IAM general vice president of transportation, he presided over about 100,000 airline and rail workers as well as a staff of collective bargaining specialists, strategists, financial analysts, communicators, and administrators. Pantoja came to the U.S. as an 11-year-old boy on a Freedom Flight from Havana to Miami. His story is an immigrant success story, and he did not take well to being stripped of his career after devoting his life to a cause he believed in.

It is said that you catch more flies with honey than you do with vinegar. In general, Pantoja adopted this approach, although he was known to pound the table if he needed to. He negotiated often with Jerry Glass, whom he called "one of the toughest negotiators I ever faced," noting "Jerry Glass and I went toe to toe dozens of times. But at least we knew where we stood. I knew I could make a deal with him. He knows a handshake with me is as good as any contract ever written. He knows I am not going to lie, and I know he is not going to lie. You need to have relationships with the companies you represent. It's good business and it yields back benefits. Really, it's the same with other unions too. I never bashed another union. I had issues with some of them, but we addressed that in private settings, never in public."[2]

The airline industry is a small world. Pantoja and Glass first met as investors battled for TWA in 1991. A decade later, TWA was in bankruptcy and a half dozen parties were bidding for the airline or parts of it. By then, Glass represented America West Airlines, one of the bidders. "We had several meetings," Pantoja said. "It didn't work because America West mechanics at the time had a contract with the Teamsters that had very loose scope." Union scope clauses govern how much work is done by union members. Under the IAM's contract with TWA, "all the work was done in-house; very little was farmed out," Pantoja said. "For us, the AWA contract was a non-starter."[3] At TWA, he noted, mechanics—not lower paid fleet service workers—oversaw the receipt and dispatch of aircraft when they were on the ground between arrival and departure. Neither side would agree to a change. In the end, American acquired TWA for about $500 million in April 2001. Five months later, after the September 11 terrorist attacks, the value of TWA declined precipitously. After acquiring the St. Louis hub, American dismantled it.

Another aspect of Pantoja's broad influence was a positive relationship with the media. This was a longtime IAM practice that distinguishes it from other national union leadership—particularly the Teamsters—that took pains to keep reporters at arm's length. On a local level, reporters who covered various industries often formed relationships with union leaders, part of the intricate web of community journalism that has been lost in the decline of the newspaper industry. But the IAM nationally stood out. During the union's struggle with Eastern Airlines in the 1980s, John Peterpaul, IAM vice president for transportation, talked regularly with *Washington Post* airlines reporter Frank Swoboda. Later, Roach talked regularly with *Wall Street Journal* airlines reporter Susan Carey. Subsequently, Pantoja and Joe Tiberi, his chief of staff, spoke regularly with me. "It was smart to have a few friends in the media, and it was ill-advised not to," Pantoja said.[4]

Pantoja, born in Havana in March 1957, was the son of a marble mason. He was among the quarter of a million 265,000 refugees who fled Cuba for Miami between 1965 and 1973. He arrived in Miami on a flight with his three sisters. Six months later, his two brothers "escaped with my dad in a raft he built," Pantoja said. "They got picked up off the Keys in Florida after four days."[5] After a few weeks in Miami, Pantoja went to Park Slope, Brooklyn, where his grandmother lived and where he grew up. He attended Catholic schools and then Aviation High School in Queens. He graduated in 1976 with an Aviation Maintenance Technician powerplant license, which enabled him to become a mechanic. After graduation, he returned for an extended twelfth grade, earning a second license so that he could also work on airframes. He left school in January 1977, worked briefly at a Long Island plant that made 747 flaps, then went to work for TWA in July 1977. He spent 32 years at the airline, retiring in 2009, when TWA was part of American.

An incident in the winter of 1979 put Pantoja on a path to union activism. He was driving a tug that skidded on the ice, damaging the Boeing 707 he was towing. "I was making a turn," Pantoja recalled. "The tug skidded. It jackknifed and the tow bar hit the nose landing gear of the 707. The flight had to be canceled, costing the carrier a lot of money. I felt terrible. I felt that I had screwed up and that I would get fired. I was 24 or 25 and I felt my life was over. I was subjected to a discharge hearing; the penalty was three days off without pay and a letter in my file. But the union assured me I would not get fired because it wasn't my fault; it was an accident due to the weather conditions. So I stayed on, and eventually, during the grievance process, I got my pay back and the letter was expunged. This opened my eyes that the union was there to protect workers so I started going to union meetings once a month. A couple of years later, I became a shop steward."[6]

In 1989, Pantoja transferred to St. Louis, where TWA had its second maintenance base. His salary when he arrived was around $40,000. "Missouri was a very nice family place, a great place to raise kids, and very affordable with my salary," he said.[7] He had married Claire Doherty, an Irish-American from Brooklyn, in 1982. She was his high school sweetheart; they met at a Bay Ridge block party in 1977. While he attended Aviation High, she attended Our Lady of Perpetual Help High School in Brooklyn. The couple and their two children moved to St. Peters, Missouri, northwest of St. Louis. Today, daughter Emily is an attorney for the Teamsters and son Richard is an economist for the TWU, after previously working for the IAM. After their children were grown, the Pantojas moved to Arlington, Virginia in 2005.

The St. Louis maintenance base, where the IAM represented about 1,000 mechanics, offered a more relaxed environment than the JFK base. "The Midwest employees let the company get away with a lot of stuff that it wouldn't get away with in Newark or LaGuardia or JFK," Pantoja said. "TWA didn't always follow safety protocols. Sometimes they didn't have the proper safety equipment. They would use a floor jack to take off a landing gear brake, which weighed 300 pounds. You should have a brake removal hoist for that job. They also got away with not having the proper number of people moving an aircraft, things like that. I quickly came to be seen as a radical union guy once I got there. I spoke up every day. I refused to do jobs without the proper safety equipment. I was known as a troublemaker, and I became popular. I ran for election as trustee for the local and I won. I never lost an election after that and I kept moving up. I became a grand lodge rep, then a safety rep, then grievance committee chairman."[8]

In the years following World War II, TWA and Pan Am were the leading U.S. trans–Atlantic carriers. Pan Am was the flag carrier, operated from the landmark Pan Am building in New York City, with routes throughout the world; TWA was a secondary flag carrier and the airline of the stars,

Sito Pantoja speaks in Charlotte at a 2004 rally against outsourcing work on U.S. Airways Airbus jets (courtesy Sito Pantoja).

best known because its logo invariably showed up in movies that showed flights between Los Angeles and New York. This was unsurprising, given that Howard Hughes, a film producer and Hollywood presence, owned the carrier from 1939 until 1960. In 1969, after Hughes gave up control, TWA's new owners merged the carrier with Hilton International for diversification. Pan Am and TWA were weakened by the Airline Deregulation Act of 1987, which led to the growth of the hub system, favoring carriers that could assemble large numbers of passengers at their domestic hubs. Over time, the successful carriers—principally American, Continental, Delta, Northwest, United and U.S. Airways—gained rights to operate international flights from those hubs. After that happened, why fly to JFK to cross the Atlantic?

The 1980s saw continuing and eventually frantic efforts to save failing carriers Braniff, Eastern, Pan Am and TWA. Eventually all four fell into bankruptcy and saw their best assets absorbed by the surviving carriers. In the case of TWA, the board of directors agreed in 1985 to sell the airline to Frank Lorenzo's Texas Air Corporation, but TWA's unions objected because Lorenzo's business model included battling unions for cost savings. They preferred financier Carl Icahn.

In the late 1980s TWA had a few successes. It acquired St. Louis-based Ozark Airlines in 1986, made a profit in 1987 and carried more than half of U.S. transatlantic passengers in 1988. But in retrospect, these were all false positives. Icahn took the carrier private in a leveraged buyout in 1988, boosting the debt. In 1990, he sold TWA's Heathrow operation to American and in 1992 TWA filed for bankruptcy protection. The next year, Icahn was ousted, but the carrier was hampered by a deal in which he could buy tickets at a 45 percent discount and then resell them. In 1995, TWA again sought bankruptcy protection. Meanwhile, both TWA and Pan Am were weakened by tragic crashes: Pan Am Flight 103 over Lockerbie in 1988 and TWA Flight 800 over the Atlantic in 1996.

"When I got there in 1977, TWA was a premier airline," Pantoja said. "TWA, Pan Am, Eastern and Northwest Orient controlled all the international flights. But TWA was mismanaged by leadership, including Howard Hughes, who at the end took a lot of money for other ventures." Icahn later did the same, but Pantoja said he doesn't regret backing the decision to sell to Icahn instead of Lorenzo. "When the unions intervened, we made a deal with Icahn and gave him concessions so he could make an offer to the board that they couldn't refuse," Pantoja said. The choice may have been "between two devils," but Pantoja gives Icahn credit because "he kept TWA alive for 14 or 15 years." In fact, by 1999, when American was negotiating with TWA, some unions—including the IAM—thought that Icahn represented a better alternative, since a merger with American would put TWA workers at the bottom of seniority lists. Secret talks with Icahn began. Pantoja was not yet a high level IAM negotiator, but he attended a meeting in Icahn's Mount Kisco, New York office, the only time he met Icahn. "We knew that with American our membership would take a beating, so we tried to negotiate to see if he would maybe buy TWA back," Pantoja said.[9] The effort failed.

Might it have been better to sell to Lorenzo? He didn't get along with his unions, but he did build airlines. At Continental, he built hubs in Houston, Newark and Denver: all three are now premier assets for United. Meanwhile, American dehubbed St. Louis after acquiring TWA. Asked in 2023 what he might have done in St. Louis, Lorenzo responded, "We thought we could make St. Louis work then. We thought it had a good local market and was well-placed geographically."[10]

Pantoja stepped to the forefront in the IAM in 1997. That year, TWA reported small operating profits in the third and the fourth quarter. The IAM sought raises. "The company was making a bit of a profit and we felt we had made enough concessions," he said. "We wanted raises—not much, but some—and I was directed to make some noise in the biggest hub." On December 9, 1997, the union staged a wildcat strike at Lambert Field St. Louis. From 4 to 6 p.m., normally the time of TWA's largest bank of flights, every employee walked out. This included agents, mechanics, fleet service and cleaners. "We told everybody to say they were going to lunch," Pantoja said. "They couldn't tell us not to go to lunch. The airport was shut down. They couldn't marshal flights, so airplanes circled for two hours and had to divert to Kansas City or Chicago. They got the message, loud and clear and we refused to return to work until the carrier assured us that not a single member would be disciplined in any manner. We settled that contract two or three months later, with 8% pay increases"[11] for the carrier's approximately 14,000 workers.

As he emerged in the IAM, Pantoja came to know Joe Tiberi, a mechanic at JFK as well as a writer and editor for union publications. "Joe is one of the smartest guys I know," Pantoja said. "He is intelligent, hardworking and loyal, the kind of guy that would lay down on the tracks for you if you treat him right. Also, he is as smart as they come. I always wanted to surround myself with people who are smarter than me. Good leaders surround themselves with smart people because they are not intimidated by staff members being smarter than they are."[12]

Between 1992 and 1999, Pantoja was elected to four consecutive

22. From a Freedom Flight to the Airline of the Stars   159

two-year terms on the grievance committee and later as committee chair. He was part of tickets that ran on "white ballots" with no opposition. Then he was elected grand lodge representative, the top office in St. Louis. In 2005, he was named chief of staff for the transportation department and he moved to the Washington, D.C., area. In 2012, he succeeded Robert Roach as general vice president of transportation. His first move was to promote Tiberi to be his chief of staff.

23

Sito Takes a Seat at the Table

As the IAM's general vice president for transportation, Sito Pantoja wanted to be fully involved in negotiations. That represented a change from the approach of his predecessor, Robert Roach, who was more active on Capitol Hill and who would enter negotiations only when necessary. During 10 years in the office, starting in 2013, Pantoja oversaw negotiations for about two dozen contracts at 17 carriers. "When I came in, I wanted to be hands-on, and I put myself in charge of all the contracts," Pantoja said. "We had gone through all the bankruptcies in the 1990s and the early 2000s. The airlines had absolutely decimated our contracts, and now they were making billions. I thought it was time for our members not only to get back what they lost, but also to go a step forward. So I assembled a team of experienced negotiators and got involved in negotiations."[1]

One goal Pantoja had was to improve a United contract negotiated in 2012. That opportunity came in 2016, when the contract opened. "When I sent my guys in, we decided that we would not only get a better deal but also we would insource work we had lost," he said. "We were able to get an industry leading contract with an unprecedented defined benefit pension increase, and then we got good contracts in all our other negotiations that came afterwards, at Alaska and American."[2]

To Pantoja, wages were important, but so was bringing back union work. Union jurisdiction not only extended wage gains to more people, but also assured those gains would continue in the future. "United had farmed out 14 stations and we had gotten a B-scale wage," he said. "The first thing I did was to bring these stations back in-house with a full scale."[3] The new contract brought back about 500 United Express fleet service and passenger service agent jobs at Los Angeles International and

23. Sito Takes a Seat at the Table

San Francisco International airports. It also indefinitely extended union protection, which had been scheduled for review, to 10,000 United Express jobs at United hub airports and to jobs at 23 non-hub airports, including Boston Logan and Washington National. Additionally, all of the 30,000 IAM workers at United received 18.4 percent salary increases in 2016, with an additional 30 percent through 2021.

Pantoja said that Oscar Munoz, who became CEO in 2015, "became very amicable to labor. He didn't want to engage in a big dispute with the Machinists since we were the biggest union on the property. We were becoming more militant, trying to get back things we had given up in the bankruptcy years, and he didn't want to get into a big fight with us, and I didn't want to get in a big fight with him."[4] He said that United tried to end the defined benefit pension plan, which IAM, unlike United's other unions, had preserved during bankruptcy. But the effort failed.

Beyond the impact at United, the contract set the tone for contracts at other airlines. "It was a new era, with companies making billions in profits," Pantoja said. "It was time for us to share some of those profits."[5] Following the United deal, Pantoja negotiated deals at McGee Air Services, a newly formed subsidiary of Alaska, and United Ground Services, a United subsidiary. The former brought 1,500 jobs to IAM; the latter brought 4,000.

At Alaska, Pantoja established relationships with CEO Brad Tilden and future–CEO Ben Minicucci. "It was the same thing, same blueprint as United. I said, 'You need a union and let's not get into a fight. Everybody's making money and I'm going to give you a fair deal. Let's figure out how we can satisfy the needs of the company and also satisfy the employees.' "We added those jobs through negotiations; I didn't spend a dime on organizing."[6]

The deals reversed a decades-long trend for airlines to outsource ground services work. "What happened in the airline industry is that back in the 1970s and 1980s, all this work was performed by airline employees," Pantoja said. "But when the bankruptcies accelerated, the companies said 'we will weaken your scope clause [so] we can farm out the work.' Then these companies were able to hire workers at $7 an hour with no benefits [and] they found out that with thousands of employees with very low pay, they had operations that were not as efficient. They had workers who didn't care and they suffered as a result."[7]

The deal with American Airlines in 2020 was the biggest. When U.S. Airways merged with American in 2013, the IAM had no members at American—but it had a long history with U.S. Airways. In fact, in

Ted Reed speaks at IAM transportation conference in Las Vegas in 2017. Sito Pantoja is at right (author's collection)

1992, it staged the only strike in U.S. Airways' history, taking out 8,300 mechanics for six days. Still, the relationship survived many mergers, as U.S. Airways went through a half dozen of them.

Following the merger with American, IAM and TWU joined together in an association to negotiate for their combined membership of 31,000. Pantoja and Alex Garcia, TWU international executive vice president, jointly led the association. "I have to give credit to Alex Garcia," Pantoja said. "We came together like fingers in a hand making a fist. We were a powerhouse in those negotiations; we stood shoulder to shoulder and never had a disagreement. We were going up against Jerry Glass, the most formidable negotiator in the world. People don't know what it's like to go up against Jerry Glass until they go up against Jerry Glass. He knows what he's doing." Both Garcia and Pantoja are Cuban. Asked whether that contributed to their compatibility, Pantoja responded, "That had a lot to do with it."[8]

Merger negotiations are complex because, typically, one contract is better in one area and the other contract is better in some other area. For instance, U.S. Airways' IAM mechanics and fleet service workers retained their defined benefit pension plan, just as IAM members at United did, while American mechanics and fleet workers had defined contribution plans. U.S. Airways workers also had a better health care package, one that cost the carrier about $18 million annually. American, after the merger, wanted to go to a cheaper package like the one its workers had. Pantoja wouldn't have it. "I used to tell Jerry Glass, ' You make $2.4 billion profit and you lose $18 million on health care and you still make $2.4 billion profit,'" he said. "It's hard to argue with that. I thought I was a good negotiator because I became a hard ass when I needed to. At the same time, to be a good negotiator, you have to know how to make a deal. You have to know what the big prize is and not sweat the little stuff. And you have to know whether the company has the ability to pay and be able to prove that. You can't drive a company into bankruptcy. In my deals, I wanted a contract that would make the company more profitable because the more profitable they are, the better off my workers are going to be."[9]

Negotiations were both lengthy and bitter, leading to a work slowdown and a court battle and contributing—along with the grounding of the Boeing 737 MAX—to American's extremely poor summer operating performance in 2019. But eventually, the two sides moved closer. The final round of talks took place early in 2020. As a member of the United Airlines board of directors, a position that came with his leadership of IAM's airline division, Pantoja understood that covid was already impacting travel in China. He anticipated that the same thing could happen in the United States. "I knew we had to get a deal done right away," he said. "We settled that in January 2020, and by March flights were being canceled," Pantoja said.[10]

In a ratification vote, the agreement passed by 95 percent, with 82 percent of the members voting. The deal was announced January 30, 2020. The first headline in *Forbes* read "American Airlines Reaches $4.2 Billion Deal with Mechanics and Fleet Service That Boosts Profit Sharing and Caps Offshore Work." In a joint statement, Pantoja and Garcia declared, "The negotiating team had the option of accepting an inferior contract quickly, or doing the hard, time-consuming work of fighting for the best contract possible. Together, after more than four years, the terms of these agreements are proof that we took the right path and achieved the best contracts in the airline industry."[11]

The deal included five separate agreements covering mechanics and fleet service workers. Besides protections against outsourcing, the deal included signing bonuses ranging from $3,000 to $6,000, wage increases ranging from 4 percent to 18 percent and pay rate increases between 23 percent and 56 percent, and increased profit sharing. "No one has ever heard of that before in the airline industry," Pantoja said. "We brought in work, we secured our jobs, we got a 56% pay increase and they couldn't lay off anybody, not even during the pandemic. Ultimately the best contract is not about money. The best contract is the one with job security. That is priceless, knowing you will make $100,000 or $150,000. You can make $200,000 a year, but if you don't have a job, it doesn't mean anything."[12]

Within months, Pantoja was ousted, part of a purge based on internal union politics. Early in 2021, Pantoja opposed an incumbent candidate, favored by IAM President Robert Martinez, for secretary treasurer in the union's April election. (The candidate denied charges that she tried to cover up her sister's theft of union funds.) In March, Martinez removed Joe Tiberi as Pantoja's chief of staff, and in June, he removed Pantoja himself. In a letter to members, Martinez then installed Pantoja as the leader of a newly established "national apprentice strategic initiative" that would promote organizing. Pantoja viewed that as a "make work" assignment. In August, he sued IAM and eight top officers in U.S. District Court in Washington, D.C., alleging that he and Tiberi were demoted because he supported an opposition candidate for secretary/treasurer. The two parties eventually settled the suit. Said Pantoja, "I could have kept quiet. But I'm proud I stood my ground, I didn't bend my knee for anybody, and I never took a penny from anyone. I went out with dignity and my morals intact."[13]

24

"Going into a war zone, you're not giggling"[1]

By the numbers, the Allied Pilots Association is a very small union. It represents 16,000 American Airlines pilots—less than a quarter of the number of pilots represented by ALPA at 43 U.S. and Canadian airlines. In fact, as 2024 began, some members were campaigning to move American pilots to ALPA. In the meantime, unlike ALPA, with its broad constituency, APA speaks for a relatively unified group of like-minded pilots. That made it able to respond decisively to the Boeing Max catastrophe.

Another asset, in terms of being an influential presence in the airline industry, has been APA's spokesman Dennis Tajer. Like the AFA's Sara Nelson, Tajer has mastered the art of public relations. He is sought out by reporters and he often appears on television news and financial programs. He is also frequently quoted by newspapers, wire services and websites. Like Nelson, Tajer has been accused of running towards every camera, but both leaders have causes which they embrace and which obviously benefit from their amplification. Additionally, both enjoy talking with other people, which is hard to fake; they understand that the words they choose are important and they can speak knowledgeably about the airline industry after long aviation careers. Nelson has been a United flight attendant since 1996, a union spokeswoman since 2001, and union president since 2014. Tajer has been an American pilot since 1992 and APA's principal spokesman since 2007.

In some ways, Tajer is as much a factor in American Airlines' image as American's corporate communications department, which is subject to continual turnover. It has no one who has been at the airline since 1992. An advantage for Tajer is that communications is a second job. A Chicago-based Boeing 737 captain, he continues to fly about 500 hours a year, about half a typical pilot's schedule. Regular flying keeps him in close touch with the people he speaks for. It also means he could easily step aside if he chose to—or if he is ousted from his communications job, which is always a possibility since many people believe they are skilled at communicating with reporters. Tajer has served six APA presidents, from confrontational Lloyd Hill in 2007 to outspoken, but practical, Ed Sicher, who was elected in 2022. All have made the decision that while they lead the union, they might as well turn external communications over to Tajer.

Tajer concedes he has made mistakes working with reporters. An early one came in 1989. In general, while reporters do not hunt controversy, it is both an obligation and a privilege to ask provocative questions. Tajer first confronted this reality as a 26-year-old captain on the KC-135R, the Air Force's principal refueling aircraft. Based at Altus Air Force base in southwestern Oklahoma, he was interviewed by a local newspaper reporter for a story about crew living conditions. "Every three weeks, we lived for a week in a building at the end of a runway and we waited until an alert went off, and then like firefighters we would scramble to the aircraft," Tajer said of the alarm used to ensure crew nuclear readiness during the Cold War. "Then we would wait to take off while the navigator decoded whether it was a launch code or just an exercise code. The reporter sat down with a crew to talk about what it was like out there. We told him that we got used to it, but there was an inherent stress in running to the aircraft thinking 'Is this one real?' Then the reporter noticed that we had an outdoor pool, a gym and standard living facilities. He said, 'This doesn't look too bad.' So I said some of those same accommodations are also offered to people who are incarcerated in prison. I said, 'Even prisons have gyms.'"[2]

The remark was innocent but flippant. For a reporter, it was irresistible. The story ran on Sunday morning, when newspapers traditionally published their biggest editions and commanded their highest circulations. Fellow crew members complimented Tajer. But the base commander was not pleased that he had seemingly compared his assignment to being in prison. In a subsequent meeting with superiors, he apologized, and he was told to apologize publicly to about 100 people at the next squadron meeting. "I said something stupid and I had to pay my penance and I did," Tajer said. "This still happens in my job. But it was fine, I learned that you have to be careful what you say to a reporter. Reporters are just trying to do a job, but also they are trying to get intriguing information for their story. You are obligated to respond, but with the discipline to be sure that what you say will not be taken the wrong

24. "Going into a war zone, you're not giggling" 167

way by a reader. Reporters are trying to fly their jet and you are trying to fly yours. Just because they turn their heading towards you does not mean they want to collide with you."[3]

Tajer was born in 1962 on the Bremerhaven Army Airfield in Germany. His father, a Chicago native, was an Air Force radar specialist, posted to the base, and his mother was Danish. When he was a year old, the family moved back to the United States. Tajer grew up in Northwest Chicago, graduating from high school in 1981. Trying to decide what to do in life, he said, "I knew I didn't want to ride a train to work and read about the news in the newspaper. I knew I wanted to be in the news. I had contempt for the ordinary life. Of course now, as an older man, I want the ordinary life."[4]

Many of the markers in Tajer's early life pointed towards the military. He sought guidance, mainly from veterans. "I was surrounded by vets every step of the way when I was young," he said. One complication was that many World War II and Korean War vets didn't want to talk about it. However, two of his father's friends were from the more talkative generation of Vietnam vets. Both encouraged him to join the

Dennis Tajer flew a T-38 pilot training aircraft at Vance Air Force Base in Enid, Oklahoma, in 1986 (courtesy Dennis Tajer).

military, but as an officer with a college degree rather than as an enlisted man. One brought out photos from his tour in Vietnam. He said, "If you're in the jungle, there are bugs all over, it's humid, you're all wet, you stink and it's miserable," Tajer recalled.. "But on an Air Force base, the food is good and everybody smells good. So if you're going to war, go in comfort. Go as an Air Force officer."[5] Tajer applied to ROTC at the University of Illinois Urbana–Champaign and followed the ROTC recruiter's first suggestion: Get a haircut. He graduated in 1985 with a degree in education, a commission as a second lieutenant and a slot to train as an Air Force pilot. That got him to Altus, and later to Grissom in Indiana, closer to Chicago.

In August 1990, Iraq invaded Kuwait. Grissom's air tanker supply crews were deployed to Riyadh, Saudi Arabia, as part of Operation Desert Shield. There, the KC-135s were used to refuel B-52 bombers. Both planes were Boeing products. The B-52s pulled up behind the tankers and connected their fuel hoses. Sometimes this occurred over Iraq, but the refueling pilots weren't specifically told where the B-52s were going. However, at one squadron meeting, they were told that if any of the tankers did not make it to their refueling spot, they would be assumed to have been lost, and fuel load deliveries would have to be recalculated. "The loss assumption was that at least one in four airplanes would not be successful in fulfilling the mission," Tajer said. "That was a pill we had to swallow. It was called 'failure to maintain station.' We all knew it meant that we could be shot down. A refueling aircraft was a high value target. We were sitting in school chairs at a table. I looked over at my crew. They were somber. If you're 25 years old, and you're going into a war zone, you're not giggling."[6]

Tajer flew about three dozen missions. He was never shot at. He was in Desert Storm and then Desert Shield, each with a six-month tour separated by a month at home. "The U.S. military delivered exactly what it said: overwhelming force," he said. "We controlled the skies over Iraq."[7] By his last tour, the Air Force decided it had too many pilots. In a tent in Riyadh, he recalled, release forms were distributed. Every pilot there took one. Tajer was released in December 1991, ending an Air Force career that lasted just over six years. In August 1992, he was hired by American Airlines. It was a happy moment, at least until he went to an introductory dinner where two dozen newly hired pilots were told they would likely be furloughed the following year. Tajer went to Miami, the most junior base, to start his career as a flight engineer in the Boeing 727's three-person cabin. Furloughed after a year, he became a math teacher at Scammon Elementary School in Northwest Chicago, the same elementary school he had attended.

Teaching made a big impact on Tajer. Scammon, when he attended, had mostly blue-collar white students who were Irish, Italian, or Polish. By the 1990s, the students were mostly Black and Hispanic. "They lived in the same flats where I had lived—I still lived in Chicago, but two miles away—and it was cool to be able to say, 'I don't know what you're going through, but I know what I went through when I lived here,'" he said. "I bonded with a lot of kids."[8]

One morning, Tajer described a classroom incident to me. Maria, a Mexican-American teenager, was consistently late to class. The day came when he questioned her repeated tardiness and said she would have to report to the principal. After class, other students approached Tajer to confide in him that Maria's father was violent with her mother and that Maria was afraid to leave her mother at home alone. "I remember feeling terrible," Tajer said. As we talked he began to cry, remembering that moment three decades earlier when he was confronted with a horrid situation. After speaking with Maria, Tajer had consulted with the school social worker, who said the school was keeping an eye on the girl. "I had come out of the military with this 'I'm good to go' approach to everything, but being back at Scammon taught me that there are bad things happening too," Tajer said.[9] Going to the social worker was, unfortunately, all he could do.

After three years as a teacher, Tajer was recalled by American in 1996. The callback was welcome, but it came at a difficult time as the young pilot's marriage was deteriorating. His first marriage ended in divorce, as did his second. He has three children. His son, the oldest, works for Duke Energy; his younger daughter works in criminal justice, and his older daughter is a pilot, accumulating flight hours at a small airline.

Shortly after being recalled, Tajer found a spot in Chicago as a first officer on the Fokker 100, then a mainline aircraft. He eventually flew the Boeing 737 and the MD-80, making captain in 2013. Meanwhile, his APA communications career began in 2007. That year, he was angered by the airline's proxy statement, which showed 2006 executive compensation led by $10.2 million for CEO Gerard Arpey and more than $4.5 million for four additional executives. In fact, as American earned $231 million, its first profit since 2000, its 874 top executives received more than $150 million in stock bonuses. American's line workers, by contrast, still felt the impact of cuts they had accepted in 2003 to keep the airline out of bankruptcy. Pilots had agreed to concessions worth $550 million as well as 2,500 layoffs and TWU had agreed to concessions worth $620 million accompanied by layoffs for 1,400 ground workers and flight attendants had agreed to concessions of $340 million. In an April 2007 story, Peter Pae of *The Los Angeles Times* wrote, "When the airline industry went into a deep slump after the 2001 terrorist attacks, American Airlines' pilots, flight attendants and mechanics agreed to billions of dollars in cuts in wages and benefits to keep the carrier afloat. As for the 57,000 rank-and-file employees, they're seeing red."[10]

Tajer recalls being struck by the contrast in remuneration. "I thought I'm not trained in business, but I've been a school teacher and an Air Force pilot, and I saw this as a gross exploitation of us trying to save the airline. It came after we cleared off the kitchen table and gave 23% back. So I wrote a piece and sent it to my local, and they sent it to APA national. Then I got a call from one of our negotiators and he said, 'We saw what you wrote, are you interested in doing more work?' I said sure, and I started writing content for APA Flight Line. I wrote all kinds of pieces. It was like a Montessori School; if you were a self-starter and wrote something, they would use it. I got paid in the joy of flying with someone who would say, 'Hey, did you see what management is doing?' And their perspective was exactly what I had written. That told me that what we were writing was worth writing. It was resonating with our target audience."[11]

Tajer attended media training, which involved undergoing mock interviews and writing mock stories, but he still wasn't fully prepared for a live interview he did with a FOX-TV reporter during contract talks in March 2008. He was on a Chicago picket line when American grounded its MD-80 fleet after the FAA required that maintenance workers reinspect wire bundles. The agency said workers had failed to follow proper procedures in restraining the wires. Tajer was asked about the grounding, a sensitive situation because it involved flight safety. "They had to bundle the wires, and if the wires were not bundled properly, it could cause chafing," he said. "If there was enough chafing, the wires could spark, and that would cause a fire under the wheel well and that could lead to a catastrophic loss of the airplane. I got on the phone with our attorneys and said 'What do I say? The airplanes are not safe, but we have to be responsible here.'" The conclusion was that Tajer would discuss the safety margin, that he would say, "the airplane is safe, but the safety margin is under pressure." It is a construct he has used repeatedly since then.[12]

25

Flight Attendant Leader Treasures Her Dad's Union Pins

From 1982 until 1987, Julie Hedrick worked as a flight attendant for AirCal, a small, regional and now cherished airline that existed for only 20 years. The airline embodied her dreams then and now. When she was 18, Hedrick did what hundreds of thousands of young people have done: She left her small town and went to Los Angeles to start her adult life. Today, as president of the largest single-airline labor union, Hedrick—like many in the airline industry—looks back fondly on the first airline to employ her. Those airlines share many characteristics. They were small and family-like, they were often benevolent towards employees, they are defunct due to mergers that folded them into bigger airlines and they are central to revered chapters of both industry and personal histories. For Hedrick the differences between then and now are particularly stark. Life for flight attendants has obviously become harder, a result of not only corporate penny-pinching but also of the societal change that has transformed commercial flying into what is often an unpleasant experience.

Based in Newport Beach, California, AirCal began operations in 1967. Its inaugural route was from Orange County Airport, now John Wayne Airport, to San Francisco. At the time, the route was unserved. Following deregulation, in 1978, AirCal began to expand into other states. By 1986, it operated around 200 daily departures, and was increasingly attractive to airlines seeking to buy a bigger West Coast presence. Delta bought Western, U.S. Airways bought PSA and American bought AirCal for $225 million.

At AirCal, "we were treated wonderfully," Hedrick recalled. "We

Julie Hedrick was re-elected APFA president in 2024 with 61 percent of the vote (courtesy APFA).

had a good contract. If we worked more than 10 hours and 20 minutes in a day, we went to double time for the entire day. Orange County was our main base, but sometimes they would van us to the other LA airports, and we were paid for that time. When American bought us, I knew it wouldn't be the same. It was apples and oranges as far as how things work. Looking back on how it was when I started, that is a big part of my fight for the flight attendants. I would definitely say that the industry has gone backwards."[1]

Hedrick was born in July 1960 in Bellevue, Ohio, and graduated from high school in Huron, Ohio. "I grew up in little towns by the lake," she said. Hedrick and a Huron High School classmate discussed moving to Southern California, but when her friend backed out, Hedrick went anyway. She took Amtrak, not surprisingly, since her father worked for the Nickel Plate Road, a predecessor to Norfolk Southern Railway. "I have his union pins at my apartment in Dallas," she said. "I wear or carry his union pins with me for pickets and big events. He started working for the railroad at 15 and retired at 60."[2]

In California, Hedrick attended Orange Coast Junior College. Tuition was free, but she delivered sandwiches and salads for a restaurant to pay expenses. Her delivery area included the AirCal offices at the

25. Flight Attendant Leader Treasures Dad's Union Pins   173

airport. In 1980 she went to work for the airline as a part-time reservations agent, working 8 p.m. to midnight, and in 1982 she applied to be a flight attendant. Her training class turned out to be the last one that was slotted for A-scale pay. "When American Airlines bought us, they brought in B-scale," she said.[3]

A plus of working at AirCal was that Hedrick met her husband Craig at a company-sponsored softball tournament in Phoenix in 1986. He played for the men's team because his brother worked for the airline. The couple married in 1988 and had two sons. Today, all four are union members: Craig drives a school bus for special needs children, one son is a firefighter paramedic and the other is a mailman.

In 2007 Hedrick became involved in union work. She had been running a small business called a "trip trade service," helping other San Francisco–based flight attendants to schedule and trade their trips. She started the business in 2000: Increasingly, she found herself answering her peers' questions about the union contract. Her high level of contract knowledge led to her decision to run for APFA's San Francisco base vice president on a ticket with Larry Salas, who ran for base president. (Salas is now APFA national vice president.) The pair served four terms. In 2013, Hedrick left the elected post to become a union negotiator, engaged in the complex work of combining American and U.S. Airways contracts after the merger. Afterwards, she stayed on as part of a committee "that made sure the intent of the contract was followed through implementation," she said. "We went through every sentence of the contract multiple times; negotiating and implementing the joint contract took five years."[4] By the end, Hedrick knew as much about the contract as anyone. She ran for APFA president in 2020 and was narrowly elected. When she ran for re-election in 2024, she got 61 percent of the vote.

Hedrick's first day on the job was April 1, 2020, a day when just 118,302 passengers cleared security, down 94 percent from the previous year due to the pandemic, according to the TSA. Among her first acts was to sign a letter, along with Sara Nelson and Lyn Montgomery—the leaders of AFA and Southwest flight attendants respectively—urging the Trump administration not to seek ownership stakes in airlines in return for the grants Congress had approved in its $2 trillion economic relief package. The package included grants of $25 billion for passenger airlines to pay workers as well as $25 billion in loans and loan guarantees for the carriers.

"These are the most challenging times in the history of our profession," Hedrick wrote at the time, in an email to APFA members. "I intend to do whatever it takes to keep our members safe and working. It is critical that flight attendants from all airlines speak with a unified voice when everything is on the line."[5] The APFA and AFA had been rivals, and the three signatures marked the start of a close working relationship between Hedrick, Nelson and Montgomery. The three women were from three different unions—APFA, AFA and TWU. Their collaboration became increasingly important as American, United and Southwest all moved into 2024 with open contracts.

Why do American flight attendants have their own union, as opposed to being AFA members? This question is best answered in a 2022 book, "The Great Stewardess Rebellion: How Women Launched a Workplace Revolution at 30,000 Feet." It tells the story of how American flight attendants, led by a gritty group of women, revolted against the sexist standards encouraged for decades by both the airline and the

(From left) Julie Hedrick, Lyn Montgomery and Sara Nelson were the key flight attendant leaders in 2024 (courtesy AFA).

25. Flight Attendant Leader Treasures Dad's Union Pins 175

TWU. Author Nell McShane Wulfhart was a *New York Times* columnist, specializing in light-hearted columns about what celebrities packed in their carry-on luggage, when she learned of the struggle. "I've always been interested in labor and feminism," she said. "I found that stewardesses had changed their whole workplace."[6] Wulfhart reached out to the women who led the effort at American, which roughly paralleled the efforts of the flight attendants at United at the time

Initially, both American and TWU were on the wrong side of the emerging women's movement. "The 1970s was a time of women's liberation and feminism and that helped wake up some of the flight attendants to the indignities of the job," Wulfhart said. For instance, on some carriers, women wore hot pants and go-go boots. "I don't know if you can imagine serving hot coffee to 140 passengers while wearing hot pants," she said. "It undermines you as a person and a worker." In fact, the entire experience seemed designed to humiliate. Weigh-ins were required, often in front of pilots and male managers. Doctors handed out amphetamines to help flight attendants lose weight. Girdles were required, and "a pilot could get a free feel while conducting a girdle check to make sure a flight attendant was wearing a girdle," Wulfhart said.[7] Also, on some Continental and American flights, flight attendants had to kiss departing passengers, she said.

At the time TWU was led by male subway workers and bus drivers who thought "that flight attendants weren't in it for a career" like they were, Wulfhart said. Those leaders "had never been flight attendants; they didn't look like flight attendants. They didn't respect flight attendants. They didn't understand that flight attendants needed pensions and benefits and all the things male workers were getting."[8] The assumption was that flight attendants would work for a few years until they married and became pregnant, at which point they would leave the airline either by choice or because they were no longer allowed to work there. Obviously, today's TWU is far different, even though the international union is led by a former subway worker.

The book also calls attention to the sexist airline advertisements of the time. A Delta ad proclaimed, "No floor show, just a working girl working," and showed a flight attendant serving beverages in a knee-length dress. A United ad said, "The Natives Are Friendly" and showed flight attendants smiling at a male customer. Another United ad showed a flight attendant pinning a rose on a male customer's lapel. "She even straightened your boutonniere," it said, touting the "extra care" flight attendants provided. "Come Back Soon."

A particularly cringey American ad proclaimed, "Think of her as your mother." It showed a slim, young woman sitting in a chair with her legs curled beneath her, wearing a cape-like jacket over a short uniform. She held her chin in her hand as she gazed directly into the camera. The text said, "She only wants what's best for you. A cool drink. A good dinner. A soft pillow and a warm blanket. This is not just maternal instinct. It's the results. Training in service, not just a beauty course. Service, after all, is what makes professional travelers prefer American. And makes new travelers want to keep on flying with us." Wulfhart, in her book, called the ad, part of a campaign launched by American in 1968, ill-conceived. The women who led the flight attendants' nascent union movement were horrified, she wrote, but most members of the workforce "weren't in the habit of finding such things repugnant" and didn't complain.[9]

One big win for American's flight attendants came in 1976, when they finally won the right to have single-room accommodations during trips, after twice voting down contracts that didn't provide them. (Pilots and male flight attendants already had them.) But the big victory came on May 10, 1977, when APFA ousted TWU in a union election. Overall, flight attendants' successful efforts to create two unions dominated by women were a major component of the women's movement. Nevertheless, five years later when Julie Hedrick joined the airline, "stewardesses" still faced indignities. "When I was hired, I was weighed," she said. "That continued for quite a long time, even after the birth of my children."[10]

According to the APFA's online archives, "For decades, American Airlines maintained a weight policy that was based entirely upon a Flight Attendant's appearance and was unrelated to his/her ability to perform the job." The policy was modified under a 1991 agreement between the union, the carrier and the Equal Employment Opportunity Commission, but it was not eliminated until 1995. "Over the years many FAs were suspended and some even terminated for being 'overweight,'" APFA said.[11] The union also fought against smoking on airplanes. In 1988, smoking was banned on domestic flights of less than two hours. The ban was extended to six hours in 1990 and then to all flights in 2000. "I was here during the smoking years and I was part of that battle," Hedrick said. "Flight attendant unions have had to fight for a long time, and we will continue to fight for what we deserve."[12]

Hedrick did not choose an easy time to be APFA president. The pandemic pushed many flight attendants to retire, so when the airline industry rebounded, carriers had to hire new people—including about

6,000 flight attendants at American. Although APFA's contract became amendable in 2019, American like most carriers put off labor negotiations. Then they all negotiated their pilot contracts first. It wasn't until 2024 that the labor spotlight shined on flight attendant contracts.

Additionally, although the merger with U.S. Airways was done, introducing 6,000 U.S. Airways flight attendants who were formerly members of AFA to their new union, was a gradual process that continued into Hedrick's term. With the size of the union nearly doubling due to new hires and former U.S. Airways employees, Hedrick decided that it was important to make the union's activities more transparent to members. So APFA, long opaque, became a union leader in transparency. Its website now provides members with information about events ranging from grievances to contract talks to negotiations.

"We brought in so many new flight attendants and they would go to the website, and there was hardly any information there," Hedrick said. "So we decided to make sure that when flight attendants need to know about the contract, it is in hotlines and in pages on the website. It was at their fingertips. That was a huge undertaking, but we knew it was worth it. What has made me happiest when I look back is to see the level of engagement by our members. They have brought new life to this union."[13] As for the lingering conflicts between disparate employee groups that were merged into American, Hedrick said, "I don't talk about legacies anymore. At one time, a lot of conversations had legacies in them, but we don't hear it very often any longer. Like many of the flight attendants, I came from a different airline, but we are past that now. We are all one."[14]

When Hedrick looks back, she sees herself as someone who grew up in a small town and learned the importance of working hard. She worked hard when she was in college, she worked hard to learn the contract and she works hard as union president. She regrets the changes in her profession. "These jobs are not the same jobs they were when we started," she said. "That's what we've been trying to convey to the public and to management. The job today and the stress, the long hours, the not knowing what you will face,—it has all changed dramatically. I don't think I ever went to work worried that someone was going to hit me. When I was in [reservations], I talked to people on the phone and sometimes they yelled at me. When I became a flight attendant, I thought this is great: people won't yell at me anymore."[15]

26

The Not So Strange Case of Laura Glading

It is part of the history of airline unions that, almost inevitably, leaders involved in signing groundbreaking deals are later excoriated for not making even better deals. Laura Glading, who headed the Association of Professional Flight Attendants from 2008 to 2015 is an example. Glading was the labor leader most engaged in enabling the 2013 merger between American and U.S. Airways, which ensured a sustainable future for both airlines and their employees. For that, she became an outcast among some factions of union leadership, although it's not clear that union membership took the same view.

When Glading left APFA in 2015; she was satisfied with what she had done during a 37-year-career as a flight attendant, including the last eight as union president. She then took up a second career as executive director of labor and employee relations for the Federal Aviation Administration, where she oversaw 15 contracts with eight unions. "I survived as executive director for almost seven years—which included three changes in (U.S. presidential) administration, countless union elections, a myriad of labor agreements and the pandemic," Glading said in a 2023 interview. "It was extremely complex, but it was a blast."[1] Glading has always seen herself as a conciliatory leader who worked to bring parties together, whether it be American and its flight attendants, the disparate parties on the airline's creditors committee during the bankruptcy, or the FAA and its unions. At the end of her tenure as APFA leader, her desire for consensus got her in trouble with more disputatious union members.

Glading retired from the FAA at age 66, in January 2023. While the AFA's Sara Nelson is easily recognized as the most important flight attendant of the 21st century, and likely as the most important flight

26. The Not So Strange Case of Laura Glading

attendant ever, it is also true that Glading's career was extremely impactful in terms of her influence on the airline industry. The two were generally rivals, certainly not fond of one another, at least partially because Nelson has long sought a merger of the two largest flight attendant unions while Glading wanted them to remain separate. That conflict reached a peak in 2013, when thousands of AFA flight attendants from U.S. Airways became American flight attendants and APFA members in the merger. The two unions agreed on the arrangement because the far larger APFA was very likely to have won an election.

Asked her thoughts on a merger of the two unions in 2023, Glading made clear they have not changed. "I hope they don't," she said. "I don't think that flight attendants are ready to vote for it and I don't think they would vote for it." Of Nelson, Glading said, "She wanted to merge. I did not want to merge. Also, there was a deal, which AFA reneged on, that we would not have an election."[2]

In 2013, AFA started to do "road shows" where it presented a case for replacing APFA at American. Said Nelson, "Of course we were trying to preserve the value of contracts and protect seniority and make sure they had the best representation. US Airways had a better contract, but [APFA] was going to use the agreement they made as a baseline. We had to protect the value of the US Airways contract." Had the two unions merged, Nelson said, "It would have created an incredibly powerful force to represent American flight attendants. Keeping the flight attendants apart was the exact wrong move at a moment when the industry had consolidated its power by merging. We should have done the same."[3]

By early 2024, Glading was retired to her home in Waccabuc, New York, a small town about 50 miles north of Manhattan. She enjoyed recalling her career as a flight attendant, a union president and an FAA executive. Although she left APFA amidst controversy, "I never felt excoriated," she said. "I did the right things for the right reasons. You can't put a price on that. I loved every second of the American Airlines experience. I loved being a flight attendant; I loved the profession. Being APFA president was tough. You had to be very thick-skinned. Everything I did was to protect the profession and protect jobs. God knows I gave it everything I had."[4]

In her second career with the FAA, Glading flew a lot and often ran into American Airlines flight attendants. "They say they appreciate what I did," Glading said. "I protected their jobs and they get their pension checks, and they understand. The merger seems to have worked. I was the first union leader who really supported it. It was the right thing to

Laura Glading has been a flight attendant, a union president and an FAA executive (courtesy Laura Glading).

do and it was the only thing to do, the only chance that American flight attendants had to survive."[5]

Glading joined American after attending St. John's College in New York. Thirty years later, in 2008, she was elected to her first term as APFA president. She quickly began to participate in the quarterly meetings between American executives and labor leaders. By 2011, she said, "I knew that things were going south financially. [American CEO] Gerard Arpey was trying desperately not to go to bankruptcy, and it seemed that if American could get what they wanted from the pilots, they could kick the can down the road a little farther. But they expected more from the pilots than I thought the pilots would give, and I didn't think they had a viable business plan."[6] When American filed for bankruptcy protection, Glading was trying to decide whether to run again for president, a demanding job that detracted immensely from her time with her husband and son. The filing convinced her to run again. "I said I could live with the fact that the flight attendants didn't want me back, but 10 months down the line, I didn't want to face, 10 months down the line, knowing that I had walked away."[7] The airline filed for bankruptcy protection in

26. The Not So Strange Case of Laura Glading

November 2011. In February 2012, Glading was narrowly re-elected to be president with 51 percent of the vote. The margin was 150 votes; she won 4,434 to 4,284.

Glading's role in the bankruptcy was widely applauded. But in October 2015, as she came to the end of her second term, the tide was turning against her. Her opponents argued that she had grown too close to management. In response to mounting criticism, Glading announced in October that she would resign on December 2. In her resignation letter, she wrote of the disunity in the 25,000-member union. She said, "Today our voice is not unified and I believe some appear to have lost sight of our duty to represent and advocate for our fellow flight attendants." She said that most of the union's board opposed efforts "to better serve our members, including educating new hires on the whys and wherefores of unionism generally and APFA specifically." Amidst talk of a recall, she wrote: "I can't imagine exposing our union to this turmoil when all that this ballot, if successful, would do is reduce my term by no more than a few months."[8] In 2023, Glading said, "I don't think membership would have booted me. I don't know if I was actually disliked. But l got frustrated with the board. Some of them seemed to feel that if you got too much attention, if you were too successful, that was the worst thing you could do."[9]

Those who already saw Glading as too close to management became apoplectic on January 7, 2016, when an email to APFA members disclosed that she had been asked to work as a consultant for the airline. Her role was to seek better enforcement of U.S. Open Skies treaties, which generally expand international access to U.S airports, so that they did not result in the loss of jobs for union members. At the time, in a now largely forgotten controversy, the big three U.S. carriers battled the big three Middle East carriers—Emirates, Etihad and Qatar—over the billions in subsidies they received from their governments while taking advantage of Open Skies agreements to fly from their hubs to the hubs of U.S. carriers. The subsidies totaled around $50 billion, according to a report by a lobbying group that represented American, Delta and United. The conflict was largely resolved in 2018: Today, American has a codeshare with Qatar and United has a codeshare with Emirates. Of course, such arrangements were unforeseeable in 2016.

The 2016 email to APFA members from Marcus Gluth, Glading's successor, began with this sentence: "I am writing to you this evening to inform you of a disgusting betrayal." He said Glading's hiring as an American consultant was "the ultimate display of disloyalty from a former APFA national president." He called an emergency meeting of the union board and he launched an investigation "to determine whether any quid pro quo was offered by the company" when Glading worked as union president.[10] The next day, the APFA board of directors wrote another letter that said, "We view her traitorous actions as having cast a dark shadow on the credibility of our entity."[11]

It was too much. Glading decided to retire as a flight attendant even though, had she continued, her high seniority would have brought a favorable schedule and top-scale pay.

Glading said American sought her out for the consulting job because she was already actively opposing the Middle East airlines' U.S. expansion. The three major carriers hired lobbyists and pursued a very public battle. However, they were essentially doomed to lose because the UAE and Qatar had strategic defense importance that took precedence over what their airlines were doing. A leader of the U.S. airlines' effort was Will Ris, American's senior vice president for government affairs, who was about to retire. Glading was viewed as a well-connected, informed advocate who could step in. "I was going to do what I had been doing all along," Glading said.[12]

It was a difficult period, made worse when her father suffered a stroke: After a few months, she resigned from the consulting job to take the FAA job. When American management learned that she was applying to the FAA, she said, someone asked, "How can we help?" and she responded, "You can keep out of it." One thing that amused Glading during her FAA career was that sometimes APFA officers would visit Washington and ask her to lunch. But they didn't want anyone to know about it. "I would visit with them, and so many of them said it was on the sneak," she said. "I thought what the hell am I meeting with them for if they wanted it to be on the sneak?"[13]

Late in 2022, when Glading was preparing to retire, a health scan revealed something ominous: Her doctors diagnosed her with lung cancer. That led to three months of treatment, during which one of her lungs was removed. Then it turned out that she did not have lung cancer after all. She did not sue anyone. But the experience was stressful. One day her brother recommended that to shift her attention, she should visit the National Memorial for Peace and Justice, informally known as the National Lynching Memorial, in Montgomery, Alabama. She went in May 2023. "It helped me mentally to get over the cancer scare," she said. "I came to terms with it. I decided that the best thing to do is to stop feeling sorry for myself, because there are people in the world who lived through a real hell."[14]

27

Unions Big and Small Find Spots in the Airline Industry

Union engagement in the airline industry does not stop with the half dozen major unions devoted primarily to airlines. The industry also has representation by both the Service Employees International Union and the International Brotherhood of Teamsters, the second and fourth largest U.S. unions with 1.9 million and 1.34 million members respectively, as well as by Unite Here with about 300,000 members and the Professional Airline Flight Control Association, which represents groups of several hundred controllers at the three largest airlines and has about 2,000 total members. This chapter and the next one will examine their roles, starting with the IBT, which is generally referred to as the Teamsters.

The IBT is the only union to represent workers in every labor segment in the airline industry. Its total airline membership is about 40,000; about a fourth of whom are United mechanics.. Also, with the CWA, IBT jointly represents about 20,000 American Airlines agents. The director of the Teamsters Airline Division is Joe Ferreira, whose long airline career started at People Express, which was merged into Continental in 1987. Ferreira's story is unusual because after 40 years in management, he joined the union in 2021. He retired in 2024.

Ferreira spent his career at United overseeing maintenance at various levels, rising from supervisor to vice president. In 2010, United and Continental merged and it took until 2015 to combine the separate Teamsters mechanics' contracts at the two careers. Ferreira left United not long after to run a Houston-based maintenance consulting firm. In 2021, he got a call from Clacy Griswold, a longtime Teamsters official, whom he knew from negotiations. Griswold said the union's airline division director post was open and United mechanics—they are also called "technicians—had a good impression of him. "He said, 'The technicians really respect you, Joe; they would be very happy if you became a Teamster.' I told him I still had a little fuel left in the tank and I'd give it a shot,'" Ferreira recalled.[1]

As a manager, Ferreira sought to be sensitive to the workers he oversaw. He had a policy regarding disagreements, which was that "if there was a 50–50 call on a dispute, I felt we should just go along with the employee. It goes a long way to making sure that people are happy and like to come to work." His core belief, he said, was, "to do what's right, from the employee perspective and from the safety perspective. I've always had a motto that I tell people, 'Fix it right the first time; that will create a lot less pain than doing it the second time.'"[2] His story demonstrates that management and labor can work together if they choose to.

At the age of five, Ferreira emigrated with his family from Portugal to Newark, New Jersey. At the time, Newark attracted many Portuguese, even acquiring the nickname "Little Portugal." Ferreira graduated from high school, obtained his airframe powerplant license and joined the Army. He spent time as a helicopter pilot and mechanic, but when he left the service in 1981, a recession meant the domestic market for his skills had dried up. The job opportunities had been concentrated in the oil industry, where helicopters serviced offshore oil rigs in the Texas gulf. "The oil bust eliminated a lot of jobs," Ferreira said.[3] He took a job as a helicopter mechanic in Saudi Arabia.

Four years later, he went home to a job as a

Joe Ferreira was a United Airlines executive before becoming director of the Teamsters airline division (courtesy IBT).

maintenance manager for People Express, a young, growing Newark-based airline. That brought him to the U.S. commercial airline industry in 1985, and he never left. Like most airline industry lifers, he spent part of his career at a carrier that no longer exists. A fortunate aspect of social media is that extinct carriers all have Facebook pages; the People Express page is called "PeoplExpress Airlines Alumni." The carrier "brought a viable travel option to millions of passengers who were new to air travel," the site says.[4]

People Express operated for just seven years, but made a big impact. It began flying in 1981 as a low-cost provider flying domestic routes. Its big moment came when it began low-cost service to London Gatwick, using a leased Boeing 747. Fares started at $149 each way and many flights sold out. At the time, transatlantic travelers from the New York area had to fly out of Kennedy, where Pan Am and TWA operated hubs. People Express changed the face of travel, becoming an airline for students, backpackers and the youth market. Its fleet eventually grew to 81 aircraft.

Despite its popularity, People Express had operational issues—some called it "People Distress"—and it soon stopped making money. In 1987, Texas International, headed by Frank Lorenzo, acquired it and merged it into Continental. That enabled Continental to expand its Newark hub, which has been a profit center ever since. The Newark hub, now essential to United, is just one more sign that Lorenzo—despite his hostility to unions—was a visionary who assembled some of the industry's most important building blocks. "People Express went into airports that were underutilized, in the U.S.—Newark was underutilized—and then Gatwick," Ferreira said. "The business was growing when I went and airplanes were being delivered. Then cash flow became a problem." With the Continental merger, Ferreira moved to the Houston headquarters and became vice president of technical operations, overseeing 8,000 technicians. He has little to say about Lorenzo, but praises Gordon Bethune, Lorenzo's eventual successor. Bethune, Ferreira said, "was a great man. I worked with him and met him many times. He was more my style of working together."[5]

In Houston, Ferreira oversaw the merger of two Teamsters contracts. Putting contracts together is among the most difficult aspects of an airline merger, even for Continental and United mechanics, who were represented by the same union. "We had two different operating certificates with two different contracts," Ferreira said. "Moving to a single operating certificate was done in 2010, but we ran different day-to-day operations for five years," he said. "That's how long it took to amalgamate the contracts. There was a lot of antiquated language left over."[6] When the work was completed, he left the carrier.

Today, Ferreira takes a dim view of mergers. "Mergers in my opinion never work out, regardless of which side you're on, " he said. "Somebody always gets hurt from them, and it takes a long time for people to come together and work through the differences between companies."[7] Airline history is filled with tales of fractious mergers: Pan Am with National, U.S. Air with Piedmont—and Lorenzo's combination of Continental, Eastern, Frontier, New York Air and People Express. Some view today's industry as an end point, with four major carriers that carry 80 percent of the traffic. But additional consolidation would surprise no one.

As a Teamster leader, Ferreira spent most of his time on contract negotiations, generally involved in three or four at the same time. Face-to-face talks can be the most productive, he said; the contrast to video conferencing, which predominated during the pandemic, is clear. The United contract became amendable in 2023 and he looks forward to negotiating a new one. "I have a lot of tribal knowledge of what was negotiated there in the past," he said. "That helps." As far as being on the other side of the table from people he used to work with, he said, "The people I know were mostly in the technician ranks. At the table, there's only a handful left from when I was there."[8]

Professional Airline Flight Control Association

Craig Symons' parents met when both worked in National Airlines' cargo offices at Miami International Airport. His mom worked in office administration; his stepdad worked in accounting. In 1980, Pan Am acquired National so they became employees of Pan Am, where even the accountants had union representation. Symons' stepdad became a Teamster. Today, Symons is not only an airline legacy but also a union legacy. He is a United Airlines dispatcher and president of the United chapter of the Professional Airlines Flight Controllers Association.

PAFCA is small and little known outside the airline industry. Perhaps the most attention it routinely gets is when a reporter somewhere writes that only the pilots and dispatchers are organized at Delta. Otherwise, "PAFCA runs under the radar," Symons said. "We're always part of the union coalitions at United, but typically we are not a high-profile union." PAFCA has about 2,000 members: 400 to 500 each at American,

Delta, and United and about 65 at Spirit. At other carriers—including Alaska, Southwest and UPS—dispatchers are represented by TWU. (FedEx and JetBlue dispatchers were not represented in early 2024.) PAFCA unions don't have administrators. "We all work the contracts we negotiate,"[9] Symonds said.

Outside the industry, many people don't know what dispatchers do. Before every flight, dispatchers consult with pilots on weight, weather, and routing. Subsequently, the two parties jointly issue a flight plan, and dispatchers communicate with the pilots during the flight. While employed by the airlines, dispatchers are charged by the FAA with ensuring that each flight is planned and operated safely in accordance with the agency's regulations. PAFCA dispatchers work primarily in the operations control centers for the major airlines in Atlanta, Chicago and Dallas.

Symons was born in Miami in 1970. In 1993 he graduated from the University of Illinois Urbana–Champaign, where he majored in history. For two summers, he was an intern in Pan Am's accounting office in Miami. His job was to audit the billing for tickets by foreign travel agencies. "If the audits were easy, all you had to do was verify the exchange rate and you were done," he said. "But some would take two days." Under the Teamster contract, whether the audits were easy or hard, an auditor could only do two a day. So Pan Am began assigning some of the audits to the intern. To accumulate more hours, some interns would come in early. "I needed to buy beer at college, so I started coming in at five,"[10] Symons said. But when Teamster officials learned of the practice, they disallowed it, since Pan Am paid straight time not overtime for extra hours. To the young college student, the union's action provided an early indication that unions protect workers. He liked airline work, and he liked union jurisdiction of the work. So he was hooked. He still has a letter in which Pan Am offered him a job when he graduated. But by 1993, Pan Am no longer existed.

Symons' first job was at charter carrier Miami Air. It was set up by former Eastern Airlines managers who were not union members. "They were the anti–Kiwi," Symons said, referring to the carrier that was established by Bob Iverson, a former Eastern pilot and striker who was a firm opponent of Eastern management. While Iverson hired pilots who struck, Miami Air hired former Eastern pilots who had crossed the picket line and, as a result, could not get jobs at ALPA carriers. Symons started at Miami Air as a ground handling coordinator but soon decided to become a dispatcher. He earned a license after taking a course in dispatch at Miami Dade Community College, then set his sights on moving to United in Chicago, his wife's hometown. After a year working for an aircraft leasing company, he was hired by United in May 1999. He was first elected to be the representative for his shift in 2001. "I was elected because I have a big mouth," he said. "I was on the midnight shift and I had a lot of opinions, and the union president at the time told me to put them to use."[11] Symons was elected in 2006 to the first of nine successive two-year terms.

Symons' take on United's leadership, past and present, is mixed. He said CEO Glen Tilton was interested only in finding a merger partner, while Tilton's successor, Jeff Smisek, was embroiled in scandal. Oscar Munoz, who arrived in 2015, was "the right guy for the job because he wanted to put the airline back together; he wanted to heal wounds, and he did a good job." As for Scott Kirby, Symons said, "He is the first CEO who actually wanted to run an airline. Everybody else had a different agenda, but this is what Kirby wants to do."[12]

Unite Here

Unite Here represents about 300,000 workers in various industries including hotels, gaming, food services, manufacturing and airports. About 45,000 workers who work in concessions and catering at about 60 airports are represented by the airport division. "Our members are among both the friendly faces who greet you when you land in a new city and the unseen army responsible for the preparation and delivery of tens of thousands of in-flight meals each day," the union's website says.[13]

Alisa Gallo, the union's airport director, primarily oversees contracts with catering companies Gate Gourmet, LSG Skychef and HMS Host, which operates restaurants in airports and other travel venues. In Charlotte, for example, Unite Here has two contracts. One is with LSG Sky Chefs, which operates a catering operation for the airlines and employs a few hundred people. The other is with HMS Host, which employs about 1,200 people.

Gallo said the union has been growing consistently and quietly. "In the South, generally you don't want to trumpet that you've just had a union victory because you don't want to invite the trolls to mess with your success," she said.[14] Unite Here represents airport workers in most of the region's busiest airports, including Atlanta, Charlotte, Dallas, Houston and Miami.

Since 2020, the airport division has added about 3,000 people, largely through its national contracts. "It's not like we've had a

27. Unions Big and Small Find Spots in the Industry 189

Sara Nelson speaks to Senate cafeteria workers fighting for a contract (courtesy AFA).

concentrated organizing drive at one particular airport," Gallo said. "But organizing is happening very broadly. We've been able to use relationships at both the corporate level and at the airport administration level to secure labor peace for workers, without the airports worrying that we will jeopardize smooth operations at the airport. It just sort of happens, and we don't broadcast when we have labor peace. We talk to workers and organize for our union and we move forward."[15]

Gallo graduated from Brown University, where she majored in urban studies. As a student, she supported workers both on and off campus. In 1994, the year after she graduated, she went to work for Unite Here. "It occurred to me that workers needed to learn how to work together and to learn how to make more money," she said. "Then I realized that's what unions do."[16] She attended the AFL-CIO Organizing Institute, then returned to Brown's hometown, Providence, Rhode Island, to work for the union. After living in various cities in New England and Canada, she found herself in Houston, working to organize United Airlines' catering workers. In Houston, she met her husband Hany Khalil, also a Brown graduate, and currently executive director of the Texas Gulf Coast Area Labor Federation.

28

Justice for Janitors Cleans Up at Airports

While the familiar professions at the top of the airline industry hierarchy have long been organized, the workers on the industry's outskirts have often been denied that advantage. So it is that the pilots, flight attendants, mechanics, dispatchers and fleet service workers at major airlines earn livable wages and sometimes enviable benefits, while the janitors, security screeners, airport cleaners and wheelchair assistants very often do not. The discrepancy has drawn the attention of the Service Employees International Union, whose longtime focus on low-paid service workers in healthcare, the public sector and property services has shifted in recent years to include the airline industry.

What unites SEIU workers, at airports or elsewhere, is that they serve people face-to-face and that many of them are women, Black, brown, or members of other minority groups that have faced burdensome economic challenges, said SEIU President Mary Kay Henry. "I've had many workers that I've had the privilege to stand beside who care more about the care they provide for a patient, or in this case for a passenger, then they do for themselves," said Henry, who became SEIU president in 2010. "They use their union to improve their own job conditions but also to improve the jobs they do for the public," Henry said. "They are at the forefront of service to the public." During the pandemic, she said, union efforts to organize such workers have gained ground. "It's been a moment like I have never seen" during a SEIU career of 45 years, mostly spent organizing health care workers. she said. "Workers are ready to take major risks, including losing their jobs at Starbucks, Amazon, and in health care. I'm proud of the way they are raising demands for unions in order to build an equitable economy."[1]

By 2023, SEIU had organized about 36,000 airport service workers at 43 airports. Out of necessity, the union's airline industry organizing approach has differed from the traditional path where, for instance, a flight attendant union organizes flight attendants at a new airline. Rather, SEIU has used the influence enabled by its large size and political savvy to run campaigns to convince elected officials to raise the minimum wage in their localities. Then it seeks to ensure that the higher wage extends to workers, including airport workers. The SEIU has a particular skill for devising distinctive slogans, including "Fight for $15" as well as "Justice for Janitors" which have been used in its campaigns.

In 2012, the union stepped up its airport organizing. Henry said airlines had used a variety of strategies—including outsourcing the service jobs largely held by minority workers—to dodge unions and labor standards. Outsourcing was often a part of the airline bankruptcies in the early part of the 21st century. The SEIU challenged the strategy by seeking to organize the displaced workers. According to Bureau of Labor Statistics data analyzed by SEIU, airlines directly employed 75 percent of their baggage handlers and skycaps as late as 2002. But by 2017, contractors employed 96 percent of those same workers. Similarly, in 2002, airlines employed 59 percent of wheelchair and cart attendants; by 2017, contractors employed 97 percent of them. As outsourcing increased, wages decreased. Additional BLS data, adjusted for inflation by the SEIU, shows that in 2018 the baggage handlers and skycaps who worked for airlines had a median hourly wage of $27.18, while those who worked for contractors were paid a median wage of $11.39 an hour.

A countervailing trend has been for SEIU to work to boost wages for the lowest paid workers. In the 1990s, living wage laws were enacted in Los Angeles and San Francisco. "This created conditions where our janitors in downtown centers, who were winning gains, to talk to janitors at airports," Henry said. "It raised their expectations."[2] The SEIU organized janitors at Los Angeles International Airport and San Francisco International Airport in the 1990s as part of the Justice for Janitors campaign and then organized the security officers at both airports after the September 11 attacks. By 2023, SEIU represented about 7,200 California airport workers including agents for smaller airlines, security officers, sky caps, cabin cleaners, janitors and fleet service workers who handle baggage.

A similar story took place in the Pacific Northwest. In 2013, residents of Sea Tac, a city of about 31,000 that surrounds the airport, voted to boost the minimum wage to $15 an hour for hospitality and transportation workers. A year later, Seattle became the first big city in the country to increase its minimum hourly wage to $15. Opponents included Alaska Airlines, the largest carrier at Seattle Tacoma International Airport, which is owned and operated by the Port of Seattle. In 2016, about 1,000 airport workers voted to join SEIU. "The first airport workers in the country to win a $15 minimum wage are now the latest to declare victory in the fight for union rights," SEIU said at the time. "The Sea-Tac workers organizing with SEIU Local 6 are part of a growing movement of airport workers across the country calling out the low-bid contracting system which has lowered standards across the country—and building conditions for responsible contractors to raise standards."[3] The workers included baggage handlers, cabin cleaners, cart drivers, wheelchair agents, unaccompanied minor escorts and lavatory and water service fillers.

Minimum wage increases in the Northwest did not stop there. In September 2020, six months after the pandemic began, the Port of Portland approved a new minimum wage requirement for companies that employed about 900 baggage handlers, security officers, wheelchair agents, and airplane and terminal cleaners at Portland International Airport. Minimum wage went to $15 an hour by July 2021 and $16.55 by January 2022. Again, the move illustrates the SEIU strategy, as Henry has said, "to use local political power to influence contracting at local airports, which are controlled by port authorities, mayors and government-appointed people."[4]

During the pandemic, SEIU members also became beneficiaries of the CARES Act. The first tranche of the bill in 2022 provided $32 billion in direct grants to pay as many as 750,000 airline industry workers through September 2020. Of the total, $25 billion was allocated for passenger airlines, $4 billion for cargo airlines, and $3 billion for contractors, including those who employed caterers and airport workers. "We were able to lobby and get help for contracted workers," Henry said. "They didn't have paid sick time, health care coverage or personal protective equipment, and what the pandemic did was to nationalize our fight. Where we had been organizing airport by airport, the pandemic took the fight national. We wanted to make sure that some of those dollars went to the frontline workers who were the most invisible."[5]

Another SEIU focus has been workers at American Airlines hubs. In May 2023, the union said that it had won an election at Charlotte Douglas International Airport to organize about 500 workers, including ramp agents, cabin cleaners, lavatory and water agents and high lift truck drivers. They worked for Jetstream Ground Services, a Jupiter,

Florida–based contractor which offers airport services at about a dozen airports.

Meanwhile, in 2021, the City of Dallas raised its minimum wage to $15.50 hourly for city workers, but efforts to extend the increase to airport workers have stalled. In Chicago, in 2022, the city council approved an ordinance-boosting minimum wage for about 6,500 contracted airport workers including caterers, de-icers, baggage handlers, aircraft cleaners and wheelchair attendants. By 2023, the wage had increased to $18 hourly, up from $15 when the ordinance passed. "We think American sets a standard for the sector," Henry said. "Because Charlotte and Dallas and Chicago are American hubs, we feel like the biggest challenge is to hold American accountable. American has received billions from federal taxpayers, it is making record profits, and its CEO is doing fine, but workers are moving between couches and homelessness."[6]

Mary Kay Henry grew up in a United Auto Workers environment. She was born in July 1957 in Detroit, went to Bloomfield High School and graduated from Michigan State University with a dual major in urban studies and labor in 1979. While in college, she supported herself

Mary Kay Henry speaks at a union rally in Chicago in March 2023 (courtesy SEIU).

by doing health care jobs, including nursing assistant for the Red Cross and surgical supply aid at St. Joseph Hospital in Pontiac. At the hospital her mentor was Marge Bursee, an older Black woman and "a veteran who taught me everything and who protected me when the surgeons were abusive to us if we didn't move fast enough," Henry said. "She didn't take shit off anybody. If somebody would come in and scream at me, she would talk to me afterwards. She said, 'What did you notice about that situation?' I said 'They didn't scream at you. That's probably because they're afraid to.' She said, 'You have to bark back at them.'" One night, as part of a UAW campaign to organize the hospital workers, Bursee asked Henry to compile a list of the names of the hospital workers. "I would do anything she wanted me to, so I stayed late," Henry recalled. "She said 'I want you to go to the switchboard operator on the third floor and get the clerical workers' names and phone numbers.' I was writing down the names when a supervisor asked me what I was doing. Then she took the list out of my hands and she fired me."[7]

Getting fired was a shock to the 22 year old, but Henry was not deterred. She subsequently sought a job with UAW, but it became clear that an idealistic young person with a health care background and labor union aspirations might find a better match at SEIU. In May 1980, SEIU hired her in Washington, D.C., as a research specialist, and sent her to a San Francisco training program for college students. There, her teachers were two early SEIU leaders. The first was Richard Liebes, who had bargained the union's first contract with health care provider Kaiser Permanente in the 1940s. Henry shadowed Liebes during bargaining, grievance hearings and organizing. She also conducted wage case studies research for health care workers, racetrack workers, and janitors. "It was incredible training," she recalled. "He taught me that the most important job in the union is organizing. I did six months in San Francisco, then six months in Los Angeles."[8]

In Los Angeles, Henry trained under George Hardy, who started at SEIU as an organizer in 1936, when the union was formed. Hardy then rose to become union president from 1971 to 1980. After his presidency, he returned to Los Angeles, where he taught Henry from the ground up. "He would tell me to meet him at 2 a.m. at a nursing home, because that was when people would take smoke breaks," Henry said. "I didn't have a car, so I would have to go to the nursing home on the bus, which would take two or three hours." It was a key to learning about the lives of the working poor. "He would be there in his car, smoking a cigarette, and he would hand me leaflets and tell me to go to the back door where people took their smoke breaks. When dawn broke, and people went home, there would be more workers than I could handle, and he would help me. I got to hear how he talked to people, and today I stand on the shoulders of people like Richard and George, who paved the way for us to help workers who have to fight to be included, primarily due to race and gender."[9]

Chapter Notes

Introduction

1. Airlines for America, airlines.org/jobs/, 2023.
2. Lane Windham, quoted by Natalie Kitroeff, "The Shutdown Made Sara Nelson Into America's Most Powerful Flight Attendant," *New York Times*, Feb. 22, 2019.
3. Doug Parker, speech to the Wings Club Awards Gala, Oct. 22, 2021, wingsclub.org.
4. Sara Nelson interview, July 14, 2023.
5. Airlines for America, U.S. Airlines Traffic and Capacity, airlines.org/dataset/annual-results-u-s-airlines-2/.
6. Sara Nelson interview, July 14, 2023.
7. Airlines for America, airlines.org/dataset/annual-results-u-s-passenger-airlines/.
8. Doug Parker, quoted by Dan Reed, "Airlines Won't Ever Lose Money Again? Boasts by American's CEO Dismiss History," *Forbes*, Oct. 24, 2017.
9. Lisa Farbstein, quoted by Ted Reed, "How a Single Statistic Helped Shape TSA's Image During the Pandemic," *The Points Guy*, Nov. 23, 2021.
10. Andrew Didora, quoted by Ted Reed, "Airline Industry Heads Back to Normal as Analyst Sees 'Insatiable' Demand," *Forbes*, March 14, 2022.

Chapter 1

1. Sara Nelson interview, Feb. 14, 2023.
2. *Ibid.*
3. Bennett Hall, "The Last Mom and Pop," *The Corvallis Gazette-Times*, Sept. 18, 2010.
4. Sara Nelson interview, Feb. 14, 2023.
5. *Ibid.*
6. *Ibid.*
7. *Ibid.*
8. *Ibid.*
9. *Ibid.*
10. *Ibid.*
11. *Ibid.*
12. *Ibid.*
13. *Ibid.*
14. *Ibid.*

Chapter 2

1. Sara Nelson interview, March 16, 2023.
2. *Ibid.*
3. *Ibid.*
4. Sara Nelson interview, July 14, 2023.
5. *Ibid.*
6. *Ibid.*
7. Sara Nelson interview, March 13, 2023.
8. *Ibid.*
9. *Ibid.*
10. *Ibid.*
11. Dave Carpenter interview, July 16, 2023.
12. Sara Nelson interview, July 14, 2023.
13. Dave Carpenter interview, July 16, 2023.
14. Craig Symons interview, Nov. 1, 2023.
15. Sara Nelson interview, July 14, 2023.
16. *Ibid.*
17. *Ibid.*

Chapter 3

1. Sara Nelson interview, March 13, 2023.
2. *Ibid.*
3. Pat Friend, quoted by Ted Reed, "Veteran Flight Attendant Leader Steps Down," *TheStreet*, Dec. 8, 2010.
4. *Ibid.*
5. *Ibid.*
6. Email from Sara Nelson, Feb. 8, 2024.
7. Mike Flores interview, June 22, 2023.
8. *Ibid.*
9. Sara Nelson interview, June 14, 2023.
10. Veda Shook, quoted by Ian Kullgren, "The New Union Label: Female, Progressive and Very Anti-Trump," *Politico*, Feb. 12, 2019.
11. Sara Nelson interview, Feb. 14, 2023.
12. Sara Nelson interview, July 14, 2023.
13. *Ibid.*
14. Sara Nelson interview, March 13, 2023.
15. *Ibid.*

Chapter 4

1. Natalie Kitroeff, "The Shutdown Made Sara Nelson Into America's Most Powerful Flight Attendant," *New York Times*, Feb. 22, 2019.
2. Sara Nelson, quoted by Bob Hennelly, "The Single Most Important Pro-Labor Speech of the Shutdown Was Not Given by AOC," *Salon*, Jan. 27, 2019.
3. Bob Hennelly, "The Single Most Important Pro-Labor Speech of the Shutdown Was Not Given by AOC," *Salon*, Jan. 27, 2019.
4. Sara Nelson, quoted by Bob Hennelly, "The Single Most Important Pro-Labor Speech of the Shutdown Was Not Given by AOC," *Salon*, Jan. 27, 2019. Statement by AFA, ALPA and NATCA, Jan. 23, 2019.
5. Sara Nelson, shown and quoted in X post by Now This Impact, Jan. 24, 2019.
6. Natalie Kitroeff, "The Shutdown Made Sara Nelson Into America's Most Powerful Flight Attendant," *New York Times*, Feb. 22, 2019.
7. Lane Windham, quoted by Natalie Kitroeff.
8. Kim Kelly, "Sara Nelson's Art of War," *The New Republic*, May 13, 2019.
9. *Ibid.*
10. Jennifer Gonnerman, "Flight Attendants Fight Back," *The New Yorker*, May 23, 2022.
11. Lesliey Stahl, *60 Minutes*, CBS, Sept. 1, 2019.
12. Sara Nelson, quoted on *60 Minutes*.
13. Sara Nelson interview, July 14, 2023.

Chapter 5

1. Doug Parker, speech to the Wings Club, Oct. 22, 2021.
2. *Ibid.*
3. *Ibid.*
4. Joe Tiberi, quoted by Ted Reed, "How Labor Unions Won Historic Pay Protection for Aviation Workers," *Forbes*, May 26, 2020.
5. Sara Nelson, quoted by Ted Reed, "How Labor Unions Won Historic Pay Protection for Aviation Workers," *Forbes*, May 26, 2020.
6. Sara Nelson interview, July 14, 2023.
7. *Ibid.*
8. IAM District 141 post, quoted by Ted Reed, "What About Sara Nelson as Joe Biden's Running Mate?" *Forbes*, May 1, 2020.
9. Sara Nelson, quoted by Ted Reed, "What About Sara Nelson as Joe Biden's Running Mate?" *Forbes*, May 1, 2020.
10. Sito Pantoja, quoted by Ted Reed, "How Labor Unions Won Historic Pay Protection for Aviation Workers," *Forbes*, May 26, 2020.
11. Lori Bassani, quoted by Ted Reed, "How Labor Unions Won Historic Pay Protection for Aviation Workers," *Forbes*, May 26, 2020.
12. Email from Sara Nelson, Feb. 10, 2024.

Chapter 6

1. Sara Nelson interview, March 13, 2023.
2. *Ibid.*
3. Joe Biden video, posted on Twitter, Feb. 28, 2021, and since removed.
4. Sara Nelson interview, March 13, 2023.

5. *Ibid.*
6. Sara Nelson, quoted by Alex Press, "Flight Attendants' Leader Sara Nelson: 'You Have to Look for Your Next Flight,'" *Jacobin*, March 19, 2021.
7. *Ibid.*
8. Sara Nelson interview, March 13, 2023.
9. Alexandria Ocasio-Cortez, quoted by Sara Ashley-O'Brien, "A Second Amazon Election Begins in New York," CNN, April 25, 2022.
10. Sara Nelson, quoted by Alex Press, "The Class War Is Waging at Amazon's Staten Island Complex," *Jacobin*, April 25, 2022.
11. *Ibid.*
12. Sara Nelson interview, March 13, 2023.
13. *Ibid.*

Chapter 7

1. Taylor Garland interview, Aug. 10, 2023.
2. *Ibid.*
3. *Ibid.*
4. *Ibid.*
5. *Ibid.*
6. *Ibid.*
7. *Ibid.*
8. *Ibid.*
9. *Ibid.*
10. *Ibid.*
11. *Ibid.*
12. *Ibid.*

Chapter 8

1. Sara Nelson quoted by Ted Reed, "Flight Attendants Move to Center Stage in U.S. Labor Battles," *Forbes*, Nov. 17, 2023.
2. Pat Friend quoted by Frank Swoboda, "Flight Attendants Reject Delta Union," *The Washington Post*, Feb. 2, 2002.
3. Rodney Ward, "Delta Flight Attendants Vote 98% for Union—and Lose," *Labor Notes*, March 1, 2002.
4. Pat Friend, quoted by John Welbes, *Twin Cities Pioneer Press*, May 28, 2008.
5. Pat Friend, quoted by Ted Reed, "Veteran Flight Attendant Leader Steps Down," *TheStreet*, Dec. 8, 2010.
6. Ted Reed, "Labor Dream Team Calls on Delta's Detroit Hub," *Forbes*, Feb. 16, 2024.
7. Sara Nelson, in text to Ted Reed, Nov. 22, 2023.

Chapter 9

1. John Samuelsen interview, Oct. 14, 2022.
2. John Samuelsen interview, Jan. 6, 2023.
3. *Ibid.*
4. John Samuelsen interview, Sept. 16, 2022.
5. *Ibid.*
6. Upton Sinclair, *The Jungle* (New York: Signet, 1960), page 101. This book was originally published in 1908.
7. John Samuelsen interview, Sept. 16, 2022.
8. *Ibid.*
9. *Ibid.*
10. *Ibid.*
11. *Ibid.*
12. Joe Samuelsen interview, Dec. 6, 2023.
13. *Ibid.*
14. John Samuelsen interview, Sept. 16, 2022.
15. *Ibid.*
16. *Ibid.*
17. Joe Samuelsen interview, Dec. 6, 2023.
18. *Ibid.*

Chapter 10

1. John Samuelsen interview, Oct. 14, 2022.
2. *Ibid.*
3. *Ibid.*
4. *Ibid.*
5. Joe Samuelsen interview, Dec. 6, 2023.
6. Chris Rock, quoted by Joe Samuelsen and also by Kalefah Sanneh, "The Duke of Doubt," *The New Yorker*, Nov. 3, 2014.
7. John Samuelsen interview, Oct. 14, 2022.
8. Joe Samuelsen interview, Dec. 6, 2023.
9. John Samuelsen interview, Oct. 14, 2022.
10. *Ibid.*

11. *Ibid.*
12. *Ibid.*
13. Joe Samuelsen interview, Dec. 6, 2023.
14. John Samuelsen interview, Oct. 14, 2022.
15. John Samuelsen interview, Oct. 18, 2022.
16. *Ibid.*
17. *Ibid.*

Chapter 11

1. John Samuelsen interview, Oct. 14, 2022.
2. *Ibid.*
3. John Samuelsen interview, Sept. 16, 2022.
4. *Ibid.*
5. John Samuelsen interview, Oct. 14, 2022.
6. John Samuelsen interview, Oct. 18, 2022.
7. *Ibid.*
8. *Ibid.*
9. *Ibid.*
10. *Ibid.*
11. *Ibid.*
12. *Ibid.*
13. *Ibid.*
14. *Ibid.*
15. *Ibid.*
16. *Ibid.*
17. *Ibid.*

Chapter 12

1. Roberto Ramirez interview, Feb. 9, 2023.
2. John Samuelsen interview, Oct. 18, 2022.
3. Martin Luther King, Jr., quoted by Ryle Dwyer in "Mike Quill. The Irishman Martin Luther King described as 'A Man the Ages Will Remember,'" *Irish Examiner*, Jan. 26, 2016.
4. Mike Quill, quoted by L.H. Whittemore, *The Man Who Ran the Subways* (New York: Holt, Rinehart and Winston, 1968), p. 290.
5. John Samuelsen interview, Oct. 18, 2022.
6. L.H. Whittemore, *The Man Who Ran the Subways*, p. xi.
7. L.H. Whittemore, *The Man Who Ran the Subways*, p. xii.
8. Hank Whittemore interview, June 21, 2022.
9. *Ibid.*
10. Roger Toussaint interview, Jan. 20, 2023.
11. Jimmy Breslin, quoted by Strauss News, "Union Mean and Irishmen: Remembering Labo Hero Mike Quill," *New York Herald Tribune*, Feb. 16, 2015.
12. Hank Whittemore interview, June 21, 2022.
13. *Ibid.*
14. *Ibid.*
15. *Ibid.*
16. TWU Local 100 website, "It's the 40th Anniversary of TWU's 1980 Citywide Strike," April 1, 1980.
17. *Ibid.*
18. John Samuelsen interview, Sept. 8, 2022.
19. Roger Toussaint interview, Jan. 14, 2023.

Chapter 13

1. Roger Toussaint interview, Jan. 14, 2023.
2. *Ibid.*
3. Roger Toussaint interview, Jan. 20, 2023.
4. *Ibid.*
5. *Ibid.*
6. *Ibid.*
7. Theodore T. Jones, quoted by Thomas J. Lueck, "Transit Union Leader Sentenced to 10 Days in Jail Over Strike," *New York Times*, April 11, 2006.
8. Jeremy Ohshan, "Marching on Tombs Day—Roger's Jail Production," *New York Post*, April 25, 2006.
9. Roger Toussaint interview, Jan. 20, 2023.
10. John Samuelsen interview, Jan. 6, 2023.
11. *Ibid.*
12. Roger Toussaint interview, Jan. 20, 2023.
13. John Samuelsen interview, Jan. 6, 2023.
14. *Ibid.*
15. *Ibid.*

Chapter 14

1. John Samuelsen interview, Jan. 12, 2023.
2. *Ibid.*
3. *Ibid.*
4. *Ibid.*
5. *Ibid.*
6. *Ibid.*
7. Incident described by Emma G. Fitzsimmons, "Mayor de Blasio's Traffic Law Vilifies Bus Drivers, New York Says," *New York Times*, Feb. 19, 2015.
8. John Samuelsen interview, Jan. 12, 2023.
9. Emma G. Fitzsimmons, "Mayor de Blasio's Traffic Law Vilifies Bus Drivers," *New York Times*, Feb. 19, 2015.
10. John Samuelsen interview, Jan. 12, 2023.
11. Ad cited in "TWU Local 100 Goes After Mayor DeBlasio's Traffic Plan with Ad Blitz," CBS News, May 26, 2015.
12. John Samuelsen interview, Jan. 12, 2023.
13. Email from John Samuelsen, Feb. 4, 2024.
14. John Samuelsen interview, Jan. 12, 2023.
15. *Ibid.*
16. *Ibid.*
17. John Samuelsen, "New Year, New Battles," "As I Was Saying" column, *Transport Workers Bulletin*, Dec. 2014.
18. John Samuelsen interview, Jan. 12, 2023.
19. Tweet by Andrew Cuomo, March 19, 2019.
20. John Samuelsen, quoted by Ted Reed, "New York Governor Cuomo Backs Union Campaign To Organize JetBlue Flight Attendants," *Forbes*, March 21, 2018.
21. John Samuelsen, quoted by J. David Goodman, "A Secretive Dinner Where $25,000 Buys Access to Governor Cuomo (and Filet Mignon)," *New York Times*, March 27, 2019.
22. John Samuelsen, quoted by Emma G. Fitzsimmons, "Why Overtime and a Trump Comparison Are Fueling Threats of a Subway Strike," *New York Times*, May 14, 2019.
23. John Samuelsen interview, Jan. 12, 2023.

Chapter 15

1. John Samuelsen in video, "TWU President Samuelsen Takes Contract Fight to AA President Isom's Face," YouTube, May 21, 2019.
2. *Ibid.*
3. *Ibid.*
4. *Ibid.*
5. Robert Isom in video, "TWU President Samuelsen Takes Contract Fight to AA President Isom's Face," YouTube, May 21, 2019.
6. John Samuelsen, quoted by Ted Reed, "New American Airlines CEO Can Run Operations. Can He Lead An Airline," *Forbes*, Dec. 10, 2021.
7. Roberto Ramirez interview, Feb. 9, 2023.
8. Ted Reed, "American Airlines Encounters Labor Slowdowns Due to Slow Pace of Contract Talks," *Forbes*, July 14, 2018.
9. Dennis Tajer, quoted by Ted Reed, "American Airlines Encounters Labor Slowdowns Due to Slow Pace of Contract Talks," *Forbes*, July 14, 2018.
10. Ross Feinstein, quoted by Ted Reed, "American Airlines Encounters Labor Slowdowns Due to Slow Pace of Contract Talks," *Forbes*, July 14, 2018.
11. John McBryde, in *American Airlines vs. Transport Workers Union of America et al.*, opinion filed in U.S. District Court Northern District of Texas, Aug. 12, 2019, page 10.
12. Sito Pantoja interview, June 8, 2023.
13. Alex Garcia and Sito Pantoja, statement quoted by Ted Reed, "Is American Airlines Nearing a Deal with Mechanics and Fleet Workers?" *Forbes*, Sept. 11, 2019.

Chapter 16

1. Jason Ambrosi interview, Oct. 16, 2023.
2. *Ibid.*
3. *Ibid.*
4. *Ibid.*
5. *Ibid.*
6. *Ibid.*
7. *Ibid.*
8. *Ibid.*
9. *Ibid.*
10. *Ibid.*

11. *Ibid.*
12. *Ibid.*

Chapter 17

1. Dennis Tajer interview, Nov. 20, 2023
2. Michael Michaelis on transcript of meeting between APA and Boeing, Nov. 29, 2018.
3. Todd Wissing on transcript of meeting between APA and Boeing, Nov. 29, 2018.
4. Dennis Tajer interview, Nov. 20, 2023.
5. *Ibid.*
6. *Ibid.*
7. *Ibid.*
8. *Ibid.*
9. *Ibid.*
10. *Ibid.*
11. *Ibid.*
12. *Ibid.*
13. *Ibid.*
14. *Ibid.*
15. *Ibid.*

Chapter 18

1. Jason Ambrosi, quoted in ALPA Press Release, "ALPA Joins Families and Clarence Center Volunteer Fire Company to Honor Memory of Flight 3407 Victims," Feb. 10, 2023.
2. Jason Ambrosi interview, Oct. 16, 2023.
3. *Ibid.*
4. *Ibid.*
5. IATA in Press Release, "IATA Welcomes Telcos' Agreement to Extend 5G Mitigations But More Is Needed," May 2, 2023.
6. Jason Ambrosi interview, Oct. 16, 2023.
7. C.B. "Sully" Sullenberger, quoted by Ted Reed, "Hero Pilot from 2009 Remains a Hero Today, Fighting Threats to Airline Safety," *Forbes*, Jan. 14, 2023.
8. *Ibid.*
9. *Ibid.*
10. *Ibid.*
11. Jason Ambrosi, quoted in ALPA Press Release, "ALPA Vows to Fight Efforts to Remove Pilots fom Flight Deck on Anniversary of the 'Miracle on the Hudson,'" Jan. 12, 2023.
12. Jason Ambrosi interview, Oct. 16, 2023.

Chapter 19

1. Bureau of Transportation Statistics at https://www.transtats.bts.gov/employment/.
2. Jerry Glass interview, May 2, 2023.
3. *Ibid.*
4. *Ibid.*
5. *Ibid.*
6. *Ibid.*
7. *Ibid.*
8. Jerry Glass interview, May 5, 2023.
9. *Ibid.*
10. *Ibid.*
11. *Ibid.*

Chapter 20

1. Jerry Glass interview, May 5, 2023.
2. Jerry Glass interview, May 2, 2023,
3. Jerry Glass interview, May 5, 2023.
4. *Ibid.*
5. Ted Reed, "AMR Pilot Leader Bates Held an Impossible Job," *TheStreet*, Aug. 13, 2012.
6. Jerry Glass interview, May 5, 2023.
7. Jerry Glass interview, May 2, 2023.
8. Jerry Glass interview, May 5, 2023.
9. *Ibid.*
10. *Ibid.*
11. *Ibid.*
12. *Ibid.*
13. *Ibid.*

Chapter 21

1. Dave Bates, quoted by Ted Reed and Dan Reed, *American Airlines, U.S. Airways and the Creation of the World's Largest Airline* (Jefferson: McFarland, 2014), p. 164.
2. Dennis Tajer interview, Sept. 1, 2023.
3. *Ibid.*
4. *Ibid.*
5. Scott Kirby, quoted by Ted Reed and Dan Reed, *American Airlines, U.S. Airways and the Creation of the World's*

Largest Airline (Jefferson: McFarland, 2014), p. 166.
  6. Laura Glading, quoted by Ted Reed and Dan Reed, *American Airlines, U.S. Airways and the Creation of the World's Largest Airline* (Jefferson: McFarland, 2014), p. 166.
  7. Jim Little, quoted by Ted Reed and Dan Reed, *American Airlines, U.S. Airways and the Creation of the World's Largest Airline* (Jefferson: McFarland, 2014), p. 165.
  8. Laura Glading, quoted by Ted Reed and Dan Reed, *American Airlines, U.S. Airways and the Creation of the World's Largest Airline* (Jefferson: McFarland, 2014), p. 161.
  9. *Ibid.*, p. 160.
  10. Dave Bates, quoted by Ted Reed and Dan Reed, *American Airlines, U.S. Airways and the Creation of the World's Largest Airline* (Jefferson: McFarland, 2014), p. 153.
  11. Dennis Tajer interview, Sept. 1, 2023.

Chapter 22

  1. Sito Pantoja interview, June 5, 2023.
  2. *Ibid.*
  3. *Ibid.*
  4. *Ibid.*
  5. *Ibid.*
  6. *Ibid.*
  7. *Ibid.*
  8. *Ibid.*
  9. *Ibid.*
  10. Frank Lorenzo, email to Ted Reed, June 12, 2023.
  11. *Ibid.*
  12. *Ibid.*

Chapter 23

  1. Sito Pantoja interview, June 8, 2023.
  2. *Ibid.*
  3. *Ibid.*
  4. *Ibid.*
  5. *Ibid.*
  6. *Ibid.*
  7. Sito Pantoja, quoted by Ted Reed, "Union Says It Organized Ground Service Workers at United and Alaska Subsidies," *TheStreet*, April 17, 2017.
  8. Sito Pantoja interview, June 8, 2023.
  9. *Ibid.*
  10. *Ibid.*
  11. Alex Garcia and Sito Pantoja, quoted by Ted Reed, "American Airlines Reaches $4.2 Billion Deal with Mechanics and Fleet Service That Boosts Profit Sharing and Caps Offshore Work," *Forbes*, Jan. 30, 2020.
  12. Sito Pantoja interview, June 8, 2023.
  13. *Ibid.*

Chapter 24

  1. Dennis Tajer interview, Sept. 1, 2023.
  2. *Ibid.*
  3. *Ibid.*
  4. *Ibid.*
  5. *Ibid.*
  6. *Ibid.*
  7. *Ibid.*
  8. *Ibid.*
  9. Peter Pae, in "Unions Pressuring Airlines on Bonuses," *Los Angeles Times*, April 14, 2007.
  10. Dennis Tajer interview, Sept. 18, 2023.
  11. *Ibid.*
  12. *Ibid.*

Chapter 25

  1. Julie Hedrick interview, Dec. 8, 2023.
  2. Julie Hedrick interview, Jan. 20, 2024.
  3. Julie Hedrick interview, Dec. 8, 2023.
  4. *Ibid.*
  5. Julie Hedrick, quoted by Ted Reed, "Flight Attendant Leaders, Newly Unified, Say Mnuchin Could Scuttle Plan to Pay Airline Workers," *Forbes*, April 1, 2020.
  6. Nell McShane Wulfhart interview, Jan. 31, 2024.
  7. *Ibid.*
  8. *Ibid.*
  9. Nell McShane Wulfhart, *The Great Stewardess Rebellion: How Women Launched a Workplace Revolution at 30,000 Feet* (New York: Doubleday, 2022), p. 83. The texts of the advertisements are also quoted in the book.

10. Julie Hedrick interview, Dec. 8, 2023.
11. APFA website at apfa.org/departments/archives-department/.
12. Julie Hedrick interview, Dec. 8, 2023.
13. *Ibid.*
14. *Ibid.*
15. *Ibid.*

Chapter 26

1. Laura Glading interview, Aug.16, 2023.
2. *Ibid.*
3. Sara Nelson interview, Feb.26, 2024.
4. Laura Glading interview, Aug. 16, 2023.
5. *Ibid.*
6. Laura Glading, quoted by Ted Reed and Dan Reed, *American Airlines, U.S. Airways and the Creation of the World's Largest Airline* (Jefferson: McFarland, 2014), p. 154.
7. *Ibid.*
8. *Ibid.*
9. Laura Glading interview, Aug. 16, 2023.
10. Marcus Gluth quoted by Ted Reed, "American Hires Former Union Leader as Consultant, Stirring Controversy," *Forbes*, Jan. 9, 2016.
11. APFA board, quoted by Ted Reed, "American Hires Former Union Leader as Consultant, Stirring Controversy," *Forbes*, Jan. 9, 2016.
12. Laura Glading, quoted by Ted Reed, "American Hires Former Union Leader as Consultant, Stirring Controversy," *Forbes*, Jan. 9, 2016.
13. Laura Glading interview, Aug. 16, 2023.
14. *Ibid.*

Chapter 27

1. Joe Ferreira interview, Nov. 6, 2023.
2. *Ibid.*
3. *Ibid.*
4. PeoplExpress Airlines Alumni, Facebook page.
5. Joe Ferreira interview, Nov. 6, 2023.
6. *Ibid.*
7. *Ibid.*
8. *Ibid.*
9. Craig Symons interview, Nov. 1, 2023.
10. *Ibid.*
11. *Ibid.*
12. *Ibid.*
13. Unite Here website, unitehere.org/industry/airports.
14. Alisa Gallo interview, Feb. 26, 2024.
15. *Ibid.*
16. *Ibid.*

Chapter 28

1. Mary Kay Henry interview, Aug. 15, 2023.
2. *Ibid.*
3. SEIU, "Sea-Tac Airport Workers Win Recognition of Their Union," press release, Oct. 21, 2016.
4. Mary Kay Henry interview, Aug. 15, 2023.
5. *Ibid.*
6. *Ibid.*
7. *Ibid.*
8. *Ibid.*
9. *Ibid.*

Bibliography

Interviews

Jason Ambrosi, Oct. 16, 2023.
Dave Carpenter, July 16, 2023.
Joe Ferreira, Nov. 6, 2023.
Mike Flores, June 22, 2023.
Alisa Gallo, Feb. 26, 2024.
Taylor Garland, Aug. 10, 2023.
Laura Glading, August 16, 2023.
Jerry Glass, May 2, 2023, and May 5, 2023.
Julie Hedrick, Dec. 8, 2023, and Jan. 20, 2024.
Mary Kay Henry, Aug. 15, 2023.
Sara Nelson, Feb. 14, 2023; March 13, 2023; March 16, 2023; June 14, 2023; July 14, 2023; Feb. 8, 2024; Feb. 14, 2024; and Feb. 26, 2024.
Sito Pantoja, June 5, 2023, and June 8, 2023.
Roberto Ramirez, Feb. 9, 2023.
Joe Samuelsen, Dec. 6, 2023.
John Samuelsen, Sept. 16, 2022; Oct. 14, 2022; Oct. 18, 2022; Jan. 6, 2023; Jan 12, 2023; and Feb. 4, 2024.
Craig Symons, Nov. 1, 2023.
Dennis Tajer, Sept. 1, 2023; Sept. 18, 2023; and Nov. 20, 2023.
Roger Toussaint, Jan. 14, 2023, and Jan. 20, 2023.
Hank Whittemore, June 21, 2022.
Nell McShane Wulfhart, Jan. 31, 2024.

Books

Reed, Dan, and Ted Reed. *American Airlines, U.S. Airways and the Creation of the World's Largest Airline*. Jefferson: McFarland, 2014.
Sinclair, Upton. *The Jungle*. New York: Signet, 1906.
Whittemore, L.H. *The Man Who Ran the Subways*. New York: Holt, Rinehart and Winston, 1968.
Wulfhart, Nell McShane. *The Great Stewardess Rebellion: How Women Launched a Workplace Revolution at 20,000 Feet*. New York: Doubleday, 2022.

Periodicals and Websites

The author has quoted from stories he has written for *Forbes, The Points Guy* and *TheStreet*.
Newspapers cited include the *Los Angeles Times*, the *New York Daily News*, the *New York Herald-Tribune*, the *New York Post* and the *New York Times*.
Other publications cited are the *Irish Examiner, Jacobin, Politico, Salon, The New Yorker* and Strauss News.

Broadcast

References are made to broadcasts on CNN and CBS.
Robert Isom in video, "TWU President Samuelsen Takes Contract Fight to AA President Isom's Face," YouTube, May 21, 2019.

Court Ruling

John McBryde, in American Airlines vs. Transport Workers Union of America et al, opinion filed in US District Court Northern District of Texas, Aug. 12, 2019, page 10.

Index

Adams, Eric 107, 109
AFL-CIO 41, 42, 51, 63, 151, 189
Air Canada 122
Air Line Pilots Association (ALPA) 1, 2, 8, 70, 118–123, 130–135, 139, 141, 143, 149, 165
Air Wisconsin 138, 139
Airbus 133
AirCal 171
Aircraft Mechanics Fraternal Association (AMFA) 73, 117
Airlines for America (A4A) 7, 48
Alaska Airlines 33, 67, 121, 128, 160, 161, 187, 192
Allegheny Airlines 136
Allied Pilots Association (APA) 1, 4, 123–129, 133, 148, 149, 152, 165, 169, 170
Amazon 38, 53–58, 104, 190
Ambrosi, Jason 3, 8, 118–122, 130, 134, 135
America West Airlines 33, 138, 139, 141, 143, 145, 146–148, 151, 154
American Airlines 1, 3, 7, 8, 11, 12, 23, 33, 34, 67, 72, 73, 112–117, 120, 123–128, 138, 142, 143, 145, 148, 149, 151, 153–155, 157, 158, 160–163, 165, 167–181, 187, 192, 193
American Trans Air 148
Arpey, Gerard 169, 180
Association of Flight Attendants (AFA) 2, 5, 8, 9; history 30–37, 41, 42, 50, 59–63, 66–70, 139, 141, 145, 146, 174, 177, 179; at United 20–29
Association of Professional Flight Attendants (APFA) 1, 4, 33, 34, 48, 67, 148, 152, 171–181
Atlantic Coast Airlines 138, 139
Atlantic Southeast Airlines 120

Basani, Lori 48
Bates, Dave 4, 148, 149, 151, 152
Bensinger, Richard 41
Bethune, Gordon 185
Boeing 63, 120, 121, 123–129, 134, 135, 155, 163, 165, 167, 169, 185
Borer, David 24, 25, 33
Braniff 31, 138, 157
Breznau, Ryan 70
Bryan, Charlie 3

CARES Act 9, 45–51
Carey, Dan 124, 127, 128
Carey, Susan 155
Carpenter, Dave 4, 25, 26
Chapman, Tony 149
Clinton, Hillary 59, 60
Colgan Air 130, 131
Communications Workers of America (CWA) 32–34, 76, 141
Continental Airlines 34, 62, 147–149, 158, 175, 183, 185, 186
Corvallis Gazette Times 15, 16
Crandall, Robert 4, 11
Cuomo, Andrew 107, 109, 110

Dallas Morning News 124, 127
De Blasio, Bill 107–109
De Fazio, Peter 47, 48, 49
Delta Air Lines 2, 7, 12, 28, 41, 66, 68–70, 118–121, 140, 142, 147–149, 157, 171, 175, 187
De Pete, Joe 8

Eastern Air Lines 1, 2, 3, 12, 138, 154, 157, 186, 187
Ethiopian Airlines 124, 127, 129

Fain, Shawn 8, 36, 66, 69, 70
Farbstein, Lisa 13

207

Federal Aviation Administration (FAA) 2, 29, 32, 39, 40, 63, 127, 128, 131–134, 178, 181, 187
FedEx 8, 133
Ferreira, Joe 183–186
Flores, Mike 33
Franke, Bill 138, 145, 146
Friend, Pat 4, 31–33, 62, 67, 68, 141
Frontier Airlines 142, 186

Gallo, Alisa 188, 189
Garcia, Alex 116, 117, 153, 162–164
Garland, Taylor 5, 36, 59–63
Genoese, Bill 4
Glading, Laura 4, 148–152, 178–181
Glass, Jerry 136–146, 154, 163
Griswold, Clacy 183–184

Hardy, George 194, 195
Hawaiian Airlines 64, 65
Hedrick, Julie 67, 171-174, 176, 177
Henry, Mary Kay 190–195
Hill, Lloyd 156
Hochul, Kathy 107, 109

Ichan, Carl 157, 158
Insler, Todd 118, 119
International Association of Machinists (IAM) 1, 4, 45, 48, 54, 68, 75, 76, 112, 117, 139, 141, 144, 153–164
International Brotherhood of Electrical Workers 76
International Brotherhood of Teamsters (IBT) 1, 4, 8, 36, 68, 75, 76, 156, 183–187
International Union of Operating Engineers 83
Isom, Robert 3, 73, 112–114, 145, 147, 148
Iverson, Bob 187

JetBlue 110, 121, 141, 142, 187
Johnson, Steve 138

Kelly, Kim 41
Kerkorian, Kirk 144
Kerr, Derek 148
Kirby, Scott 138, 147–149, 152, 188
Kiwi International Air Lines 187
Kuhn, Corey 59

Lake Central Airlines 136
Lakefield, Bruce 143
Liebes, Richard 194, 195
Lion Air 124, 125
Little, Jim 148, 151
Lorenzo, Frank 138, 157, 158, 185, 186

Martinez, Robert 164
McGlashen, Bill 33
Miami Air 187
Michaelis, Michael 124–126, 129
Minicucci, Ben 161
Montgomery, Lynn 67, 173, 174
Moore, Rosemary 25, 27
Munoz, Oscar 31, 161, 188

National Airlines 186
National Labor Relations Board (NLRB) 55, 56
National Mediation Board (NMB)14, 33, 68
Nelson, Carol 15–17, 24
Nelson, Don 15, 18, 24
Nelson, Sara 4, 8, 9, 11; Delta campaign 66–71, 119, 144, 165, 173, 174, 178, 179, 189; early years 15–20; fights Amazon 51–65; United flight attendant 21–29, 31–36; works in Washington 37–52, 55
New York Mets 76, 77
New York Times 127
Northwest Airlines 33, 68, 70, 117, 147, 149; Northwest Orient 157

O'Brien, Sean 8, 36
Ornstein, Jonathan 148
Ozark Airlines 157

Pacific Southwest Airlines 134, 136, 171
Pan American World Airways 1, 4, 12, 72, 120, 138, 156, 185, 186
Pantoja, Sito 3, 4, 48, 116, 117, 144, 145, 153--164
Parker, Doug 8, 9, 12, 44–46, 48, 50, 65, 138, 146–148, 151
People Express 183, 185, 186
Peterpaul, John 155
Piedmont Airlines 186
Pollock, Bill 143, 144
Primaris Airlines 121
Principia College 18–20
Professional Airline Flight Control Association 26, 182, 183, 186–188

Quill, Mike 3, 92–98

Railway Labor Act 14, 112, 113
Ramirez, Roberto 92, 114
Retail, Wholesale and Department Store Union (RWDSU) 55, 56
Rikers Island 72, 80, 81, 85
Ris, Will 181
Roach, Robert 141, 144, 159, 160
Roberts, Cecil 51

Index

Salas, Larry 173
Samuelsen, Joe 76, 77, 79, 81
Samuelsen, John 3, 51, 52, 72, early days 73–80; as international president 72–73, 112–117, 145; as Local 100 official 89–93, 95, 98, 99, 101, 103–105, 109–111; at Rikers 80–88
Samuelsen, Lisa 82, 83, 105, 106
Samuelsen, Theresa Foy 75, 76
Samuelsen, Warren Christian (Bunky) 74, 75
Sept. 11 attacks 22, 23, 35, 45, 67, 120
Service Employees International Union (SEIU) 183, 190–195
Shook, Veda 33, 34, 67
Sicher, Ed 166
Siegel, Dave 140
60 Minutes 41
Skiles, Jeff 133–135
Smalls, Christian 56–58
Smisek, Jeff 188
Song (airline) 27
Southwest 7, 12, 67, 72, 136, 140, 142, 147, 173, 174
Spirit (airline) 117, 121, 142, 187
Sullenberger, C.B. "Sully" 133–135
Swoboda, Frank 155
Swoop (airline) 122
Symons, Craig 26, 186–188

Tajer, Dennis 4, 5, 115, 119, 124–129, 148, 149, 152, 165; military service 166–170
Ted (airline) 27, 28
Tiberi, Joe 3, 45, 155, 158, 159, 164
Tilton, Glenn 23, 25, 26, 28, 188

Tilden, Brad 161
Toussaint, Roger 90, 91, 95, 98–103, 105, 106
Trans State Airlines 139
Transport Workers Union (TWU) 1, 3, 52, 67, 72, 79, 84–117, 139, 145, 148, 151–153, 156, 162, 170, 174, 176
Transportation Security Administration (TSA) 12–14, 39, 63, 173
TWA 31, 137, 138, 144, 145, 148, 153–158, 185

Unite Here 188, 189
United Airlines 2, 4, 7, 8, 12, 20, 21, 22; bankruptcy 23–32, 34, 41, 62, 67, 118, 120, 121, 137–139, 142, 148, 149, 157, 160, 161, 163, 165, 174, 175, 181, 183–188
United Auto Workers (UAW) 8, 36, 66, 69, 193, 194
United Food and Commercial Workers 75
United Mine Workers of America 51, 54
US Airways 2, 28, 33, 34, 112, 133, 134, 136, 140–143, 146–148, 151, 157, 161–163, 171, 177, 179
US Airways Airline Pilots Association (USAPA) 2, 146

Western Airlines 171
WestJet 122
Whittemore, Hank 94–97
Wissing, Todd 125
Wolf, Stephen 140
Wulfhart, Nell McShane 175, 176

Zack, Jeff 22, 25

www.ingramcontent.com/pod-product-compliance
Lightning Source LLC
Chambersburg PA
CBHW032044300426
44117CB00009B/1179